A HANDBOOK OF SECOND LANGUAGE ACQUISITION FOR BIBLICAL STUDIES

INSIGHTS OF MODERN LANGUAGE INSTRUCTION FOR TEACHING BIBLICAL LANGUAGES

CW01497598

A HANDBOOK OF SECOND LANGUAGE ACQUISITION FOR BIBLICAL STUDIES

INSIGHTS OF MODERN LANGUAGE INSTRUCTION FOR TEACHING BIBLICAL LANGUAGES

Jennifer E. Noonan

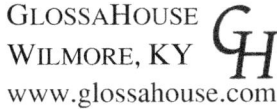
GLOSSAHOUSE
WILMORE, KY
www.glossahouse.com

A Handbook of Second Language Acquisition for Biblical Studies: Insights of Modern Language Instruction for Teaching Biblical Languages

GlossaHouse, LLC
110 Callis Circle
Wilmore, KY 40309
www.GlossaHouse.com

Noonan, Jennifer E.
A Handbook of Second Language Acquisition for Biblical Studies: Insights of Modern Language Instruction for Teaching Biblical Languages / Jennifer E. Noonan — Wilmore, KY: GlossaHouse © 2022

xviii, 284p. 15.24cm. —
Original work

ISBN-13: 978-1-63663-0434

Library of Congress Control Number: 2022921050

Corrected Version 3 (January 2023)

Cover design by T. Michael W. Halcomb

Text layout and book design by Andrew J. Coutras and Fredrick J. Long

Volume Editing by Andrew J. Coutras and Fredrick J. Long

The fonts used to create this work are available from
www.linguistsoftware.com/lgku.htm

For Ben and Katy, my two favorite language scholars.

TABLE OF CONTENTS

ACKNOWLEDGMENTS

I am deeply grateful for so many individuals who are part of my life, without whom this project would not have been completed.

First and foremost, I would like to thank my husband Ben for his ongoing support and encouragement throughout the process. His belief in me and in the work represented here have been invaluable. I am also grateful for his depth of knowledge and his editorial skills in reading the manuscript and making insightful suggestions along the way. I am also grateful for my daughter Katy, whose constant devotion and admiration have given me the courage to press forward and whose joy for life has reminded me to play along the way.

I would also like to thank Andrew Coutras and the team at Glossa-House. I am so grateful for their guidance and expertise, helping me to develop ideas, communicate them clearly, and bring everything to print.

Thank you also to Jessie Udall for her editorial skills and encouragement. I am so grateful for her time and care in reading many of the early chapters and helping me launch the work. I have also had many, many cheerleaders along the way who have listened to my ideas, encouraged me, and believed in me. Several deserve specific mention: Jessica Bechtel, David Croteau, Lee Fields, Paul Overland, and Brian Schultz. Their support has meant more than they may realize.

I am also indebted to Kimberly Buescher Urbanski for allowing me special access to her dissertation, which gave me the opportunity to include a very useful teaching example.

Finally, I am grateful to God who alone is worthy of all praise and glory. I am honored to be working under His grace.

ABBREVIATIONS

ACTFL	American Council on the Teaching of Foreign Languages
LAD	Language Acquisition Device
L1	First language
L2	Second language
PI	Processing Instruction
SALVI	Septentrionale Americanum Latinitatis Vivae Institutum
SLA	Second Language Acquisition
TOEFL	Test of English as a Foreign Language
TPR	Total Physical Response
UG	Universal Grammar
ZPD	Zone of Proximal Development

A
HANDBOOK
OF
SECOND
LANGUAGE
ACQUISITION
FOR
BIBLICAL
STUDIES

CHAPTER 1: INTRODUCTION

In the modern period, the fields of linguistics and psychology have flourished with a parallel growth and development in approaches to teaching languages. More specifically, the field of *Instructed Second Language Acquisition* (SLA) has seen substantial growth in the last forty years, beginning with the work of Stephen D. Krashen in the 1980s. Subsequently, modern language instruction has changed significantly because of this research. While this growth in knowledge and expertise has not influenced biblical and ancient language instruction to the same degree, in the past decade or two, instructors of biblical and ancient languages have shown greater interest in the developments in SLA research and their implications for teaching Hebrew, Greek, and Latin.

To appreciate where we are in ancient language pedagogy, then, we need to understand where we have come from. Therefore, a brief history of modern linguistics and language pedagogy is in order, followed by a general overview of the discipline of SLA research. Only then can we address the current state of biblical and ancient language instruction and the focus of this volume.

A Brief History of Modern Linguistics and Language Teaching

Language teaching is an ancient art that may be as old as the Tower of Babel. Modern language teaching, however, probably began in the late Middle Ages as Latin died out as a living language and became an object of study rather than a popular mode of conversation and interchange. With Latin as an object of study, language instructors focused on the discipline of memorizing Latin vocabulary and paradigms with translation serving as the main form of both student practice and assessment. This approach to language instruction, commonly called the *Grammar-Translation Method*, continued to be used for modern languages into the early 1900s.[1] The remainder of this section presents a brief overview of

---

[1] Alice Omaggio Hadley, *Teaching Language in Context*. 3rd ed. (Boston: Heinle & Heinle, 2001), 106–7; Jack C. Richards and Theodore S. Rodgers, *Approaches and Methods in Language Teaching: A Description and Analysis* (Cambridge: Cambridge

the recent history of linguistics and language teaching beginning with the early 1900s as research and practice moved away from the Grammar-Translation Method, focusing on three general approaches to language learning: *environmentalist, innatist,* and *interactionist.*[2]

The Environmentalist Approach to Language Learning

The structural school of linguistics, promoted by Ferdinand de Saussure in Europe and Leonard Bloomfield in the United States, and the behaviorism of B. F. Skinner led to a shift in linguistics and in language instruction in the early twentieth century.[3] The structural school of linguistics understood language as an abstract system and focused on such elements of language as phonemes, morphemes, words, and sentence types. According to this perspective, the various language elements are related to each other linearly. The goal of language learning, then, was to master all the language elements and the rules governing their combinations and interactions.

Skinner's classic conditioning with stimulus-response chains added the perspective that all learning is associative learning or habit-formation. Behaviorism focuses on the role of the environment, to the near exclusion of internal mental processes. For the behaviorists, language learning was a simple stimulus-response-reinforcement change, leading to habits of language.

For the environmentalists who combine structural linguistics and behaviorism, language instruction meant getting the student to imitate and practice the same structures over and over until they were habits. Teachers were expected to be explicit and focus their instruction mainly on the

---

University Press, 1986), 1–5.

[2] The discussion below is adapted from Esther Usó-Juan and Alicia Martínez-Flor, "Approaches to Language Learning and Teaching: Towards Acquiring Communicative Competence Through the Four Skills," in *Current Trends in the Development and Teaching of the Four Language Skills,* ed. E. Usó-Juan and A. Martínez-Flor (De Gruyter, 2006), 3–25.

[3] See Ferdinand de Saussure, Charles Bally, and Albert Sechehaye, *Cours de Linguistique Générale* (Paris: Payot, 1916); Leonard Bloomfield, *Language* (New York: Holt, Rinehart & Winston, 1933); and B. F. Skinner, *Verbal Behavior* (New York: Appleton-Century-Crofts, 1957). In the US, structuralism was also known as American Descriptivism.

more difficult structures. This type of language instruction is called the *Audio-Lingual Method*, and it held a place of prominence for a few decades.[4] However, the environmental approach to language learning eventually gave way to the innatist approach to language learning.

The Innatist Approach to Language Learning

Several major changes in linguistics and psychology in the 1960s led to a corresponding shift in language teaching. For those who did not agree with the perspective of structural linguistics, with its focus on the surface forms of language, a new approach emerged: generative linguistics. This new approach acknowledged both surface forms and underlying abstract structures in a language while acknowledging and even emphasizing the creative nature of human language, in contrast to the stimulus-response perspective of the behaviorists.

Noam Chomsky initiated a significant change in perspective with what he called "Transformational-Generative Grammar."[5] He believed that children were born with a *Language Acquisition Device* (LAD), which was later replaced by the idea of *universal grammar* (UG). According to this theory, all children have an innate ability to learn any grammar.

Parallel changes in psychology also contributed to a shift in approaches to language instruction. Around the same time as Chomsky, the new field of psycholinguistics emerged with a focus that was both mentalistic and dynamic in contrast to the simple stimulus-response view of the behaviorists. Children were now seen as active participants in learning with an ability to understand and interact with the language system being learned. Language was understood as rule-governed and internal, not something that was developed as a habit. Moreover, language development in children came to be understood as incremental and going through stages that were similar and predictable across learners, a consistent order of acquisition.

---

[4] Hadley, *Teaching Language*, 110–13; and Richards and Rodgers, *Approaches and Methods*, 44–63.

[5] Noam Chomsky, *Syntactic Structures* (The Hague: Mouton de Gruyter, 1957).

Two contrasting methods of language teaching grew out of the innatist approach to language learning. The first method, the *Cognitive Anti-Method*, attempted to recreate "natural" learning processes in the classroom.[6] The opposing view was called the *Cognitive-Code Method* and developed from Chomsky's competence-performance distinction. This method held that students need to understand and analyze language rules to develop competence.[7]

The Interactionist Approach to Language Learning

Further shifts in linguistics and psychology in the 1970s led to another shift in language instruction. The field of linguistics saw an increase in focus on discourse, understood as language beyond the sentence and connections between sentences. At the same time, more attention was given to the function of language in social contexts and how this determines form. In reaction against Chomsky, functionalism emerged, with M. A. K. Halliday's being one of the most common functionalist approaches.[8] He identified seven functions of language, all of which are social in nature. Relatedly, the focus moved from analysis of the formal structures of the language to a more "contextualized perspective followed by systemic-functional linguistics."[9]

In the 1970s, changes in the field of psycholinguistics also contributed to changes in theories about language learning. With the development of cognitive psychology and then cognitive linguistics shortly thereafter, researchers and practitioners sought to understand the mental processes involved in language learning. Other new disciplines also aided in the shift of perspective in language learning, including sociolinguistics, which was a reaction against Chomsky. Sociolinguists

---

[6] Hadley, *Teaching Language*, 113. See Leonard Newmark and David A. Reibel, "Necessity and Sufficiency in Language Learning," *International Review of Applied Linguistics in Language Teaching* 6 (1968): 145–64.

[7] Hadley, *Teaching Language*, 113. See Kenneth Chastain, *Developing Second Language Skills: Theory and Practice*, 2nd ed. (Chicago: Rand McNally, 1976).

[8] M. A. K. Halliday, *Learning How to Mean: Explorations in the Development of Language* (London: Arnold, 1975).

[9] Usó-Juan and Martínez-Flor, "Approaches," 9.

elevated the importance of communicative competence and the appropriate use of language in specific social contexts.

These shifts in linguistics and psychology led to further changes in language instruction that continue to influence modern language classrooms. After seeing so many language teaching methods come and go over the past century, many contemporary practitioners eschew methods altogether, preferring to focus on guiding principles and strategies for teaching language.[10] The new approach to language learning incorporates the role of both environmental and innate factors. In other words, instructors see the environment as interacting with the learner's innate predisposition to language development. Therefore, language learning is understood to be social, dynamic, and communicative, thus giving the name *Communicative Approach* to this type of instruction.[11] The Communicative Approach is too broad to be considered a method, but rather refers to a philosophy of instruction that incorporates various principles and strategies under its umbrella. Instructors using this approach focus on developing the communicative competence of their learners, while emphasizing the cognitive abilities that learners bring to the process.

To summarize, modern language instruction has changed in many ways over the past century, being influenced by changes in linguistics and psychology. Beginning with the Grammar-Translation Method of the early twentieth century, language teaching has seen several transformations, moving from environmentalist approaches through innatist approaches to interactionist approaches. Additionally, SLA research came into its own in the 1980s, beginning with the work of Krashen, who set the stage for significant growth in research specifically focused on the teaching and learning of languages in a classroom setting.[12] The next section introduces some of the basic questions that SLA researchers

---

[10] See, e.g., B. Kumaravadivelu, "The Postmethod Condition: (E)merging Strategies for Second/Foreign Language Teaching," *TESOL Quarterly, 28* (1994): 27–48.

[11] Hadley, *Teaching Language*, 116–18; Richard and Rodgers, *Approaches and Methods*, 64–86.

[12] Stephen D. Krashen, *Principles and Practice in Second Language Acquisition* (New York: Pergamon, 1982); Stephen D. Krashen, *The Input Hypothesis: Issues and Implications* (New York: Longman, 1985).

seek to answer as they pursue greater understanding of language learning and instruction.

The Discipline of Instructed Second Language Acquisition

The field of instructed SLA seeks to better understand what language instruction can and cannot do, providing a basis for how to do language instruction well. As an introduction to the discipline of SLA, this section presents some of the important questions that SLA researchers attempt to answer, including the following: the initial state of the learner, the possibility of achieving native-like proficiency in a second language, implicit and explicit learning, acquisition orders, the role of language instruction, and constraints on language learning.[13]

The first question that concerns SLA researchers is the initial state of a language learner when he or she first begins to learn a second language (L2). Some hold that the learner's first language (L1) is the initial state.[14] This is called the full transfer position. According to this perspective, the learner must replace or overwrite his or her L1 assumptions with L2 grammar, vocabulary, morphology, etc. Others at the opposite end of the spectrum believe that L2 learners begin with a blank slate like children learning L1, having universals and internal mechanisms to guide them rather than assumptions from their L1. This is called the no transfer position. There are others, however, who hold to a partial transfer position on the issue, believing that "learners transfer the lexicon and its syntactic properties ... but not the functional features of language related to things such as tense, person-number, agreement, and so on."[15] While the evidence is not conclusive, there seems to be more support for the full or partial transfer position rather than the no transfer position.[16] An instructor's view on this issue will necessarily affect his or

---

[13] Adapted from Bill VanPatten and Alessandro G. Benati, *Key Terms in Second Language Acquisition* (London: Continuum, 2010), 11–57.

[14] See, e.g., Bonnie D. Schwartz and Rex A. Sprouse, "L2 Cognitive States and the Full Transfer/Full Access Model," *Second Language Research* 12 (1996): 40–72.

[15] VanPatten and Benati, *Key Terms*, 14. See, e.g., Anne Vainikka and Martha Young-Scholten, "The Gradual Development of L2 Phrase Structure," *Second Language Research* 12 (1996): 7–39.

[16] For a summary and evaluation of these issues, see VanPatten and Benati, *Key Terms*,

her approach to teaching L2 and how the L1 is or is not used in the classroom. Principles related to types of language knowledge and instruction will be addressed in chapters 2 and 3.

A second question addressed by SLA is, "Can L2 learners achieve a level of proficiency that is native-like?" Like the question above, answers fall on a continuum from "yes" to "no," and everything in between. The research seems to suggest that non-natives can become native-like, but the occurrences are quite rare.[17] Related to this question is the issue of whether there is a critical period, that is, a developmental period during which the language must be learned to achieve a significant level of proficiency. This question will be addressed in greater detail in chapter 12. Again, an instructor's pedagogy will necessarily be affected by his or her assumptions on the potential for his or her students to achieve native-like proficiency.

The relative importance of implicit and explicit learning is another area that interests SLA researchers. Many hold that language acquisition is largely or entirely implicit.[18] While few believe that SLA is entirely explicit, some do see a role for both explicit and implicit learning.[19] Chapters 2 and 3 address this issue in further detail.

Researchers in SLA also address questions of L2 language development over time and the effects of instruction on L2 acquisition, particularly acquisition orders.[20] Researchers note that learners exhibit a stage-like development in the learning of a single language structure or feature. Learners must pass through these developmental sequences or stages, and instruction seems to have little or no effect on changing or

---

11–15.

[17] See summary and analysis by VanPatten and Benati, *Key Terms*, 20.

[18] This is the view of a number of scholars, including Krashen, *Principles and Practice*; and Nick C. Ellis, "At the Interface: Dynamic Interactions of Explicit and Implicit Language Knowledge," *Studies in Second Language Acquisition* 27 (2005): 305–52.

[19] See, e.g., Robert DeKeyser, "Skill Acquisition Theory," in *Theories in Second Language Acquisition*, 2nd ed., ed. B. VanPatten and J. Williams (New York: Routledge, 2015), 94–112; and Richard Schmidt, "Attention," in *Cognition and Second Language Instruction*, ed. P. Robinson (Cambridge: Cambridge University Press, 2001), 3–32.

[20] This question is particularly concerned with the acquisition of a language, that is, the learning of implicit knowledge, rather than explicit learning or memorization of rules and paradigms. For further discussion on the distinction, see chapter 2.

reordering the stages themselves.[21] Research indicates that the relative order in which learners acquire different structures is also somewhat fixed.

This, then, begs the question of whether instruction has any effect on a learner's acquisition of L2. First, it must be understood that SLA researchers do not address the question of instruction to language learning issues like vocabulary and reading skills, but rather to the learning of formal properties of the language, such as morphology and syntax. Views on this issue range from "instruction makes no difference"[22] to "instruction is constrained"[23] to "instruction is necessary."[24] Many see instruction as something that speeds up the language learning process, even though it does not change the order of developmental sequences.[25] Principles related to this issue, specifically course structure and design, will be addressed in chapter 11.

Another perspective on the question of instruction is emerging in the field. As discussed in chapter 4, *comprehensible input* is almost universally accepted as a necessary ingredient for successful language acquisition. Therefore, the trajectory of SLA research is shifting from "Does instruction make a difference?" to "Does manipulating input make a difference?"[26] Once again, answers to these questions will have a significant impact on an instructor's approach to language teaching and learning. Principles related to input will be addressed in chapters 4, 5 and 6.

One last question that SLA researchers investigate is, "What constraints are there on acquisition?" According to Bill VanPatten and

---

[21] See, e.g., Manfred Pienemann, *Language Processing and Second Language Development: Processability Theory* (Amsterdam: John Benjamins, 1998); and Manfred Pienemann, "An Outline of Processability Theory and Its Relationship to Other Approaches to SLA," *Language Learning* 65.1 (2015): 123–51.

[22] See, e.g., Krashen, *Principles and Practice*; and Vivian Cook, *Second Language Learning and Language Teaching*, 5th ed. (New York: Routledge, 2016).

[23] See, e.g., Pienemann, *Language Processing*.

[24] See, e.g., Michael H. Long, "Does Second Language Instruction Make a Difference?" *TESOL Quarterly* 17 (1983): 359–82; and John M. Norris and Lourdes Ortega, "Effectiveness of L2 Instruction: A research Synthesis and Quantitative Meta-analysis," *Language Learning* 50 (2000): 417–528.

[25] See the summary and evaluation by VanPatten and Benati, *Key Terms*, 51–52.

[26] VanPatten and Benati, *Key Terms*, 52.

Alessandro G. Benati, "SLA is complex and a variety of linguistic, psycholinguistic, and contextual factors interact that shape and constrain the course of acquisition."[27] As researchers come to understand these constraints, they can better understand how to promote instruction that works with the constraints rather than against them, ultimately improving student outcomes. The question of constraints particularly affects the development of L2 skills, which are addressed in chapters 8, 9, and 10.

The State of Biblical and Ancient Language Instruction and Research

Having explored the history of modern language learning and the discipline of SLA, we turn to the current state of biblical and ancient language teaching and research. Historically, biblical and ancient language instruction has been heavily influenced by the early approaches to language learning described above. Even in modern times, the primary approach being used for these languages is the Grammar-Translation Method with a focus on explicit learning of rules, memorization of vocabulary and paradigms, and practice in the form of translation, primarily from L2 to L1. For example, a recent survey indicates that most Hebrew instructors use the Grammar-Translation Method or some variation of this method.[28] Similarly, a review of Hebrew textbooks indicates that most of these are based on the Grammar-Translation Method.[29]

However, in the past decade or two, instructors of ancient languages have become more interested in approaches to language teaching that are informed by SLA principles. For example, the Applied Linguistics and Biblical Languages Group in the Evangelical Theological Society has been delivering papers on SLA-informed instructional practices for the biblical languages for about a decade. Relatedly, a few recent introductory grammars include communicative elements and a few others attempt to employ a more thorough communicative approach for the

---

[27] VanPatten and Benati, *Key Terms*, 57.

[28] Jennifer Elizabeth Quast, "Using Processing Instruction to Teach Biblical Hebrew Grammar" (PhD diss., Hebrew Union College-Jewish Institute of Religion, 2009), 34–36.

[29] Jennifer E. Noonan, "Recent Teaching Grammars for Biblical Hebrew: A Review and Critique," *Ashland Theological Journal* 43 (2011): 99–118.

biblical and ancient languages.[30] Scholarly and peer-reviewed publications related to teaching biblical and ancient languages using SLA principles are not as plentiful, but more are showing up all the time.[31]

Bringing SLA to Biblical and Ancient Language Teaching

In response to the changes in teaching biblical and ancient languages noted above, this book is intended to promote and inform the movement of increased interest in SLA among instructors of biblical and ancient languages. To this end, the current volume presents a limited number of carefully selected principles drawn from research and practice in the

---

[30] See, e.g., Randall Buth, Brian Schultz, Scott McQuinn, and Benjamin Kantor, *Living Biblical Hebrew* (Jerusalem: Biblical Language Center, 2019); John A. Cook and Robert D. Holmstedt, *Beginning Biblical Hebrew: A Grammar and Illustrated Reader* (Grand Rapids: Baker, 2013); Hélène M. Dallaire, *Biblical Hebrew: A Living Language*, 2nd ed. (Hélène M. Dallaire, 2017); Paul Overland, *Learning Biblical Hebrew Interactively*, rev. ed. (Sheffield: Sheffield Phoenix, 2016); Travis West, *Biblical Hebrew: An Interactive Approach* (Wilmore, KY: GlossaHouse, 2016); T. Michael W. Halcomb, and Jordan Day. *The Path to Learning Greek* (Wilmore, KY GlossaHouse, 2013); T. Michael W. Halcomb, and Fredrick J. Long, *Speak Koine Greek: A Conversational Phrasebook* (Wilmore, KY: GlossaHouse, 2014); Paula Saffire and Catherine Freis, *Ancient Greek Alive* (Chapel Hill: University of North Carolina Press, 1999); James Tabor and Randall Buth, *Living Koine Greek* (Jerusalem: Biblical Language Center, 2002); Karen Moore and Gaylan DuBose, *Latin Alive!* (Camp Hill, PA: Classical Academic Press, 2008); John C. Traupman, *Conversational Latin for Oral Proficiency*, 4th ed. (Wauconda, IL: Bochazy-Carducci, 2007).

[31] See, e.g., John Gruber-Miller, ed. *When Dead Tongues Speak: Teaching Beginning Greek and Latin* (Oxford: Oxford University Press, 2006); Mair E. Lloyd and Steven Hunt, eds, *Communicative Approaches for Ancient Languages* (London: Bloomsbury Academic, 2021); Jennifer E. Noonan, "Teaching Biblical Hebrew Grammar," in *"Where Shall Wisdom Be Found?" A Grammatical Tribute to Professor Stephen A. Kaufman on the Occasion of His Retirement from Hebrew Union College-Jewish Institute of Religion*, eds. H. Dallaire, B. J. Noonan, and J. E. Noonan (Winona Lake, IN: Eisenbrauns, 2017), 317–35; Jennifer Noonan and Paul Overland, "Teaching Biblical Hebrew to Oral-Preference Learners," *Hebrew Higher Education* 19 (2017): 121–34; Paul Overland, "Can Communicative Methods Enhance Ancient Language Acquisition?" *Teaching Theology and Religion* 7.1 (2004): 51–57; Paul Overland, Steve Cook, Jennifer Noonan, Benjamin Noonan, Robert (Bob) Stallman, "Communicative Methods for Teaching Biblical Hebrew," *The Wabash Center Journal on Teaching* 2.2 (2021): 109–30; Paul Overland, Lee Fields, and Jennifer Noonan, "Can Communicative Principles Enhance Classical Language Acquisition?" *Foreign Language Annals* 44.3 (2011): 583–98; and Jeremy P. Thompson, "Word-list Size and Biblical Hebrew Vocabulary Learning," *Hebrew Higher Education* 14 (2012): 47–61.

field of SLA. These principles form the theoretical basis for much of what we know about second language learning and teaching.

Chapters 2 through 13 follow the same basic structure. Each chapter begins with a discussion of an SLA principle, including a brief overview of the research and scholarly discussion on that principle, followed by a few implications for instruction. The second part of the chapter explains how the issue relates to biblical and ancient language acquisition, including some of the unique challenges facing biblical and ancient language instructors when trying to incorporate the principle.

The last section of each chapter presents a few brief examples of how to integrate the SLA principle into biblical and ancient language classrooms, focusing on Hebrew, Greek, and Latin. The examples are not intended to be a full language course. Rather, they illustrate possible applications of that chapter's principles. Most of the examples can be adapted for teaching other languages and for teaching other target structures in each language.

This volume is intended to be an introduction and cannot cover every SLA principle or every nuance of every theory or empirical study. Because the discussions are necessarily brief, each chapter ends with a short list of resources for further reading. An interested reader is invited to continue his or her learning on the given principle by accessing those resources.

The select SLA principles are organized into four sections. Section one covers types of language knowledge and corresponding types of language instruction. Section two presents the raw materials of language learning: input and output. Section three addresses language skills with a special focus on those needed for reading and interpreting texts, including reading fluency, vocabulary acquisition, and issues related to course design and syllabus structure. The last section presents principles that address the role of the learner, including learner differences and sociocultural issues related to language instruction.

Conclusion

The field of SLA continues to grow and change, developing more refined and effective language pedagogy based on well-researched principles. Instructors of biblical and ancient languages have the unique opportunity to learn from the field of SLA and develop pedagogy that is informed by its principles. The current volume introduces some of these important SLA principles and how they can be incorporated into biblical and ancient language classrooms.

For Further Reading

Ellis, Rod. *The Study of Second Language Acquisition.* 2nd ed. Oxford Applied Linguistics. Oxford: Oxford University Press, 2008.

Gruber-Miller, John, ed. *When Dead Tongues Speak: Teaching Beginning Greek and Latin.* Oxford: Oxford University Press, 2006.

Lee, James F., and Bill VanPatten. *Making Communicative Language Teaching Happen.* 2nd ed. Boston: McGraw-Hill, 2003.

Lightbown, Patsy, and Nina Spada. *How Languages are Learned.* 3rd ed. Oxford: Oxford University Press, 2006.

Lloyd, Mair E., and Steven Hunt, eds. *Communicative Approaches for Ancient Languages.* London: Bloomsbury Academic, 2021.

Schwieter, John W., and Alessandro Benati, eds. *The Cambridge Handbook of Language Learning.* Cambridge: Cambridge University Press, 2019.

VanPatten, Bill, and Alessandro G. Benati. *Key Terms in Second Language Acquisition.* London: Continuum, 2010.

VanPatten, Bill, and Jessica Williams, eds. *Theories in Second Language Acquisition.* Mahwah, NJ: Erlbaum, 2007.

CHAPTER 2: THE BUILDING BLOCKS OF LANGUAGE PROFICIENCY: IMPLICIT KNOWLEDGE, EXPLICIT KNOWLEDGE, AND AUTOMATICITY

In English, native speakers know that the word "book" becomes "books" when there are two or more. Most people can also verbalize the rule: to indicate "more than one" of a given noun, add *-s*. This is an example of *explicit language knowledge*. Similarly, many native English speakers also know that you cannot have a "green, big, loud truck." It must be a "big, loud, green truck." However, most of us cannot verbalize the rule. We just "know." This is *implicit language knowledge*. More than that, most native English speakers can immediately recognize the error above without thinking or reflecting. This is *automaticity*.

The Principle: Language Proficiency

All three of these elements—implicit knowledge, explicit knowledge, and automaticity—are component parts of what is known as language proficiency. The following discussion will address each of these three in turn, presenting a basic explanation for each, followed by discussion of their significance for biblical and ancient language classrooms.

Language Proficiency

Language instructors may agree that they want their students to become skilled, or *proficient*, in L2.[1] However, not everyone can agree on what

---

[1] For a brief definition of proficiency, see Rod Ellis, *The Study of Second Language Acquisition*, 2nd ed. (Oxford: Oxford University Press, 2008), 976. For the purposes of this book, the term "proficiency" is to be preferred over "fluency" or "linguistic competence." According to Norman Segalowitz, fluency is "an ability in the second language to produce or comprehend utterances smoothly, rapidly, and accurately" (Norman Segalowitz, "Automaticity and Second Languages," in *The Handbook of Second Language Acquisition*, ed. C. Doughty and M. Long [Malden, MA: Blackwell, 2003], 384). This definition covers both the receptive language skills (listening and reading) and the productive skills (speaking and writing). However, in common usage, the word "fluency" often brings up the idea of spoken language fluency, which introduces a bias against reading and interpreting texts. "Linguistic

this means and how to get there. Diane Larsen-Freeman and Michael Long summarize some of the various approaches and difficulties related to defining proficiency.[2] The American Council on the Teaching of Foreign Languages (ACTFL) maintains a complex set of proficiency descriptions for various modern languages in a series of stages from "novice low" to "distinguished."[3] These descriptions are exhaustive and can be useful as a practical model for defining proficiency in biblical and ancient languages at various levels, but they are too specific and complex for the current discussion.

To address proficiency specifically in ancient languages rather than modern languages and to help us navigate the complexities of the concept, the definition by Jan H. Hulstijn works better than that from ACTFL. According to this definition, language proficiency incorporates the following three components: First, proficiency includes implicit knowledge of phonetics, prosody, phonology, morphology, and syntax. Second, proficiency involves vocabulary mastery, which is largely explicit in its form-meaning connections. Finally, the first two elements of proficiency must be combined with automaticity.[4]

Note that implicit knowledge, explicit knowledge, and automaticity are all integral parts of language proficiency, and each plays a specific role. By contrast, biblical and ancient language instruction has

---

competence" is another description sometimes used for the same concept; see, e.g., Robin C. Scarcella, Elaine S. Andersen, and Stephen D. Krashen, eds., *Developing Communicative Competence in a Second Language* (New York: Newbury House, 1990). However, "linguistic competence" refers to the internalized knowledge of L2, while "proficiency" refers to the ability to use this knowledge in various tasks, including reading and interpretation of texts (Rod Ellis, *Study of Second Language Acquisition*, 976). Therefore, "proficiency" will be preferred in this book because it maintains a focus on language skills without a bias toward one skill over another.

[2] Diane Larsen-Freeman and Michael Long, *An Introduction to Second Language Acquisition Research* (New York: Longman, 1990), 38–45.

[3] The ACTFL Proficiency Guidelines are available on its website: https://www.actfl.org/publications/guidelines-and-manuals/actfl-proficiency-guidelines-2012.

[4] Jan H. Hulstijn, *Language Proficiency in Native and Non-Native Speakers: Theory and Research* (Philadelphia: John Benjamins, 2015), 22. Hulstijn also differentiates between lower-level and higher-level language cognition, but the distinction is somewhat arbitrary. According to his definition, the higher level of language cognition only adds low-frequency items and an expanded skill set to the basic definition above.

traditionally promoted the learning of explicit knowledge, with automaticity assumed as something that comes with experience. Therefore, an understanding of these three components will be foundational in helping the instructor of ancient languages more fully understand and develop his or her classroom instruction to promote language proficiency.

Introduction to Implicit and Explicit Knowledge

Those who study languages and language acquisition generally agree that L2 knowledge is differentiated. That is, there are different kinds of language knowledge: implicit and explicit.[5] These different types of knowledge are stored separately in the brain and accessed differently. Krashen formalized this idea in his Monitor Hypothesis,[6] and language scholars continue to discuss and explore the significance of this differentiation of language knowledge.[7]

Implicit Knowledge

Implicit knowledge is the language knowledge we use every day when we communicate in our native tongue without knowing or referring to any formal rule. In the example above, native speakers of English access implicit language knowledge when deciding that "the big, loud, green truck" is correct. Implicit language knowledge is the ability to use grammatical features "in some kind of performance involving either judging the grammaticality of sentences or actual language use."[8] We don't have to think about it or concentrate or take a time-out to remember a grammar rule. We simply talk (or read or write or listen) without reflecting on the language itself.[9] Many language learners internalize this implicit

---

[5] See the review of research in Ellis, *Study of Second Language Acquisition*, 417–27.

[6] Krashen, *Principles and Practice*, 15–20.

[7] See, e.g., Rod Ellis et al., *Implicit and Explicit Knowledge in Second Language Learning, Testing and Teaching* (Bristol, UK: Multilingual Matters, 2009).

[8] Rod Ellis, "Explicit Knowledge and Second Language Learning and Pedagogy," in *Encyclopedia of Language and Education*, ed. J. Cenoz & N. H. Hornberger (New York: Springer, 2008), 6:147.

[9] It should be noted here that being quick with a rule of grammar or syntax is evidence of the automatization of explicit knowledge, not evidence of the acquisition of implicit knowledge. See Bill VanPatten, *From Input to Output: A Teacher's Guide to Second*

knowledge "without intending to and without becoming aware of the knowledge … acquired."[10] What is more, this language knowledge is usually "unconscious knowledge, that is, knowledge that is tacit and inaccessible to conscious introspection."[11] Implicit knowledge is also characterized as being developmental, meaning it is learned in "acquisitional sequences."[12] Certain forms and features must be learned before others can be acquired.

Explicit Knowledge

By contrast, explicit knowledge of a language is the conscious knowledge a learner has of the grammatical rules and patterns of a language. In the example above, English speakers access explicit language knowledge to explain that one must add -*s* to make a noun plural. Rod Ellis provides a very thorough definition of this type of knowledge:

> Explicit L2 knowledge is the declarative and often anomalous knowledge of the phonological, lexical, grammatical, pragmatic and sociocritical features of the L2 together with the metalanguage for labelling this knowledge. It is held consciously and is learnable and verbalizable. It is typically accessed through controlled processing when L2 learners experience some kind of linguistic difficulty in the use of the L2.[13]

Unlike implicit knowledge, explicit language knowledge can be consciously learned and verbalized. As indicated in the above definition, a language learner also needs vocabulary to express these grammatical rules, and therefore, he or she will often learn *metalanguage* along with

---

Language Acquisition (Boston: McGraw-Hill, 2003), 59.

[10] Patrick Rebuschat, "Measuring Implicit and Explicit Knowledge in Second Language Research," *Language Learning* 53:3 (Sept. 2013): 595–96.

[11] Rebuschat, "Measuring," 597.

[12] Rod Ellis, *Instructed Second Language Acquisition: Learning in the Classroom* (Oxford: Blackwell, 1990), 185.

[13] Rod Ellis, "The Definition and Measurement of L2 Explicit Knowledge," *Language Learning* 54 (2004): 244–45.

the explicit knowledge of the language. Metalanguage would include terms such as "participle" and "declension."

Chart Comparing Implicit and Explicit Knowledge

The following chart contrasts the two types of language knowledge:

Implicit Knowledge	Explicit Knowledge
Unconscious knowledge	Conscious knowledge
Intuitive knowledge	Formalized, articulated rules
Procedural knowledge	Declarative knowledge
Language edited by "feel"	Language edited by "monitor"
Results in language "acquisition"	Results in language "learning"
Results in knowledge "of" the language	Results in knowledge "about" the language

Which is Better?

Teachers of L2, of course, want to know which type of language knowledge is better for their students, and researchers continue to test this same question in different situations and with different languages. However, the answer is not as clear as we might like. The definition of proficiency above seems to indicate that both types of knowledge are useful, but for different aspects of language learning. One thing SLA researchers *can* tell us, however, is that neither kind of L2 knowledge is "developmentally primary—that is, the learner may acquire a particular 'rule' explicitly in the first instance and then proceed to acquire the same rule implicitly at a later point, or vice versa."[14] Even in L1, under certain circumstances the explicit learning of a rule may precede implicit learning, although it is usually the other way around, especially in the early years of language development.

When considering which type of language knowledge is better for SLA, there are three possible positions: 1. SLA is largely or exclusively implicit; 2. SLA is largely or exclusively explicit, 3. SLA consists of both implicit and explicit learning. Krashen and other experts who hold to the Universal Grammar (UG) theory of language acquisition would argue that it is only the learning of implicit knowledge that results in

---

[14] Ellis, *Instructed Second Language Acquisition*, 185.

competence.[15] In this view, explicit knowledge does not contribute meaningfully to language acquisition, with the possible exception of vocabulary learning which is necessarily explicit as we are aware that there is a connection between the object or idea and its name in L2. Other nonlinguistic, psychological accounts of learning (like connectionism) would also hold that language acquisition is largely implicit.[16] There also seems to be a strong association between implicit knowledge and automaticity as we will see below.

Considering the second view, there are virtually no scholars who would argue that SLA is largely the result of gaining explicit language knowledge, although a few think that SLA may begin with gaining explicit knowledge, particularly those that hold to the skill theory of second language acquisition (see below).[17] As VanPatten and Benati explain, "…explicit processes are relatively cumbersome and do not result in an implicit linguistic system that can be used with rapidity and ease during communication."[18] In other words, implicit knowledge can be accessed more quickly than explicit knowledge, and implicit knowledge is easier to use (see discussion below). We should also keep in mind that communication is not limited to spoken communication. It includes all forms of communication, including the reading of ancient texts.

The final position is that SLA is the result of gaining a combination of explicit and implicit knowledge. There are two major groups that hold to this position. The first group is comprised of those who hold to the skill theory perspective from general learning theory mentioned above. In this theory, students begin by learning explicit knowledge of the skill, and, with plenty of practice and exposure, knowledge of the skill becomes implicit.[19] The learner moves from declarative knowledge (explicit knowledge) to procedural knowledge (which becomes automatized, i.e. implicit knowledge). The second group theorizes that both explicit and implicit processes are at work in SLA. For example, Richard

---

[15] Krashen, *Principles and Practice*, 10–11. See also Lydia White, *Second Language Acquisition and Universal Grammar* (Cambridge: Cambridge University Press, 2003).

[16] See, e.g., Ellis, "At the Interface."

[17] VanPatten and Benati, *Key Terms*, 33.

[18] VanPatten and Benati, *Key Terms*, 33.

[19] See, e.g., DeKeyser, "Skill Acquisition Theory."

Schmidt acknowledges that learners must notice linguistic features in the language input they receive, which means that conscious awareness plays a role as learners attend to input.[20]

Interface

This leads us to a second issue: If both implicit and explicit knowledge play a role in language acquisition, how do they interact with each other? Once again, there are several possible positions on the issue.

The first position, advocated by Krashen, is the non-interface position. This position holds that implicit and explicit knowledge are entirely separate, involving different mental processes and storage. Moreover, "explicit knowledge does not convert into implicit knowledge," clearly in opposition to the skill acquisition theory mentioned above.[21]

On the other end of the spectrum is the strong interface position, held by Robert DeKeyser among others. This position is based on John R. Anderson's skill acquisition theory and posits that L2 knowledge begins as explicit/declarative knowledge and changes into implicit/procedural knowledge through practice.[22]

However, a sizeable group of experts hold to the middle position, that is, the weak-interface position. "The model allows for explicit knowledge to convert into implicit knowledge under certain stringent conditions (e.g., when a learner is developmentally ready to acquire implicit knowledge of a specific feature) and also for implicit L2 knowledge to convert into explicit L2 knowledge."[23] According to this position, explicit knowledge can function to facilitate L2 acquisition by helping learners notice forms, rules, and properties in the input that he or she might not notice otherwise.

---

[20] Schmidt, "Attention," 3–32.

[21] Krashen, *Principles and Practice*, 10–11, 83.

[22] See, e.g., Robert DeKeyser, "Beyond Focus on Form: Cognitive Perspectives on Learning and Practicing Second Language," in *Focus on Form in Classroom Second Language Acquisition*, ed. C. Doughty and J. Williams (Cambridge: Cambridge University Press, 1998), 42–63. For Anderson's skill acquisition theory, see John R. Anderson, "Acquisition of Cognitive Skill," *Psychological Review* 89 (1982): 369–406; and John R. Anderson, *The Architecture of Cognition* (Cambridge: Harvard University Press, 1983).

[23] Ellis, "Explicit Knowledge," 146.

Having covered the different types of language knowledge and some of the views regarding their relative importance, we now turn to the issue of automaticity.

Automaticity

As noted above, proficiency involves a combination of implicit knowledge, explicit knowledge, and automaticity. As an integral part of proficiency, automaticity is usually contrasted with controlled language processing, where a learner must stop and intentionally remember a rule or word before he or she can continue communicating.[24] Because automaticity is multi-faceted, it has been described in various ways.[25]

First, automaticity can be understood simply as fast processing.[26] Immediate, or nearly immediate, word recognition by a language student would be evidence of automaticity. However, automaticity is more than just faster processing. It is also a change in the way the learner carries out the processing, giving evidence of mental restructuring. This leads to a second, related aspect of automaticity, *ballistic processing.*[27] In a language context, ballistic processing means unstoppable or involuntary processing. In other words, a language student cannot help but comprehend the L2 word when language processes are automatized. This is one reason billboard advertising is so effective. Proficient readers cannot stop themselves from taking in the message.

Automaticity in language learning is also characterized by *load independent processing.*[28] In other words, language learning is automatic if the learner can continue language processing independent of the number of other processes (or distractions) going on at the same time. For example, a proficient language processor can drive her car and listen to her passenger at the same time. Relatedly, effortless processing is a

---

[24] Rod Ellis, "A Theory of Instructed Second Language Acquisition," in *Implicit and Explicit Learning of Languages*, ed. N.C. Ellis (London: Academic Press, 1994), 99.

[25] The following descriptions are a summary of a fuller discussion provided by Segalowitz, "Automaticity," 382–408.

[26] Segalowitz, "Automaticity," 385–87.

[27] Segalowitz, "Automaticity," 387–88.

[28] Segalowitz, "Automaticity," 388–90.

characteristic of automaticity.[29] For example, if a language learner is trying to complete a secondary task while performing a language task, the learner will not slow down on the secondary task if the language processes are automatic.

Automaticity in language learning is also understood as unconscious processing, again connecting automaticity with implicit language knowledge.[30] When language processing is automatic, the learner may or may not remember where his or her knowledge came from. When a language student can read and comprehend a text rapidly without needing to stop and recall a grammar rule, he or she has achieved automaticity. He or she just "knows" without having to go through a process of conscious recollection. This is another reason automaticity is seen as being closely connected with implicit, or unconscious, language knowledge.

Another characteristic of automatic language processing is that learners will shift to *instance processing*.[31] In other words, the learner will move from finding a solution by algorithm, or by a rule, to finding a solution by means of "a token or instance of the solution in stored memory" because enough instances or examples have been encountered and stored.[32] A familiar, analogous example would be learning multiplication tables. At first, the learner must use repeated addition or some sort of mnemonic device to arrive at the correct answer. However, after enough encounters, the learner can answer immediately because he or she has shifted to instance processing.

Finally, automaticity can be measured in brain activity.[33] Researchers have noted that as a learner becomes more skilled with greater automaticity, the region of the brain devoted to executing that skill actually becomes smaller because the activity requires less attention.[34]

---

[29] Segalowitz, "Automaticity," 390–91.

[30] Segalowitz, "Automaticity," 391–92.

[31] Segalowitz, "Automaticity," 393.

[32] Segalowitz, "Automaticity," 393.

[33] Segalowitz, "Automaticity," 393–94.

[34] See, e.g., Ira Fischler, "Attention and Language," in *The Attentive Brain*, ed. R. Parasuraman (Cambridge: MIT Press, 1998), 381–99; and Richard J. Haier et al., "Regional Glucose Metabolic Changes After Learning a Complex Visuospatial/Motor Task:

Conclusion

The three main elements of language proficiency are implicit knowledge, explicit knowledge, and automaticity. Most language researchers and practitioners agree that language knowledge is differentiated. Some language knowledge is implicit, or unconscious, intuitive, and procedural, while other knowledge is explicit, or conscious, formalized, and declarative. Very few, if any, would argue that explicit knowledge alone is sufficient for promoting language proficiency, but there are also only a few who would jettison explicit knowledge completely. In other words, SLA researchers do not agree on the role or the ideal proportion of explicit knowledge in language education, nor do they agree on whether the two forms of knowledge interface in language learning, and if they do, to what degree. However, these researchers do believe that implicit knowledge is the main source of language knowledge for those who are proficient in L2. Moreover, most would also agree that automaticity is an integral component of language proficiency, which is also closely connected with implicit language knowledge.

The Significance of Proficiency for Biblical and Ancient Languages

As shown above, proficiency involves implicit knowledge, explicit knowledge, and automaticity. Moreover, most language experts believe that implicit language knowledge should be the main goal of SLA, with the assistance of automaticity.[35] Explicit knowledge plays a role in promoting proficiency, but it is not the main goal. Because the primary goal of many ancient language classrooms is teaching and learning explicit language knowledge, it is important to address whether and how implicit knowledge and automaticity could benefit students of ancient languages. The discussion below highlights at least four benefits of developing

---

A Positron Emission Tomographic Study," *Brain Research* 570 (1992): 134–43.

[35] See, e.g., Rod Ellis, "Principles of Instructed Second Language Learning," in *Teaching English as a Second or Foreign Language*, 4th ed., ed. M. Celce-Murcia, D. M. Brinton & M. A. Snow (Boston: Heinle and Heinle, 2013), 31–45; and DeKeyser, "Skill Acquisition Theory."

implicit knowledge and automaticity in biblical and ancient language learners, followed by the benefits of developing explicit knowledge.

Benefits of Implicit Knowledge and Automaticity

First, an individual who has implicit knowledge of Hebrew or Greek and has developed automaticity in those languages will read and process the biblical text faster. Similarly, a proficient reader of Latin or Greek will read and process ancient texts faster. If the learner has internalized his or her knowledge of the language, he or she will not be slowed down by frequent interruptions to look up an unknown word or form. Moreover, he or she will be able to read without having to translate into L1, even internally, which also speeds up the task of reading. A faster reading rate will, in turn, increase the learner's exposure to the language, which will further facilitate language learning.

A second benefit of implicit language knowledge and automaticity is accuracy. A student with implicit knowledge of a language and greater automaticity will also be more accurate when processing that language.[36] Language processing can refer to any of the four basic language skills: reading, writing, speaking, or listening. Because automatic language processing is "immune to interference from other sources of information,"[37] language processing that has been automatized is not only faster but also more accurate than language processing that has not been automatized and must rely on explicit knowledge. A learner who has not automatized a particular verbal form, for example, will have to pause, try to remember the paradigm, and then may or may not correctly identify the verb in question. However, a learner who has automatized that same form will immediately recognize it and process it correctly without hesitation or confusion with other forms.

Third, implicit knowledge of the language and automaticity free up attentional resources for other types of processing. In some cases, this means freeing up attention to focus on learning new language forms and features. However, automaticity also frees up higher order processing skills necessary for interpretation, which is often one of the main goals

---

[36] Segalowitz, "Automaticity," 401.
[37] Segalowitz, "Automaticity," 401.

of learning a biblical or ancient language. In other words, as the lower-level processes such as phonology and syntax become automatized, the learner's attentional resources are freed up to focus on the higher-level processes, such as semantics and sociolinguistic levels of communication, also known as interpretation or exegesis.

Finally, there is a secondary benefit of increased automaticity and proficiency. Greater automaticity and proficiency increase a student's motivation for further learning. One of the more common obstacles faced by students is discouragement.[38] They think the task of reading an ancient language is impossible. However, when they can do it will ease, they are more interested in continuing. (Student motivation will be discussed in further detail with the discussion of learner differences in chapter 12.)

Explicit Knowledge

Recognizing the benefits of implicit knowledge and automaticity does not mean that we completely abandon explicit knowledge in the biblical and ancient language classrooms. First, as noted above, vocabulary knowledge is a form of explicit knowledge. Second, at least according to some language-learning models, explicit knowledge can play a role in language acquisition and in developing implicit knowledge and automaticity. Finally, as a necessary accommodation, ancient language instructors need to provide their students with at least some explicit knowledge of the ancient languages and the accompanying metalanguage needed to access the current scholarly resources and reference grammars. There may come a time, however, when some scholarly resources are also written with the fully proficient language student in mind.

---

[38] Frederick E. Greenspahn broadly addresses this obstacle for students of Biblical Hebrew in his article, "Why Hebrew Textbooks Are Different From Those For Other Languages," *SBL Forum*, n.p. [cited July 2005]. Online: http://sbl-site.org/Article.aspx?ArticleID=420. Moreover, a great deal of research has been done that addresses issues of student motivation in response to this obstacle of discouragement in language learning. See, e.g., the review of research in Kim Bower, "Explaining Motivation in Language Learning: A Framework for Evaluation and Research," *Language Learning Journal* 47.5 (2019): 558–74, and in Ellis, *Study of Second Language Acquisition*, 677–91.

Examples for Biblical and Ancient Language Classrooms

The next chapter will cover in greater detail different teaching approaches that promote the acquisition of implicit knowledge, explicit knowledge, and automaticity, complete with pedagogical examples. Therefore, this section will provide some hypothetical examples of language learners who have implicit knowledge, explicit knowledge, and automaticity in Hebrew, Greek, and Latin, offering a glimpse of the potential for promoting language proficiency in each.

Hebrew

Consider two individuals reading a passage from the Hebrew Bible in which the word order is unusual. Perhaps the object is fronted or there is a redundant subject pronoun. The first individual, Joseph, is proficient in Hebrew, possessing implicit knowledge of the language with some explicit knowledge and having developed automaticity in his language processing. When Joseph reads this passage, he reads at a steady pace without stopping to look up a word or check a point of syntax. Joseph immediately recognizes that the word order is marked because he feels it. He knows what typical word order should be, and he implicitly understands the significance of this construction. Moreover, because Joseph's lower level processes (phonology, morphology, syntax, etc.) are automatized, he still has attentional resources with which to analyze the impact that the unusual word order has on the interpretation of the passage.

By contrast, consider Hannah, who possesses a relatively large amount of explicit knowledge of Hebrew. However, her implicit knowledge and automaticity are only beginning to develop. When Hannah reads the same passage, her rate of reading is unsteady as she stops to parse verbs and occasionally look up a vocabulary item she does not know. After each interruption, she must go back over what she has read to remember what the earlier part of the passage said before moving forward again. It is possible that Hannah does not recognize the unusual word order at all, or she may not recognize it immediately. After all, a subject pronoun is necessary (i.e., not redundant) in her native language, English. Once she does recognize it, she may have to take some time to intentionally retrieve the information she has memorized about Hebrew syntax that would relate to this situation, or she may have to search a reference grammar to assist her. She can eventually reach an acceptable interpretation of the passage, but she probably finds the process tedious.

Greek and Latin

For Greek and Latin, the situation can be similar. Consider, for example, two different individuals reading a passage with a noun in the accusative case. Again, we start by considering a proficient reader, Priscilla, complete with implicit knowledge of the language, some explicit knowledge, and well-developed automaticity. When Priscilla reads this passage, she reads at a steady, reasonable pace. As she reads the sentence with the noun in question, she feels the nuance indicated by the accusative case chosen by the author. She may or may not have a label for the function of the noun case in this context, but she does not need one. She understands it implicitly. Additionally, as with Joseph, above, her lower level processes are sufficiently automatized so that she can tune into the significance of the choice of noun case as she continues to read the entire context of the passage and interpret it.

By contrast, consider Peter, who has memorized the significant explicit grammatical information of the language, but is only beginning to acquire implicit knowledge and automaticity. As Peter reads this passage, he may not notice that the noun is in the accusative, or he may incorrectly identify the case. It is also possible that he will stop reading and consult a paradigm (one in his memory or one in a book) to help him identify the case. Even if he does correctly identify the case, he may still need to stop and look up the word in a lexicon or reference grammar to be sure he has identified the correct meaning or function of the accusative in this context. In the reference grammar, he will likely be confronted with a long list of labels and functions for the accusative case, and he feels he must choose the right one to get the translation correct. Only then does he move on to interpretation. He can eventually get to the point of correctly interpreting the passage, but it takes time and effort.

While these examples are caricatures with some polarization, one can see the benefit of implicit knowledge and automaticity in reading and interpreting ancient texts.

Conclusion

Language proficiency—the ability to automatically recognize that "green, big, loud truck" is incorrect and correctly produce "big, loud, green truck" instead—includes a combination of implicit language knowledge, explicit language knowledge, and automaticity. Most SLA experts agree that implicit knowledge and automaticity contribute more to proficiency than explicit knowledge. With this in mind, the next chapter will introduce a few general approaches to language instruction and how these can aid in the acquisition of implicit knowledge, explicit knowledge, and automaticity in different ways.

For Further Reading

Ellis, Nick C. "At the Interface: Dynamic Interactions of Explicit and Implicit Language Knowledge." *Studies in Second Language Acquisition* 27 (2005): 305–52.

Ellis, Rod, Shawn Loewen, Catherine Elder, Rosemary Erlam, Jenefer Philp, & Hayo Reinders. *Implicit and Explicit Knowledge in Second Language Learning, Testing and Teaching.* Bristol, UK: Multilingual Matters, 2009.

Hulstijn, Jan H. *Language Proficiency in Native and Non-Native Speakers: Theory and Research.* Language Learning and Language Teaching 41. Philadelphia: John Benjamins, 2015.

Krashen, Stephen D. *Principles and Practice in Second Language Acquisition.* New York: Pergamon, 1982.

Rebuschat, Patrick, ed. *Implicit and Explicit Learning of Languages.* Amsterdam: John Benjamins, 2015.

Segalowitz, Norman. "Automaticity and Second Languages." Pages 382–408 in *The Handbook of Second Language Acquisition.* Edited by C. Doughty and M. Long. Malden, MA: Blackwell, 2003.

CHAPTER 3: GENERAL APPROACHES TO LANGUAGE INSTRUCTION: MEANING-FOCUSED INSTRUCTION, FORM-FOCUSED INSTRUCTION, AND PRACTICE

If you have ever spent time around a young child, you know the funny phrases that can come out of a little one. My parents still quote my eighteen-month-old self, swatting flies away from my highchair, saying, "Dumb birds!"

We often ask a child in amazement, "Where did you get that phrase?" We must marvel at the language abilities children have at such a young age. They never studied grammar. They never memorized a vocabulary list. Yet, remarkably, they can communicate very effectively. How do they do it? We may chalk it up to a young, supple mind whose neurons are ready and even eager to make synapses.

However, we also must wonder about the foreign diplomat who can easily switch between his L1 and L2, all the while preventing wars and smoothing ruffled political feathers. How does one achieve such a level of language proficiency as an adult, even in L2 (or L3 or L4)?

The Principle: Approaches to Language Instruction

The previous chapter covered the necessary components of language proficiency: implicit language knowledge, explicit language knowledge, and automaticity. Different types of language knowledge require different approaches to instruction. This chapter will discuss some of the general approaches to language teaching that will facilitate the acquisition of the three components of proficiency: *meaning-focused instruction*, *form-focused instruction*, and practice. Subsequent chapters will address various aspects of these approaches in greater detail.

Generally speaking, meaning-focused instruction lends itself to the acquisition of implicit knowledge, while form-focused instruction generally facilitates the learning of explicit knowledge.[1] However, these correlations are not always simple or neat. Regarding automaticity, it is generally believed that practice, or repetition, promotes the

---

[1] Ellis, *Instructed Second Language Acquisition*, 189.

development of this aspect of proficiency.[2] The following discussion addresses each of these in turn.

Meaning-Focused Instruction

As noted above, meaning-focused instruction is generally associated with the acquisition of implicit knowledge.[3] Meaning-focused instruction treats the L2 as a tool for communication rather than an object of study.[4] While some implicit knowledge can be learned directly through memorization—usually fixed expressions—most implicit knowledge is learned incidentally through *input* and *interaction*, which are the primary components of meaning-focused instruction.[5] In meaning-focused instruction, "the learner is engaged in communication where the primary effort involves the exchange of meaning and where there is no conscious effort to achieve grammatical correctness."[6] Acquisition of implicit knowledge, then, is a "by-product of comprehension."[7]

SLA experts speak of the learners performing L2 "tasks" in which the successful completion of the communicative task is more important than the grammatical accuracy used for the task.[8] This approach encourages semantic processing and is differentiated from form-focused instruction which encourages reflection on the formal features of the language. While meaning-focused instruction can make use of a variety of different teaching techniques, it seeks to provide the learner with two

---

[2] Ellis, "A Theory of Instructed Second Language Acquisition," 99.

[3] Some may refer to meaning-focused instruction as the communicative teaching method. However, there is no single "communicative method" of language teaching. Instead, there are several approaches that can be classified as communicative, such as the Natural Approach and immersion. See VanPatten, *From Input to Output*, 98.

[4] Raquel Criado, "Towards the Validation of a Scale for Measuring the Load of Form Focus and Meaning Focus of Textbook Activities in Foreign Language Teaching," *Revista Electrónica de Lingüística Aplicada (RAEL)* 1:15 (2016): 130.

[5] Ellis, "A Theory of Instructed Second Language Acquisition," 92

[6] Ellis, *Instructed Second Language Acquisition*, 187.

[7] VanPatten, *From Input to Output*, 26.

[8] See, e.g., Martin Bygate, ed., *Learning Language Through Task Repetition* (Philadelphia: John Benjamins, 2018); and Michael Long, *Second Language Acquisition and Task-Based Language Teaching* (New York: Wiley & Sons, 2015).

essential elements for language acquisition: input and interaction. These two important elements are covered in the following sections.

Input

Although it may seem obvious, it is worth stating that a learner must have access to authentic language samples, or input, to acquire the language. "Input is the language that a learner hears (or reads) that has some kind of communicative intent."[9] The learner's task, then, is to attempt to comprehend what is being communicated in the L2 input. Because of the essential nature of input, SLA experts have spent a great deal of time studying the role of input in language acquisition. As a result, there is general agreement regarding the type of input that is most conducive to developing language proficiency.

First, input must be meaning bearing. Input that best facilitates language proficiency does not consist of paradigms or explanation about the language, including *explicit corrective feedback*, which is given when a learner makes an error in production. Rather, the input that best facilitates language proficiency consists of actual statements made in the language that convey meaning. According to VanPatten, "...processing meaning in the input is a prerequisite for acquisition."[10] Second, the input must be comprehensible to the learner. If the input is too difficult to understand, the learner will not be able to process it or learn from it. Thus, meaning-focused instruction should be rich in meaning-bearing, comprehensible input. The next three chapters will cover various aspects of this important principle in greater detail.

Interaction

In addition to providing input, meaning-focused instruction also provides the learner with interaction, another essential for language acquisition.[11] Classroom communication results in language learning through

---

[9] VanPatten, *From Input to Output*, 25–26.

[10] VanPatten, *From Input to Output*, 90.

[11] For a summary of the Interaction Hypothesis, related research, and its significance for understanding language acquisition, see Ellis, *Study of Second Language Acquisition*, 252–60.

the process of interaction in the target language. According to Merrill Swain, "… negotiating meaning—coming to a communicative consensus—is a necessary first step to grammatical acquisition."[12] Interaction is the place in which learning takes place and is therefore a source of acquisition.[13] Language is by nature a social endeavor. One must be interacting with another person to communicate in a language, even if the interaction is mediated through writing. As learners communicate, interact, and receive feedback, they move forward in the process of language acquisition. Therefore, meaning-focused instruction incorporates interaction as an essential classroom component.

Interaction in the context of meaning-focused instruction would not include rote memorization of dialogues, a feature prominent in the audio-lingual method of language teaching.[14] For acquisition to take place, the interaction must be genuine communication, which includes some unpredictability. Most conversations can and should have some measure of regularity, but when an entire dialogue is memorized, the learners are not motivated to attend to meaning and are unlikely to acquire implicit knowledge of L2. However, when one person knows something that the other does not, both interlocutors have a vested interest in getting the message across and will, therefore, attend to meaning. This, then, is what promotes acquisition and ultimately proficiency.

In sum, meaning-focused instruction encourages learners to receive L2 input and interact in L2 while the focus is on the exchange of meaning rather than on grammatical accuracy. The outcomes include student gains in the acquisition of implicit language knowledge. Therefore, as many SLA experts say, the more input and interaction, the better.[15]

---

[12] Merrill Swain, "Communicative Competence: Some Roles of Comprehensible Input and Comprehensible Output in Its Development," in *Input in Second Language Acquisition*, ed. S. M. Gass & C. G. Madden (Rowley, MA: Newbury House, 1985), 248.

[13] Rod Ellis, *Language Teaching, Research, and Pedagogy* (Malden, MA: Wiley-Blackwell, 2012), 266.

[14] For a fuller description of the Audiolingual Method, see Hadly, *Teaching Language in Context*, 111.

[15] VanPatten, *From Input to Output*, 102–8.

Form-Focused Instruction

Form-focused instruction can be differentiated from meaning-focused instruction in that the goal of the instruction is the development of grammatical accuracy rather than meaningful communication, although the distinction is not always clear-cut.[16] In form-focused instruction, "the learner is engaged in activities that have been specially designed to teach specific grammatical features."[17] While form-focused instruction is usually associated with the learning of explicit language knowledge, it can also facilitate the acquisition of implicit knowledge in some cases. In fact, some studies suggest that a learner's acquisition of implicit knowledge can be faster and more accurate when form-focused instruction is added to meaning-focused instruction, especially if the form-focused instruction is meaning-based and not rote memorization of rules or paradigms.[18]

Within the broader framework of form-focused instruction, SLA experts recognize a variety of different approaches, although there is no consensus regarding how to organize and label these different approaches within the framework. Some differentiate between focus-on-form and focus-on-forms,[19] while others speak of implicit versus explicit instruction, not to be confused with implicit and explicit language knowledge.[20]

---

[16] Criado, "Towards the Validation of a Scale," 131.

[17] Ellis, *Instructed Second Language Acquisition*, 187.

[18] VanPatten, *From Input to Output*, 58.

[19] See, for example, Michael Long, "Focus on Form: A Design Feature in Language Teaching Methodology," in *Foreign Language Research in Cross-cultural Perspectives*, ed. K. de Bot, R.B. Ginsberb, & C. Kramsch (Amsterdam: John Benjamins, 1991), 39–52, and Catherine Doughty & Jessica Williams, eds., *Focus on Form in Classroom Second Language Acquisition* (Cambridge: Cambridge University, 1998).

[20] See, e.g., the definition in Ellis, *Study of Second Language Acquisition*, 878–89; see also Rick de Graaff and Alex Housen, "Investigating the Effects and Effectiveness of L2 Instruction," in *The Handbook of Language Teaching*, ed. M. Long and C. Doughty (Oxford: Blackwell, 2009), 726–55; Robert DeKeyser, "Implicit and Explicit Learning," in *The Handbook of Second Language Acquisition*, ed. C. Doughty and M. Long (Malden, MA: Blackwell, 2003), 313–48; and Michael Long, *Second Language Acquisition and Task-Based Language Teaching* (West Sussex, England: Wiley & Sons, 2015).The following discussion of form-focused instruction will follow the slightly more nuanced

Ellis divides form-focused instruction into reactive and proactive options for classroom activities. *Reactive form-focused instruction* involves corrective feedback from an instructor to a learner on his or her performance, especially when a mistake is made. Reactive form-focused instruction can include such strategies as direct explanation, *recasts* (restating the learner's incorrect utterance in a way that corrects the mistake), and requests for clarification. *Proactive form-focused instruction*, covered in the next section, can be further divided into *consciousness-raising* options and *language-processing* options for instruction.

Consciousness-Raising Options

Consciousness-raising is "an attempt to focus the learner's attention on the formal properties of the language" or, more specifically, "attempts to help learners understand a grammatical structure and learn it as explicit knowledge."[21] Consciousness-raising options for classroom instruction can also be referred to as *explicit grammar instruction* and can be direct or indirect. When an instructor uses *direct consciousness-raising tasks*, he or she provides the learner with an explanation of L2 features, often in the form of a short lecture that describes both the form and function of the target structure. The instructor may also point the learner to other educational materials that provide direct explicit grammar instruction, such as textbooks and paradigms. With *indirect consciousness-raising tasks*, the learners are invited to generate their own descriptions of the L2 feature, given examples of L2 input. Consciousness-raising tasks primarily facilitate the learning of explicit language knowledge.

Language-Processing Options

Form-focused instruction that involves language processing tasks reinforces the acquisition of specific L2 features through language use. This type of processing can facilitate the acquisition of implicit language knowledge, although grammatical accuracy is the focus, unlike the

---

organization put forth by Ellis. See Ellis, *Language Teaching, Research, & Pedagogy*, 276–78.

[21] Ellis, *The Study of SLA*, 958.

meaning-focused instruction discussed above. Language processing tasks can employ the learner's receptive skills through comprehension tasks (such as answering comprehension questions after listening to or reading L2 input) or their production skills through output-based tasks (such as describing an event using recently-acquired verbal forms). (Chapters 4, 5, and 6 will cover input and input-based tasks in greater detail; chapter 7 will cover output and output-based tasks.)

In conclusion, form-focused instruction encourages the learner to attend to specific grammatical features of the language and usually facilitates the learning of explicit language knowledge, although some types of form-focused instruction can also aid in the acquisition of implicit language knowledge. A typical lesson may contain a mixture of these different types of form-focused activities, along with some tasks that are meaning-focused.

Developing Automaticity: Practice

Having examined the types of instruction that facilitate the acquisition of implicit knowledge and explicit knowledge, we now turn to a brief discussion of the types of instruction that will promote automaticity in learners: practice or repetition. It is generally believed that massive practice, in the range of thousands of hours, promotes the development of automaticity. However, "properly organized practice can lead to great improvements in second language skill" in a shorter amount of time.[22] Moreover, implicit and explicit knowledge seem to require different approaches for developing automaticity.

For explicit L2 knowledge, *controlled grammar practice* activities can help the learner develop automaticity in retrieving and using this knowledge.[23] Controlled practice involves consciously rehearsing structures until they are internalized.[24] However, controlled practice does not seem to help automatize implicit knowledge. Instead, evidence shows that learners achieve control or automaticity of implicit knowledge

---

[22] Segalowitz, "Automaticity," 402.

[23] Michael Sharwood Smith, "Consciousness-Raising and the Second Language Learner," *Applied Linguistics* 2 (1981): 161.

[24] Ellis, *Instructed Second Language Acquisition*, 192.

through repetition in the context of meaning-focused instruction (described above) where they use their implicit L2 knowledge communicating in tasks that require them to focus on meaning.[25]

Ellis argues that meaning-focused instruction "provides the conditions the learner needs to activate those procedures that are responsible for both automatizing knowledge and for compensating for the lack of it."[26] There are at least two stages worthy of note in this developmental process, which takes place during free practice of L2. First, learners are confronted with a mistake in their comprehension and/or production during communication, often a communication breakdown. Second, the learner is given the opportunity to try again in the same communicative context. This, then, corrects and reinforces implicit L2 knowledge, and the learner develops automaticity as a result. Some experts recommend a balance of targeted repetition with free practice in a communicative setting as in meaning-focused instruction to promote automaticity.[27]

The development of automaticity, then, is associated with practice. However, the type of practice will determine what type of language knowledge is automatized. Controlled grammar practice is more likely to automatize explicit language knowledge, while practice that has meaning in focus is more likely to automatize implicit language knowledge.

Conclusion

The three main options for L2 instruction include meaning-focused instruction, form-focused instruction, and practice. These three approaches can lead to the acquisition of implicit knowledge, explicit knowledge, and automaticity, the foundational elements of language proficiency.

---

[25] Ellis, "A Theory of Instructed Second Language Acquisition," 99.

[26] Ellis, *Instructed Second Language Acquisition*, 192.

[27] Ellis, "A Theory of Instructed Second Language Acquisition," 99–100.

Significance for Biblical and Ancient Languages

Having covered some of the general approaches to classroom L2 instruction, the following discussion will address why these are important for consideration in the biblical and ancient language classroom.

Meaning-Focused Instruction

As discussed above, meaning-focused instruction must include input and interaction. While the importance of input for learning any language is rather self-evident, the instructor of a so-called dead language may question the value of interaction in the ancient language classroom. After all, his or her students will not have the opportunity to interact with anyone in the L2 outside the classroom. However, there are at least two reasons to consider incorporating meaning-focused instruction for ancient languages: meaning-focused instruction promotes implicit knowledge and reading is a form of interaction.

The first reason for incorporating meaning-focused instruction was discussed in the previous chapter: most SLA experts agree that implicit knowledge, which is usually acquired incidentally, is an important, if not essential, component of language proficiency. As Ellis puts it, "Ultimately, success in L2 learning depends on implicit knowledge."[28] After many years of refinement and empirical research, most SLA experts also agree that meaning-focused instruction is the primary classroom approach for facilitating the acquisition of implicit knowledge.[29] There are at least three good explanations for why this meaning-focused instruction works.

First, meaning-focused instruction provides L2 input for the learners to process as they develop their implicit, or unconscious, knowledge of L2. More specifically, meaning-focused instruction gives learners access to comprehensible input, which is essential for acquisition (see chapter 4.) As learners interact with the instructor and with each other, the *negotiation of meaning* that takes place during the course of communication—including repeating, requests for clarification, restating,

---

[28] Ellis, "A Theory of Instructed Second Language Acquisition," 98.

[29] Ellis, *Instructed Second Language Acquisition*, 190–91.

and circumlocution—ensures that the learner comprehends the input.[30] Second, meaning-focused instruction creates opportunities for the learner to produce output, which also promotes acquisition (see chapter 7.) Finally, according to sociocultural theory, interaction is the place in which acquisition takes place. According to this theory, interaction is acquisition-as-participation.[31] (Sociocultural theory will be addressed in greater detail in chapter 13.)

There is a second reason meaning-focused instruction should be considered for ancient language classrooms: reading is an interactive form of communication, albeit a much slower and more carefully thought-out form of interaction than spoken interaction. As learners read texts, they are receiving from and reacting to the ancient author in a communicative context. Because reading ancient texts is a form of communication, and because language students need meaning-focused instruction to learn how to communicate, meaning-focused instruction is important for ancient language learning.

The interactive nature of reading is worth considering from a couple angles. On one hand, meaning-focused instruction in a classroom can include written interaction, providing practice for reading ancient texts in a meaningful, communicative context. For example, students could exchange letters or brief messages with each other or with the instructor. On the other hand, the transferability of communicative interaction should also be considered. In other words, the gains that students make during spoken interaction will transfer to gains in the comprehension of written interaction. Moreover, spoken or written interaction in the classroom will give the learners opportunities to check—in real time—whether they are comprehending the message, something ancient authors can no longer do for them, and this immediate feedback can also speed up the process of acquisition.

---

[30] See study by Lester Loschky, "Comprehensible Input and Second Language Acquisition," *Studies in Second Language Acquisition* 16.3 (1994): 303–23.

[31] See Anna Sfard, "On Two Metaphors for Learning and the Dangers of Choosing Just One," *Educational Researcher* 27.2 (1998): 4–13; and Josep Artigal, "Some Considerations on Why a New Language is Acquired by Being Used," *International Journal of Applied Linguistics* 2 (1992): 221–40.

Form-Focused Instruction

As with meaning-focused instruction, form-focused instruction can also have value for biblical and ancient language classrooms because it facilitates the learning of explicit language knowledge and, in some cases, implicit language knowledge. Below are two points for consideration.

First, although meaning-focused instruction facilitates the acquisition of implicit knowledge, studies have shown that form-focused instruction can facilitate and help speed up that process.[32] Therefore, a combination of meaning-focused instruction and form-focused instruction can be very beneficial—in any classroom.

Second, there is a wide variety of form-focused teaching approaches from which biblical and ancient language instructors can choose. Traditional language instruction, especially for biblical and ancient languages, is usually limited to direct consciousness-raising activities (explicit grammar information delivered as explanations), but other form-focused options are available to promote and facilitate language proficiency. One such option is the use of indirect consciousness-raising tasks. Moreover, within the language-processing options, instructors can create activities that encourage the learners to interact with the target structure in meaning-based tasks. These types of activities can also be interactive, and they may be considered a hybrid of meaning-focused and form-focused instruction. Language-processing tasks can encourage comprehension of input or production of output or both.

Developing Automaticity: Controlled Practice and Meaning-Focused Instruction

Finally, because automaticity is also an integral part of language proficiency, biblical and ancient language instructors should consider instructional approaches that facilitate automatic processing of language data. As discussed above, instructors can encourage automatic processing of explicit language knowledge through controlled grammar practice using

---

[32] Ellis, *Language Teaching, Research, & Pedagogy*, 279. For a thorough summary of research on form-focused instruction, see Ellis, *Language Teaching, Research, & Pedagogy*, 278–305.

more traditional activities, such as manipulating verbal forms (e.g., having students change verb endings to agree with a given subject). However, one cannot assume that this kind of practice will result in automaticity of implicit knowledge. As VanPatten points out, "[simple] repetition develops … the ability to perform a particular task quickly. If the task varies, the ability slows down or disappears."[33] Therefore, for implicit language knowledge, meaning-focused instruction is, again, the best approach. According to Ellis, learners need to participate in language use under "real operating conditions" to automatize implicit knowledge.[34] Several studies show that having the opportunity to correct one's errors in the context of meaningful communication increases accuracy and thus automaticity.[35] This, then, adds yet one more rationale for using meaning-focused instruction in the L2 classroom.

Having described the various types of instruction that promote L2 proficiency and discussed why they should be considered for ancient language instruction, we now turn to a few examples.

Examples for Biblical and Ancient Language Classrooms

Below are a few suggestions for how to implement meaning-focused instruction, form-focused instruction, and automaticity development in Hebrew, Greek, and Latin classrooms.

Meaning-Focused Instruction

One of the best ways to bring meaning-focused instruction into the classroom is through communicative tasks such as questions and discussion prompts. Good questions can foster discussion in L2 that will provide both input and interaction. These questions can promote

---

[33] VanPatten, *From Input to Output*, 83. VanPatten goes so far as to say, "You can't know what you know implicitly in an L2 or perform in an advanced manner if all you did was get rules and practice them" (*From Input to Output*, 86).

[34] Ellis, "A Theory of Instructed Second Language Acquisition," 99.

[35] See, for example, Keith Johnson, "Mistake Correction." *English Language Teaching Journal* 42 (1988):89–96; and Patsy M. Lightbown, "Getting Quality Input in the Second/Foreign Language Classroom," in *Text and Context: Cross-Disciplinary Perspectives on Language Study*, ed. C. Kramsch & S. McConnell-Ginet (Lexington, MA: Heath & Co., 1992), 187–97.

teacher-to-student discussion or student-to-student discussion. Some questions are more objective with only one correct or expected answer, for example, "What is your name?" or "What do you have in your hand?" These can be good for earlier stages of acquisition as students are learning basic structures and vocabulary. However, to maximize input and interaction in the classroom, open-ended, affective questions are often better. Such questions elicit personal responses that are not always anticipated, and they allow for further discussion or follow-up questions. Affective questions might include such items as "What did you do over the weekend?" or "Which presidential candidate do you prefer?" with follow up questions like "With whom did you go to the beach?" or "Why?" Below are a few sample questions and discussion prompts for Hebrew, Greek, and Latin.

Objective Questions/Prompts (Hebrew, Greek, and Latin)

Hebrew: "How are you?"
　　　"I am well."
　　　"I am not well."
　　　הֲשָׁלוֹם לְךָ / לָךְ[36]
　　　יֵשׁ לִי שָׁלוֹם
　　　אֵין לִי שָׁלוֹם

This is a nice way to begin each class session. While this is technically an open-ended question, the responses are usually limited and predictable.

　　　Variation/Expansion: Consider making this a group activity with extra practice the first time it is introduced. The instructor can also provide other options for answers, such as עָיֵף אָנֹכִי "I am tired."[37]

Greek: "What is your name?"　　　"My name is…"
　　　τί ὄνομά σοι;　　　　　　ὄνομά μοι[38]

---

[36] This is the biblical counterpart to the modern Hebrew expression מַה-שְׁלוֹמְךָ or מַה-שְׁלוֹמֵךְ. See 2 Kings 4:26.
[37] Gen 25:30.
[38] Mark 5:9.

This is a good activity for the first week of class as students get to know each other and start learning the language. The questions and answers are relatively fixed and predictable, allowing the students to get used to speaking in L2.

Variation/Expansion: "What is his/her name?"
τί ὄνομα αὐτῷ/αὐτῇ;[39]

Latin: "What do you have?" "I have…"
Quid habes? Habeo…[40]

As an objective activity, this can be a great way to practice vocabulary. However, as the learners focus on naming their items, they are incidentally learning and practicing the grammar associated with the activity, thereby developing implicit knowledge and automaticity. Hand out various props that correspond to the vocabulary being learned. Then go around the room asking students what they have. Better yet, put the students in groups and have them ask each other.

Variation/Expansion: This could be transformed into a more affective exercise by having students hide their object, turning it into a guessing game with the student giving clues in L2 to help the others identify the hidden object or find where it is hidden.

Affective Questions/Prompts (Hebrew, Greek, and Latin)

Hebrew: "Please recount to me all the great things that the LORD has done."

סַפְּרָה־נָּא לִי אֵת כָּל־הַגְּדֹלוֹת אֲשֶׁר־עָשָׂה יהוה[41]
סַפְּרִי־נָא לִי אֵת כָּל־הַגְּדֹלוֹת אֲשֶׁר־עָשָׂה יהוה

This open-ended invitation can start an uplifting discussion of God's work in each student's life and can lead to follow-up questions.

---

[39] LXX Exod 3:13.
[40] Vulgate 1 Sam 21:3–4.
[41] Cf. 2 Kings 8:4.

Variation/Expansion: Ask another student to summarize and/or re-state the answer of the first student, perhaps in the form of a brief prayer of thanks. This serves as a comprehension check and as a reinforcement of the grammar and vocabulary introduced by the first student's answer.

Greek: "What did you do [yesterday, over the weekend]?"
τί ἐποίησας;[42]

People often like to talk about themselves. A discussion of previous activities or future plans are relatively non-threatening and require fewer attentional resources than would, say, a debate about theology or politics. This approach puts the student more at ease and allows him or her more attentional resources with which to focus on communicating in L2.[43] This type of question also lends itself to follow-up questions, such as "With whom?" or "Why?"

Variation: "What will you do [tomorrow, next week]?"
τί ποιήσεις;[44]

Latin: "What do you want?"
Quid quaeritis?[45]

As with the Greek example above, this question gives the students an opportunity to talk about themselves, which can relieve some of the added stress that comes with interaction in L2. Depending on the context, this question could elicit only a one-word answer, as in "[I want] cake." However, in a more complex context, such as a discussion of preferred vacation destinations or activities, a discussion of preferences could lead to interaction that is more involved.

Variation/Expansion: To give it a more culturally and geographically authentic feel, make this a role-playing game in which the

---

[42] John 18:35.
[43] For a discussion of lowering the affective filter, see chapter 12.
[44] LXX Jer 4:30.
[45] Vulgate John 1:38.

students pretend to live in the ancient world and discuss their favorite destinations, foods, etc.

Form-Focused Instruction

Most traditional biblical and ancient language instruction includes form-focused instruction in the form of direct consciousness-raising activities, or explicit grammar instruction. Therefore, the following examples will demonstrate a few of the other options for form-focused instruction.

Indirect Consciousness-Raising (Hebrew)

In indirect consciousness-raising activities, the instructor provides the learners with several examples of the targeted L2 feature and asks them to discover, and usually articulate, the rule(s) associated with this feature. For this activity, the target structure is the masculine plural construct, and the assumption is that the learners have not encountered it before. The instructor shows the class a picture representing the masculine plural absolute of a familiar noun (e.g., בָּנִים, "sons") saying the noun and perhaps writing the word on the board. Immediately after, the instructor shows a picture that represents the same noun in construct (e.g., בְּנֵי יַעֲקֹב "sons of Jacob") pointing to the "sons" in the picture, and again optionally providing the printed words. The instructor may repeat this process with a few more familiar nouns until he or she feels the students grasp the concept. At this point, the instructor may ask individual students to describe what the rule is or put them in groups to discuss what the rule is.

Variation/Expansion: Instead of presenting the new structure verbally, present the input in written form with enough context and/or pictures to aid in comprehension. Give the students time to examine the input, perhaps in groups, and explain the rule.

Language-Processing: Input (Greek)

In this activity, the learners are encouraged to process the target structure (aorist active indicative) through input practice. The students must choose the correct Greek word for each photo, demonstrating comprehension of the form and ability to differentiate this form from other forms in the paradigm. Most of the distractors would be different forms of the same verb, but an occasional vocabulary-based distractor can also be included with the grammar-based distractors. Adding vocabulary-based distractors would make the activity meaning based, meaning the learner must know what the word means to successfully complete the activity. Below is an example for the verb λαμβάνω.

© *Jennifer E. Noonan, used by permission*

a. ἐλάβομεν
b. ἔλαβον
c. ἔλαβε(ν)
d. ἐξέβαλες

Language-Processing: Output (Latin)

In output-based language-processing activities, the learners are encouraged to process the target structure through output practice. Because output tasks require more attentional resources than input tasks, output activities should be used to reinforce L2 features that the learner has encountered previously. Assuming that they have been introduced to noun and adjective inflection previously, learners then practice adjective agreement through the description of various items. The instructor puts a list of relevant and familiar adjectives on the board (*bonus*, *antiquus*, *clarus*, *magnus*, *novus*, etc.) and provides each pair of learners with an item or a picture. These items and pictures should also represent vocabulary that the learners already know, so they only need to focus on one aspect of language learning at a time. The learners then take turns describing their item using the terms on the board, inflecting the adjectives as appropriate for the gender of their item. After two to three minutes, the groups trade items and start again with the new item.

Variation/Expansion: Include plural items for description and/or include nouns in cases other than nominative.

Developing Automaticity: Controlled Practice and Meaning-Focused Instruction

Developing automaticity can take a couple routes, but the underlying principle is practice, or repetition. As discussed above, meaning-focused instruction is the best route to automaticity for implicit knowledge. For explicit knowledge, controlled practice will promote automaticity. Because examples of meaning-focused instruction were provided above, this section will give a brief example of controlled practice that can be applied to all three languages.

Controlled Practice (Hebrew, Greek, and Latin)

Controlled practice is more common in traditional language classrooms and would involve repetition of explicit grammar knowledge. An example of this might be instructing learners to memorize a verbal paradigm (such as Qal perfect for Hebrew or imperfect active indicative for Greek or Latin). Memorization could be facilitated through a mnemonic device or perhaps through a song.[46] Following memorization drills, the instructor gives the learners a fill-in-the-blank activity in which the learner

---

[46] Grammar-memorization songs can be found online, and some grammars include them as supplemental materials. See, e.g., the CD set that accompanies Bonnie Pedrotti Kittel, Victoria Hoffer, and Rebecca Abts Wright, *Biblical Hebrew: Text and Workbook*, 2nd ed., fully revised by Victoria Hoffer (New Haven: Yale, 2005).

must add endings to the verb base to complete the paradigm or complete a simple sentence.

Conclusion

This chapter introduced several broad approaches to language instruction, each targeted at promoting a different aspect of language proficiency. The chapter began with meaning-focused instruction, which prioritizes exchange of meaning over grammatical accuracy in communicative contexts. Input and interaction are essential to this type of instruction with learners completing communicative tasks. Meaning-focused instruction promotes the acquisition of implicit language knowledge and automaticity.

In contrast with meaning-focused instruction, form-focused instruction prioritizes grammatical accuracy over exchange of meaning and can encompass a variety of different classroom activities. For example, reactive form-focused instruction uses corrective feedback that an instructor provides to the learner to help him or her improve grammatical accuracy in language processing. Proactive form-focused instruction includes direct or indirect consciousness-raising tasks and language-processing tasks that may focus on input or output. Unlike meaning-focused instruction, form-focused instruction generally promotes the learning of explicit language knowledge, but some types of form-focused instruction can also promote the acquisition of implicit language knowledge, especially those that involve meaning-based tasks and interaction.

Finally, practice or repetition generally promotes the development of automaticity in language processing. Controlled practice is the best way to automatize explicit language knowledge, while meaning-focused instruction leads to automatic processing of implicit knowledge.

Because developing proficiency involves the acquisition of implicit knowledge, explicit knowledge, and automaticity, an ideal program of L2 study would include a combination of all the approaches discussed in this chapter, with meaning-focused instruction playing the lead. Foreign diplomats and interpreters of ancient texts all stand to benefit from such a rich approach to instruction.

For Further Reading

Bygate, Martin, ed. *Learning Language Through Task Repetition.* Philadelphia: John Benjamins, 2018.

DeKeyser, Robert. "Implicit and Explicit Learning." Pages 313–48 in *The Handbook of Second Language Acquisition.* Ed. C. Doughty and M. Long. Malden, MA: Blackwell, 2003.

Doughty, Catherine, and Jessica Williams, eds. *Focus on Form in Classroom Second Language Acquisition.* Cambridge: Cambridge University Press, 1998.

Ellis, Nick C., ed. *Implicit and Explicit Learning of Languages.* London: Academic Press, 1994.

Ellis, Rod. *Language Teaching, Research, & Pedagogy.* Malden, MA: Wiley-Blackwell, 2012.

Gass, Susan M. *Input and Interaction and the Second Language Learner.* Mahwah, NJ: Erlbaum, 1997.

Long, Michael H. *Second Language Acquisition and Task-based Language Teaching.* West Sussex, England: John Wiley & Sons, 2015.

CHAPTER 4: COMPREHENSIBLE INPUT

Imagine that you are listening to a radio broadcast or a podcast in a language completely unknown to you. You receive a flood of authentic language data, input that experts say is essential for acquisition. The problem is you do not understand a word of it. Without any kind of simplification, visual context, or the ability to ask for clarification from the speaker, the input is entirely incomprehensible, and language acquisition is virtually impossible.

Consider another scenario: You visit a foreign country where the only language spoken is one that you have never encountered before. However, in this context, you find a kind and patient guide who speaks the language. Your guide points to a glass of water and says the word for it. You get it. Suddenly, with the help of simplification, context, and a willing guide, the input is comprehensible. You have an entry point into the language, and acquisition is now possible.

The Principle: Comprehensible Input

The two main constructs in SLA research are input and *output*.[1] Input, which was introduced in the previous chapter, is language data that a learner receives through listening or reading. Output, on the other hand, is language that a learner produces. (Output will be addressed in greater detail in chapter 7). While there is some debate regarding the role and importance of output in language acquisition, the role of input is central and "indispensable for acquisition."[2] However, as the scenarios above illustrate, not all forms of input will result in acquisition.

Comprehensible Input and the Input Hypothesis

For input to facilitate acquisition, it must be comprehensible. As its name suggests, comprehensible input is "input that can be understood

---

[1] VanPatten and Benati, *Key Terms*, 36.

[2] VanPatten and Benati, *Key Terms*, 39. See also Susan M. Gass, *Input and Interaction and the Second Language Learner* (Mahwah, NJ: Erlbaum, 1997), 1; and VanPatten, *From Input to Output*, 28.

by a learner."[3] Krashen popularized the term in the 1980s and put forth the Input Hypothesis (also called the comprehension hypothesis),[4] setting a course for SLA research and practice that continues to affirm his hypothesis.[5] Using Krashen's abbreviations, a learner's acquired competence is designated i. According to the Input Hypothesis, input that is ideal for acquisition is $i + 1$, or input that is only one degree more difficult than the learner's current level of competence. As noted above, input that is too difficult will not facilitate acquisition. On the other hand, input that does not contain any new features may not promote acquisition as there is nothing new to learn.

There are at least two pedagogical implications of the Input Hypothesis. First, comprehension precedes production, meaning that learners should be allowed a silent pre-production period in which they build up competence through comprehension before trying to produce output.[6] Second, the learner must be focused on the meaning of the message, not its form, for acquisition to occur.[7] For this reason, the input must also be meaning bearing.[8] In other words, the input must convey a message. This would exclude paradigms and other types of language input that do not require the learner to understand the meaning encoded in the input.

Further, Krashen and Tracy D. Terrell distinguish between finely tuned input and roughly tuned input.[9] Finely tuned input is aimed at the specific level of $i + 1$, providing the learner with many examples of the next linguistic feature to be acquired. By contrast, roughly tuned input

---

[3] Ellis, *Study of Second Language Acquisition*, 957.

[4] See Krashen, *Principles and Practice*; Stephen D. Krashen and Tracy D. Terrell, *The Natural Approach: Language Acquisition in the Classroom* (Hayward, CA: Alemany Press,1983); Krashen, *Input Hypothesis*; and Stephen D. Krashen, "The Comprehension Hypothesis Extended," in *Input Matters in SLA*, ed. T. Piske & M. Young-Scholten (Bristol, England: Multilingual Matters, 2009), 81–94.

[5] For a summary of research on the Input Hypothesis, see Ellis, *Study of Second Language Acquisition*, 246–52; see also James F. Lee's state-of-the-field article "Comprehensible Input," in *The TESOL Encyclopedia of English Language Teaching*, ed. John I. Liontas (New York: Wiley & Sons, 2018).

[6] Krashen and Terrell, *The Natural Approach*, 78.

[7] Krashen, *Principles and Practice*, 21.

[8] James F. Lee and Bill VanPatten, *Making Communicative Language Teaching Happen*, 2nd ed (Boston: McGraw-Hill, 2003), 27.

[9] Krashen and Terrell, *The Natural Approach*, 33–5.

is language input that is just trying to make the message understood. It may contain a mix of previously acquired features and $i + 1$, $i + 2$, $i + 3$ (i.e., input with more advanced features). However, because roughly tuned input is not as comprehensible, instructors need to find ways to make it more comprehensible.

Making Input Comprehensible

Because comprehensible input is "the primary source of data in L2 acquisition,"[10] it is important to make the input comprehensible to the learner, thereby increasing the likelihood of acquisition. SLA researchers discuss several approaches to achieving this goal, including *simplification/modification of input*, providing *contextual clues*, and negotiation of meaning.[11]

Simplification and/or modification is one approach to making input comprehensible. Parents and others who care for children instinctively simplify (or modify) their speech to accommodate the developing linguistic skills of their young audience. This is sometimes called "motherese" or "caretaker speech." In a similar way, people adjust their speech when addressing foreigners ("foreigner talk"), and teachers can do the same in their classrooms both in written and spoken communication ("teacher talk").[12] These modifications include such strategies as slowing down, enunciating, adjusting vocabulary usage, adjusting syntax with shorter sentences and more repetition, and modifying discourse structure (for example, offering several options to choose from when asking a question).[13]

In addition to simplification, instructors can make input comprehensible through contextual clues. Visual aids, such as objects, models, and

---

[10] Ellis, *Instructed Second Language Acquisition*, 190.

[11] Krashen and Terrell, *The Natural Approach*, 32; Lee and VanPatten, *Communicative Language Teaching*, 29–32.

[12] Lee, "Comprehensible Input," 5.

[13] See the thorough treatment by Evelyn Hatch, "Simplified Input and Second Language Acquisition," in *Pidginization and Creolization as Language Acquisition*, ed. R.W. Andersen (Cambridge, MA: Newbury House, 1983), 64–86; see also the analysis of research on teacher talk by Craig Chaudron, *Second Language Classrooms: Research on Teaching and Learning* (Cambridge: Cambridge University Press, 1988), 50–89.

photos, are helpful for providing context and are commonly used to make communication comprehensible for both spoken and written input. Other contextual clues might include gesturing or miming actions. In the example at the beginning of the chapter, the guide pointed to water while saying the word for it to contextualize and aid in the comprehension of an unknown word.

Another approach to making input comprehensible is the negotiation of meaning that occurs in the context of communication. When communication breaks down because of misunderstanding or lack of understanding, the interlocutors must negotiate to reestablish comprehension. Such negotiation of meaning might include clarification requests, comprehension checks, and statements of confirmation, such as, "Did you mean…?" and "No, I meant…" According to Lester Loschky, "…all other things being equal, learners who are allowed to negotiate interaction while listening to the target language have a higher probability of comprehending what they hear—a point with important classroom implications."[14]

Conclusion

Comprehensible, meaning-bearing input is language data in the L2 that conveys a message and is understood by the learner. This type of input is important, if not essential, for language acquisition. Instructors have at their disposal several approaches for making language input comprehensible to the learner, including simplification/modification of the input, contextual clues, and giving learners the opportunity to negotiate meaning in the context of interaction and communication.

The Significance of Comprehensible Input for Biblical and Ancient Languages

Because comprehensible input is considered essential for language acquisition in modern language classrooms, instructors of biblical and ancient languages should give it careful consideration also. Two aspects of this issue are worthy of note. First, the essential nature of

---

[14] Loschky, "Comprehensible Input," 318.

comprehensible input for language acquisition is supported by empirical research conducted under controlled conditions.[15] Moreover, there is strong agreement among SLA experts regarding the central role that comprehensible input plays in language acquisition. According to Susan M. Gass, "The concept of input is perhaps the single most important concept of second language acquisition. It is trivial to point out that no individual can learn a second language without input of some sort. In fact, no model of second language acquisition does not avail itself of input in trying to explain how learners create second language grammars."[16]

Second, if comprehensible input is, indeed, essential for acquisition, then instructors of biblical and ancient languages should actively look for ways to make their relevant corpus comprehensible, especially for beginners. This is no small challenge to overcome. The extant texts in Hebrew, Greek, and Latin are complex and challenging, sometimes barely comprehensible for the experts, let alone beginners. There are no children's books or other authentic simplified texts to use, aside from word lists. Moreover, these languages no longer have native speakers who can guide us in creating simplified texts that are truly authentic examples of the languages we are trying to teach. However, these challenges do not mean that we should not try. Using the approaches described above, instructors of ancient languages can bring comprehensible input to their students.

As noted above, there are three basic approaches to making input comprehensible. First, instructors of biblical and ancient languages can create simplified and modified texts and classroom dialogue. Instructors should carefully search the texts we do have for authentic examples to imitate. For example, if the instructor wants to write a short story or encourage students to introduce themselves in the target language, a quick search in a concordance should provide some models to follow, even if the end result does not use the exact vocabulary of the original text. One must keep in mind that only providing input from the largely incomprehensible original text can do a disservice to the students,

---

[15] For a summary of research related to comprehensible input and language acquisition, see Lee, "Comprehensible Input," 2–3; and Ellis, *The Study of SLA*, 247–52.

[16] Gass, *Input and Interaction*, 1.

especially at the early stages of learning. Specifically, there is a great need for graded readers in the ancient languages, and this need is only beginning to be filled by innovative instructors and writers.[17]

Second, those who teach biblical and ancient languages can also use visual aids, such as photos, maps/diagrams, and props, to create context, thereby making the language more comprehensible for the students. Instructors may need to carry an additional bag to class with stuffed animals and other props that add visual context for the lesson of the day. Some language textbooks are now including pictures,[18] more like their

---

[17] For Biblical Hebrew, see the following resources: Ethelyn Simon, Irene Resnikoff, Linda Motzkin, Susan Noss, *Tall Tales Told in Biblical Hebrew* (Oakland, CA: EKS Publishing, 1994); Jesse R. Scheumann and Christine Lynn Hiegel, *Jonah: An Illustrated Hebrew Reader's Edition* (Wilmore, KY: GlossaHouse, 2017); also, the following website, produced by Aleph with Beth, includes several simplified stories: https://hebrew.bibleling.org/?fbclid=IwAR2PKKvxpdpU1UO061yHdjHu1o0FHOxlc8 j14rGE8sTcaGf9mOXIS5UQ0nk#/; Paul Overland includes a serialized story woven throughout his textbook with each episode increasing in difficulty to match the level of the corresponding unit (*Learning Biblical Hebrew Interactively*). See also Donald R. Vance, *A Hebrew Reader for Ruth* (Peabody, MA: Hendrickson, 2003); and Miles V. Van Pelt and Gary D. Pratico, *Graded Reader of Biblical Hebrew: A Guide to Reading the Hebrew Bible*, 2nd ed. (Grand Rapids: Zondervan, 2020), although note that the Hebrew text is not simplified in any way for these resources. Vance and Van Pelt and Pratico just add study helps (philological commentary, vocabulary glosses, and/or comments on syntax) for second year students. For Greek, see the Accessible Greek Resources & Online Studies (AG-ROS) series published by GlossaHouse (Wilmore, KY), a set of readers, grammars, and specialized studies that are tiered in five discrete levels for Greek students; and William D. Mounce, *A Graded Reader of Biblical Greek* (Grand Rapids: Zondervan, 1996). As with the corresponding Hebrew reader above, note that the New Testament text is not simplified in any way. Mounce just adds study helps (vocabulary glosses and comments on syntax) for second year students. For Latin, see Anne H. Groton and James M. May, *Thirty-Eight Latin Stories Designed to Accompany Wheelock's Latin*, 5th ed. (Wauconda, IL: Bolchazy-Carducci, 2004). This resource is more in line with the idea of simplified input with some authentic stories and some fabricated to help the student access comprehensible input in Latin.

[18] Aleph with Beth, in partnership with GlossaHouse, offers comprehensible Hebrew input through the use of visual aids in a video format (https://www.glossahouse.com/aleph-with-beth). As examples, the following textbooks also incorporate pictures to aid in comprehension and instruction: Cook and Holmstedt, *Beginning Biblical Hebrew*; Overland, *Learning Biblical Hebrew Interactively*. See also the Biblical Language Center materials for Hebrew, Greek, and Aramaic (https://www.biblicallanguagecenter.com/books-products/).

modern language counterparts.[19] However, much more could be done here as well. For example, a database of vocabulary words that are "glossed" with photos instead of English or another L1 would be a great resource for making in-class discussion more comprehensible and for students to use as a study tool.[20]

Finally, instructors of ancient languages should work to bring more L2 dialogue into the classroom. Through the natural flow of conversation, learners will have the opportunity to negotiate meaning, ensuring that the input is, in fact, comprehensible on a moment-by-moment basis.[21] The next chapter covers immersion strategies for maximizing comprehensible input in the classroom.

Once an instructor has worked to make his or her input comprehensible, how can he or she be sure that the input is, in fact, comprehensible for the learners? Above all, instructors must be attentive to their students, learning to read and interpret the responses of the students, sometimes on a minute-by-minute basis. In the context of oral exchanges, frequent comprehension checks and negotiation of meaning as described above can ensure that students are understanding the input in real time. For written input, where comprehension often cannot be checked in real time, SLA experts recommend that students read texts in which they know at least ninety-five to ninety-eight percent of the words.[22] Even for the more advanced learner, most authentic ancient texts have too many unknown words.[23] Once again, modified and simplified texts are needed.

---

[19] Perhaps in answer to the challenges put forth by Greenspahn, "Why Hebrew Textbooks Are Different."

[20] See, e.g., the print resource by Jesse R. Scheumann and Merissa Scheumann, *According to Their Kinds: A Biblical Hebrew Picture Dictionary* (Wilmore, KY: GlossaHouse, 2019).

[21] For example, courses offered by the Biblical Language Center (https://www.biblicallanguagecenter.com) are intentionally interactive, and other organizations and individual instructors are starting to include more interaction into their courses. See, e.g., Gruber-Miller, ed., *When Dead Tongues Speak.*

[22] For a summary of the research that supports this range of vocabulary coverage for reading, see I. S. P. Nation, *Learning Vocabulary in Another Language* (Cambridge: Cambridge University Press, 2013), 205–9. See chapter 9 for further discussion of reading instruction and chapter 10 for further discussion of vocabulary and vocabulary learning.

[23] However, see the list of "simple" passages from the Hebrew Bible, based on

Comprehensible input is something that teachers of ancient languages should take seriously. SLA experts consider it to be essential to the acquisition process, and relevant research supports its importance. Moreover, there is a significant lack of available comprehensible input for the ancient languages, a situation which needs to be remedied.

Examples for Biblical and Ancient Language Classrooms

When making comprehensible input available to the learners, an instructor should keep in mind a couple things. First, the instructor should be aware of the level of proficiency the learners have achieved. The input he or she produces needs to be comprehensible to the learners *at their level*. Second, the instructor should keep in mind the three different approaches available for making input comprehensible. Below are a few examples that describe how to make input comprehensible in biblical and ancient language classrooms, one for each of the three approaches described above. Notice that some of the activities incorporate more than one approach for making the input comprehensible.

Simplification/Modification: Simple Story or Graded Reader (Hebrew)

For those who are proficient in L2, verbal input can be modified on the fly during conversation. However, because many instructors did not learn to interact verbally in ancient languages, spoken interaction can be more challenging. Therefore, this example will demonstrate simplification of written input, a graded reader. Creating written input gives the instructor more time to double check the authenticity of the language data (while building up spoken language proficiency to use later). The following will demonstrate only the text of a graded reader with the assumption that pictures would accompany such a book, thus incorporating both simplification/modification and contextualization through visual aids. Each line below represents a separate page in the book, each with its own illustration.

---

vocabulary, compiled by Jeremy Bullard, "The 100 'Simplest' Chapters of the Hebrew Bible," *Hebrew Higher Education* 21 (2019): 1–8.

שָׁלוֹם:
שְׁמִי יוֹסֵף:
נַעַר אָנִי:
יֶשׁ לִי אָב: יֶשׁ לִי אֵם:
יֶשׁ לִי בַּיִת:
יֶשׁ לִי צֹאן:
יֶשׁ לִי אֱלֹהִים:
יֶשׁ לִי שָׁלוֹם:

Contextualization through Visual Aids: "Put the stone over the table" (Greek)

Visual aids can be used to introduce new vocabulary items, especially concrete nouns. Consider a family photo for introducing family vocabulary, a drawing of a person to help learn body vocabulary, or stuffed animals for introducing animal vocabulary. However, more complex concepts and vocabulary, like prepositions, can also be contextualized through visual aids.

For this activity, use a desk or chair and a small moveable object (like a stone) to demonstrate prepositions in Greek as you say them. For example, hold the small object over the desk or chair and say, ὑπέρ "over." Then hold the small object under the desk or table and say, ὑπό "under." Be sure to repeat the new word several times before moving to the next, checking with the students for comprehension as you do. Continue with other prepositions.

Variations/Expansions:

1. Using Greek, direct a student (or all the students) to place a small object on, under, or beside their desk, using the command θές/θέτε "put, place!"
2. Have the students divide into groups and direct each other to place an object on, under, beside, etc.
3. Change up the objects used in the demonstration (coin, bread, etc.), reinforcing familiar vocabulary as you also introduce and reinforce the prepositions.

Interaction: "I am walking" (Latin)

As noted above, verbal interaction can seem out of reach for an instructor who was never taught to speak L2. However, it is possible, even advisable, to start small and each time teaching the material add more to the repertoire of interactive activities for the class. Therefore, the following dialogue demonstrates a brief interaction for an early stage in the class, where the instructor is introducing the present active indicative. Notice that the instructor must adjust the input as part of the interaction (nonverbal on the part of the student) for the student to comprehend it before moving on.

Instructor:

Ambulō [while walking, perhaps pointing to feet and legs]
Putasne intellegis?[24] [student shakes head no]
Ambulāre [which the student already knows] … *ambulō* [verbally
      emphasizing the ending on verb, walking and pointing]
Putasne intellegis? [student nods yes]
Now it's your turn. [motion for student to get up and walk]
Ambulās [pointing to the student's feet]
Ambulō [emphasize ending and points to own feet] … *ambulās* [em-
      phasize ending and points to student's feet]
[Repeat, checking for comprehension frequently and adding forms
      and auxiliary words only as comprehension is established.]

Conclusion

Comprehensible, meaning-bearing input is language data that conveys a message that can be understood by the L2 learner, like the guide at the beginning of the chapter who points to a glass of water while saying the previously unknown L2 word for it. Because comprehensible input is considered essential for language acquisition by SLA experts, instructors of biblical and ancient languages should seek to make the input in

---

[24] Vulgate Acts 8:30. This phrase can be introduced and memorized ahead of time as a "chunk," basically as a vocabulary item, rather than as discreet, analyzed words. The next chapter will discuss immersion, including classroom navigation phrases such as this.

their classrooms more comprehensible, using the strategies discussed in this chapter. The next two chapters will present language instruction strategies that increase the quantity of comprehensible input (chapter 5) and the quality of comprehensible input (chapter 6) to improve student learning.

For Further Reading

Krashen, Stephen D. *The Input Hypothesis: Issues and Implications.* London: Longman, 1985.

Krashen, Stephen D. "The Comprehension Hypothesis Extended." Pages 81–94 in *Input Matters in SLA*. Edited by T. Piske & M. Young-Scholten. Bristol, UK: Multilingual Matters, 2009.

Krashen, Stephen D., and Tracy D. Terrell. *The Natural Approach: Language Acquisition in the Classroom*. Hayward, CA: Alemany Press, 1983.

Lee, James F. "Comprehensible Input." In *The TESOL Encyclopedia of English Language Teaching*. Ed. By John I. Liontas. New York: Wiley & Sons, 2018.

VanPatten, Bill. *From Input to Output: A Teacher's Guide to Second Language Acquisition*. Boston: McGraw-Hill, 2003.

CHAPTER 5: QUANTITY OF INPUT: CLASSROOM IMMERSION, TOTAL PHYSICAL RESPONSE (TPR), AND EXTENSIVE READING

Consider two students learning Spanish. The first one sits in a language classroom three days a week for a semester and studies an adequate amount of time in between, enough to get a respectable grade. The second student spends the same semester as an exchange student in Spain surrounded by the language. It is not difficult to guess that the exchange student will be more proficient in Spanish at the end of the semester. SLA experts would attribute much of the success of the second student to the availability of large quantities of comprehensible input.

The Principle: Quantity of Input

An immersion experience, like that of the exchange student above, is ideal. However, when such an opportunity is not available (as with ancient languages), instructors look for other ways to bring a similar experience to the student in the classroom. Because comprehensible input is considered essential for language acquisition (see chapter 4), SLA experts recommend teaching approaches that will provide as much comprehensible input to the students as possible.[1] Therefore, "The more input, the better."[2] This chapter presents three approaches for maximizing comprehensible input: *immersion in the classroom*, *Total Physical Response* (TPR) with the related *TPR Storytelling*, and *extensive reading*.

---

[1] In empirical research, teaching approaches that prioritize comprehensible input have been shown to be at least as effective and usually more effective than traditional teaching methods. See review of research by Stephen D. Krashen, "The Input Hypothesis and Its Rivals," in *Implicit and Explicit Learning of Languages*, ed. N. C. Ellis (New York: Academic Press, 1994), 54–55.

[2] VanPatten, *From Input to Output*, 102; Krashen concurs: "…the research confirms that those [teaching methods] that provide more comprehensible input are more effective" ("Input Hypothesis," 57).

Immersion in the Classroom

One teaching approach aimed at maximizing comprehensible input is to create an immersion experience in the classroom. In other words, the teacher and students use L2 as much as possible and L1 as little as possible while in the classroom, effectively teaching how to use the target language in the target language.[3] This approach can significantly increase the amount of exposure to the L2, providing plenty of comprehensible input for the students that can then be utilized for developing proficiency. According to Miles Turnbull and Katy Arnett, "There seems to be near consensus that teachers should aim to make maximum use of the [target language]."[4] The American Council on the Teaching of Foreign Languages (ACTFL) recommends that 90 percent or more of classroom time be spent in the target language. Expanding on this idea, ACTFL states, "The target is to provide immersion in the target language unless there is a specific reason to NOT use the target language."[5] This recommendation includes both L2 input and L2 output, keeping in mind that one person's output is another person's input.[6]

As with any teaching approach, instructors employing an immersion classroom environment need to be purposeful and intentional in their use of L2 in the classroom, ensuring student comprehension and participation. For example, a student performing a memorized script or an instructor delivering a monologue in L2 may not be the best approach for bringing immersion into the classroom because these activities are not interactive and may not be comprehensible. The following, then, is a summary of some strategies that support the use of L2 in an immersion setting.[7]

---

[3] Scott McQuinn, "Toward a Principled Communicative Methodology for Teaching the Biblical Languages" (Master's thesis, Fresno Pacific University, 2017), 35.

[4] Miles Turnbull and Katy Arnett, "Teachers' Uses of the Target and First Languages in Second and Foreign Language Classrooms," *Annual Review of Applied Linguistics* 22 (2002): 211.

[5] American Council on the Teaching of Foreign Languages, "Facilitate Target Language Use," https://www.actfl.org/resources/guiding-principles-language-learning/target-language, emphasis original.

[6] The role of output in language acquisition will be covered in chapter 7.

[7] The ACTFL website provides a nice discussion of classroom immersion strategies,

First, instructors should provide a language-rich environment. This means making as much L2 input as possible available to the learners in as many forms as possible, including spoken language, written language, learner output/interaction, online sources, and realia. What is clearly in view is the instructor using all four language skills—speaking, listening, reading, and writing—in the target language and expecting students to do the same. However, instructors should also consider adding other items such as posters, culturally relevant objects, and ancient artifacts or replicas, especially those with inscriptions.

Second, instructors should also support the learners as they meet the challenges of comprehension and production. This would include strategies for making input comprehensible, such as contextualization, visual aids, and gestures as discussed in chapter 4. Relatedly, it is important for instructors to do frequent comprehension checks to be sure that students are understanding the input.

Third, an immersion classroom should also encourage spontaneous use of the target language, even if it is only a single word or a gesture in response to a question. An instructor should create opportunities for the students to respond and interact in L2 and celebrate with them when they do. When a student is ready and willing to dialogue in L2, an instructor can encourage his or her attempts and continue the dialogue as long as the student is able. Keep in mind also that it is better to encourage student participation first and only later work toward accuracy.

Students can also memorize *chunks* of language that serve specific purposes. For example, instructors can teach their students classroom navigation phrases, such as, "Turn in your homework," or "Come to the board." In a similar way, instructors can also teach students how to ask for clarification or seek assistance in the target language with phrases such as, "How do you say...?" or "I have a question." These memorized chunks of language are unanalyzed words and phrases, usually beyond the students' current level of grammar and vocabulary understanding. While the phrases may be advanced, there is nothing wrong with using them. In fact, the unanalyzed chunks serve to provide an initial exposure to more advanced grammar and vocabulary items, supplying

---

many of which are summarized here. See, ACTFL, "Facilitate Target Language Use."

comprehensible input to the class as they are learned and used. Furthermore, as they are repeated, these chunks become automatized.

One last strategy for maintaining an immersion environment in the classroom is to avoid using L1 as a default for checking for meaning and/or understanding. These checks, too, should be in L2 if possible. This, then, leads to the question, "Is there *any* use for L1 in the language classroom, especially if the instructor is aiming for an immersion experience?" This question is still being explored through research and practice. However, some SLA experts say that the L1 can be used "judiciously" to aid in the acquisition process, primarily by making the classroom input more salient and by scaffolding the learning process, that is, by helping the learners get from one stage of learning to the next.[8] *Code-switching* or going back and forth quickly between L2 and L1 can be especially fruitful in this regard. Vivian Cook recommends using L1 when using the target language would be inefficient and/or problematic for the learner. Such instances might include explaining some of the finer points of grammar, organizing tasks, disciplining students, implementing tests, or when "the cost of the L2 is too great."[9]

In sum, creating an immersion environment in the classroom can be a highly effective way of providing large quantities of comprehensible input to the learners and promoting proficiency. While the L1 can be used prudently in the immersion classroom, it should not be employed as frequently as the target language. Scott McQuinn rightly notes, "The more time spent in the learners' L1 is less time spent acquiring the L2."[10]

Total Physical Response (TPR) and TPR Storytelling

An immersion setting can be particularly challenging in the earliest stages of language learning when students have not yet built up enough language knowledge to be able to interact in the L2. A remedy for this is the Total Physical Response (TPR) method developed by James J. Asher,[11] another technique for maximizing comprehensible input in the

---

[8] Turnbull and Arnett, "Teachers' Uses," 205–6.

[9] Vivian Cook, "Using the First Language in the Classroom," *Canadian Modern Language Review* 57 (2001): 402–23, esp. 418.

[10] McQuinn, "Principled Communicative Methodology," 37.

[11] James J. Asher, *Learning Another Language through Actions*, 6th ed. (Los Gatos:

classroom. In this approach, the instructor gives commands to the learners in L2, to which the learners respond through actions.

Asher models his approach on young children learning their first language.[12] Toddlers receive countless commands and instructions from their caregivers throughout the day, ranging from, "Eat your banana" to "Get down from there" to "Good job! Do it again." The toddler is expected to respond physically in most cases rather than verbally. As the toddler listens and demonstrates comprehension through actions, his or her vocabulary size increases, and his or her understanding of grammatical relationships improves—all before saying a (recognizable) word.

The TPR method is based on the belief that the situation for early L2 learners is in many respects similar to that of a toddler. Because comprehensible input and interaction are deemed important, if not essential, to language acquisition, instructors are encouraged to provide as much as possible. However, especially for early language learners, L2 output is difficult and intimidating, so basic conversation and interaction is challenging. The learners must build up enough L2 data before they are able to produce output. This is the reason Krashen and Terrell recommend a "silent period" for learners while they process and acquire L2 through exposure to comprehensible input before producing any output.[13] The TPR method provides a solution to immersion and interaction during this silent period.

In Asher's TPR method, instructors begin instruction with simple commands ("Stand up!") and then add complexity with nouns and adjectives ("Go to the open door!") and then eventually with full statements ("If Joe walks to the door, raise your hand!"). Only when they are comfortable and have developed enough language ability do the students themselves begin to use the L2.

The TPR method provides input that is both meaning bearing and comprehensible, and it also requires interaction, all essential components of meaning-based instruction. Learners listen to the L2 input and demonstrate comprehension by their actions rather than by producing

---

Sky Oak Productions, 2000).

[12] James J. Asher, "Children's First Language as a Model for Second Language Learning," *The Modern Language Journal* 56.3 (1972): 133–39.

[13] Krashen and Terrell, *The Natural Approach*, 78.

L2 output. At the same time, they are building up their vocabulary and grammar comprehension, which contributes to their internal developing language system. Moreover, the learners' reception of the language in TPR is not passive, but active. They must do something with the input, which means that they must pay attention to the meaning encoded in the input rather than just letting it wash over them.

TPR as developed by Asher can be remarkably effective, especially for developing listening and speaking skills at the earlier stages of language acquisition. However, Blaine Ray and Contee Seely have expanded the approach to promote the development of other language skills as learners progress in their language ability. This adaptation of TPR, called TPR Storytelling, combines commands with responses, reading, and acting out stories for a more well-rounded curriculum.[14] Both TPR and TPR Storytelling aim to stay in L2 for at least 90 percent of the class time using comprehensible input,[15] and the methods can be used in combination with other approaches to create an immersion classroom setting.

In the pursuit of creating an immersion environment for the language classroom, two related approaches, TPR and TPR Storytelling, can aid in meeting that goal. Both approaches maximize comprehensible input in the classroom through the use of verbal commands and student responses, and with TPR Storytelling, through the development of reading and writing skills.

Extensive Reading

Another language teaching approach that promotes an increase in the quantity of comprehensible input is to develop an extensive reading program for the L2 students. Extensive reading can be defined as "a lot of reading practice with extended texts that are not frustrating and that control the number of new words being introduced."[16] This type of

---

[14] Blaine Ray and Contee Seely, *Fluency through TPR Storytelling: Achieving Real Language Acquisition in School*, 2nd ed. (Berkeley: Command Performance Language Institute, 1998).

[15] Ray and Seely, *Fluency*, 15.

[16] William Grabe, *Reading in a Second Language: Moving from Theory to Practice* (Cambridge: Cambridge University Press, 2009), 37.

extensive reading program can be challenging to set up, especially for ancient languages, but the results are worth the effort. Besides providing exposure to large quantities of comprehensible input, extensive reading also promotes student motivation, vocabulary growth, and the development of language and literacy skills.[17]

To set up an extensive reading program, instructors need to motivate students to read large quantities of material through incentives, like course grades or other rewards. The extensive reading program should also be intentionally correlated to the language curriculum with a clear sense of what reading material is appropriate for each level. Finally, the reading program should have "appropriate structure, rationale, and goals."[18] Without intentionality and clear goals, the program is less likely to succeed.

William Grabe suggests a few specific ideas for engaging students in extensive reading.[19] For example, instructors can make available as many interesting and attractive L2 reading materials as possible for various levels of language ability, allowing students to borrow materials for at-home use. Instructors can also create opportunities in and out of class for extensive reading (also called free reading or Silent Sustained Reading). Instructors might also read interesting material to the class and give students an opportunity to discuss their reading in class.

The challenge for teachers of ancient languages, of course, is the general lack of resources in this area. The authentic ancient texts available do not qualify for extensive reading material if we are looking for texts that are not frustrating or texts that do not present too many new words, especially for beginners. As noted in the previous chapter, we have very few reading materials outside the canonical texts, let alone a full complement of graded readers. However, instructors can start with what is available and perhaps even write some of their own materials (see resources and suggestions in the examples section below).

---

[17] For a summary of research on the benefits of extensive reading, see Grabe, *Reading*, 316–22.

[18] Grabe, *Reading*, 326.

[19] Grabe, *Reading*, 327.

Conclusion

Because comprehensible input is considered essential for language learning, SLA experts encourage instructors to maximize the availability of comprehensible input for the learners. There are at least three ways to do this: immersion in the classroom, TPR with TPR Storytelling, and an extensive reading program. These three approaches aim to provide students with as much comprehensible input as possible to give the students the best chance of acquiring the L2 and developing proficiency.

Rationale for Increasing Quantity of Input in Ancient and Biblical Language Classrooms

As noted above and throughout the SLA literature, comprehensible input is essential for language acquisition and for developing L2 proficiency. Logically, then, an increase in comprehensible input provides an increase in the opportunity for L2 acquisition. This is true for any language, ancient or modern. Of the teaching approaches listed above, one can easily explain the usefulness of an extensive reading program for ancient and biblical language teaching. The more reading practice, the better, especially when reading and interpreting texts are the primary skills needed for these language programs. Understanding the benefits of an immersion classroom (including TPR) for ancient languages can be a little more challenging. However, such an approach to language instruction has some clear benefits—even for the ancient language classroom.

The main reason for utilizing an immersion classroom is that this approach provides significantly more exposure to L2 than other more traditional approaches that spend most of their class time explaining grammar in L1. This boils down to more practice and more experience with both grammar and vocabulary. Paula Saffire provides anecdotal evidence from her ancient Greek classroom in which she uses an immersion approach. In one two-minute interchange on the fourth day of her ancient Greek class, Saffire recorded 155 words (based on thirteen lexical entries) used by teacher and students with 149 of those used correctly. She also estimates that in the first two weeks of her immersion class, her students have solidly learned over fifty vocabulary words, having heard each of them about eighty times on average.[20] By comparison, in the same time period of a traditional class taught in L1 using a more traditional textbook, the students might hear or read each new vocabulary item five to ten times at most.

A second reason for using an immersion classroom is that this approach also provides interaction. Interaction is a significant component of meaning-based instruction (see chapter 3) because it is the arena in which input is made comprehensible, customized to the student, in real time, and it is also a context that encourages careful attention to the input. When a student is reading an L2 text alone, several things can occur. First, when he or she encounters an unknown word, the only approach for making that input comprehensible is to stop reading and look up the unknown word in a lexicon or reference grammar. The text will not explain itself or make itself more comprehensible as the student struggles to understand it. However, in an interactive, immersion context, an attentive instructor will do frequent comprehension checks and make adjustments as needed to be sure that the students understand and are following along, tailoring instruction to the needs of the students. In addition, those who are engaged in communication, teachers and students alike, will usually negotiate meaning on the spot, quickly making sure that the input is comprehensible before moving on. Second, when reading alone, a student's mind can wander without immediate repercussions. However, in an immersion environment, the student must attend to meaning in the L2 more carefully, which promotes acquisition. He or she is less likely to daydream while the instructor is expecting a response.

The last reason for utilizing an immersion classroom approach to teaching ancient languages comes from ACTFL. While the organization clearly advocates for immersion in the modern language classroom, it also recognizes the importance of immersion for ancient language teaching: "In Classical Languages, the instruction focus is on the interpretive mode; however, interpersonal conversations and presentational writing tasks develop fluency in looking for the 'gist' and thinking in

---

[20] Paula Saffire, "Ancient Greek in Classroom Conversation," in *When Dead Tongues Speak: Teaching Beginning Greek and Latin*, ed by J. Gruber-Miller (Oxford: Oxford University Press, 2006), 163.

'chunks' rather than reading or writing one word at a time."[21] When students work with larger amounts of language at a time, they begin to understand how the language works on a discourse level. In other words, they learn to see the texts as larger pieces rather than as collections of atomized vocabulary and grammar. This approach, then, helps the students move from basic decoding of texts to reading that is more fluent and automatized.

In conclusion, there are several good reasons for increasing the amount of comprehensible input in biblical and ancient language teaching, especially through classroom immersion. These reasons include an increase in exposure to vocabulary and grammar, an increase in interaction and the many benefits of interaction, and an increase in the ability to think about the language in larger units. The next section provides a few specific examples of how to implement some of these approaches for increasing comprehensible input for Hebrew, Greek, and Latin.

Examples for Biblical and Ancient Language Classrooms

This section presents resources and examples for increasing the quantity of comprehensible input in Hebrew, Greek, and Latin classrooms.

Immersion Resources (Hebrew, Greek, and Latin)

To work up to a more fully immersive experience in the classroom (at least 90 percent in L2), an instructor needs to build up a collection of common classroom words and phrases for everyday use. The good news is that there are resources available for Hebrew, Greek, and Latin. This list of resources is not exhaustive, but it is a good place to start.

Hebrew:

- מִלִּים לְשִׂיחָה = *Millim: Words for Conversation in the Biblical Hebrew Classroom* by Paul Overland[22]

---

[21] ACTFL, "Facilitate Target Language Use," https://www.actfl.org/resources /guiding-principles -language-learning/target-language.

[22] Paul Overland, *Millim: Words for Conversation in the Biblical Hebrew Classroom* (Wilmore, KY: GlossaHouse, 2019).

Latin and Greek:

- Classroom phrases: https://latinandgreekchats.wee-bly.com/phrasebook.html
- Neo-Latin and Neo-Greek (modern English words in the ancient languages): https://neolatinlexicon.org/

Immersion in the Classroom (Hebrew)

The following example is intended to help an instructor visualize how he or she might approach a grammatical discussion on Hebrew masculine and feminine nouns in Hebrew. Begin by writing זָכָר "masculine" on one side of the board and נְקֵבָה "feminine" on the other.[23] To make these two words comprehensible without using L1, the instructor can add the universal symbols for masculine and feminine (♂ and ♀ , respectively) next to the appropriate word, checking for comprehension along the way. Then, using vocabulary words that the students already know, start categorizing the words with the students. Start with words that are obviously masculine and feminine because of their referent, like אִישׁ "man" and אִשָּׁה "woman", and then move to words whose gender may seem more arbitrary to the students, like בַּיִת "house." Present the first word to the students through speaking, writing, or both. Then ask the students if they think the noun is masculine or feminine using a simple either-or question, "זָכָר אוֹ נְקֵבָה?" perhaps pointing to the words on the board as you say them and indicating with body language that this is a question. Once the gender of the noun has been correctly identified, write the word under the appropriate heading. Repeat with several words, creating two lists on the board. Draw attention to the הָ ending on the feminine nouns by circling, pointing, and/or vocal stress to help the students begin processing this gender marker. At this point, it may be beneficial to make judicious use of L1. Add a brief sentence or two in L1 to explain that Hebrew has only masculine and feminine nouns, which is different from English. (If the students' L1 is more similar to Hebrew in this area of grammar, there may not be any need for the L1 explanation.) Then move on to the next part of the lesson, returning to L2.

---

[23] Both Hebrew words are found in Genesis 1:27.

TPR (Greek)

The following is a sample activity for an initial Greek TPR lesson. Notice that the instructor does all the speaking and keeps the entire lesson in L2, but students are active participants. The instructor should incorporate many repetitions and do comprehension checks frequently, only adding a new element once comprehension is firmly established with the current element(s).

> ἀνάστηθι[24] "Stand up!" [Instructor stands up to model the action. Alternative: invite a more advanced student or another instructor as an assistant to model for the class.]
>
> κάθισον[25] "Sit down!" [Instructor or assistant sits down to model the action.]
>
> [Repeat as necessary, checking for comprehension.]
>
> [Turn to one of the more capable students in the class.]
>
> ἀνάστηθι [If the student does not understand or respond right away, motion for student to stand up. If the student still does not understand, model the action again and repeat the imperative.]
>
> κάθισον [To the same student.]
>
> [Repeat with the same student a couple times, establishing comprehension. Then move to other students and repeat the process, giving every student in the class the opportunity to respond if possible. Comprehension is now demonstrated (and thus checked) via the students' physical responses to the commands.]

Add a new element:

> ἀνάστητε "Stand up (pl.)!" [To indicate that the instructor is now using a plural command, motion for two or more students to stand and/or address the individuals by name: "Paul and Silas, ἀνάστητε."]

---

[24] Acts 8:26.
[25] LXX Susanna 50.

καθίσατε "Sit down (pl.)!" [To the same students.]

[Repeat with the same students and then with other students as comprehension is established and demonstrated through the actions of the students.]

[Continue adding other imperatives, one at a time, modeling first and using plenty of repetitions with many students. Add nouns, one at a time, to the imperatives to teach/reinforce vocabulary and create variety and maintain interest.]

Extensive Reading (Latin)

The first step in moving toward the incorporation of an extensive reading program for the L2 classroom is to build up a collection of simple but interesting reading materials. An internet search is a good place to start as some simple Latin stories are available electronically for free, while others are available for purchase in print or electronic format.[26] However, it is likely that the materials available are still insufficient for a robust extensive reading program.

Another option, then, is to create a diglot weave, which is a story that is written in two languages (L2 and L1). The instructor replaces the unfamiliar L2 words with an L1 gloss, removing the original L2 word so that it does not create a distraction. This ensures the student understands 95 to 98 percent of the words in the text, and the approach is versatile enough to be used at any reading level. In fact, one version of a given story could be adapted for an early beginner and a more difficult version of the same story (i.e., with fewer L1 words) made available for more advanced students. Reusing a story like this promotes reading fluency through repetition and at the same time gives the more advanced

---

[26] See, e.g., John P. Piazza, "Simple Latin Online Reading Resources," http://johnpiazza.net/latin/online-reading/. For Hebrew and Greek, more advanced students may be able to use the following for extensive reading as infrequent words are glossed in English: A. Philip Brown II, Bryan W. Smith, Richard J. Goodrich, Albert L. Lukaszewski, *A Reader's Hebrew and Greek Bible*, 3rd ed. (Grand Rapids: Zondervan, 2020).

student a sense of accomplishment, recognizing that he or she can now read the story with fewer words in L1.[27]

Once the instructor has procured a sizeable collection of reading materials, he or she needs to analyze the vocabulary and grammar of each story or article to determine its level of difficulty. As discussed above, the students should know at least 95 to 98 percent of the words in the text to be sure that the text is comprehensible and not too frustrating. Using this benchmark, determine the earliest lesson in the L2 curriculum at which the student could read the given story and understand 95 to 98 percent of the words. For example, if a student who has completed lesson ten in the L2 textbook knows enough vocabulary and grammar to understand at least 95 to 98 percent of the words in the reading material in question, but a student who only completed lesson nine will not, then the reading material should be considered something to be read with lesson ten or above. Label the item accordingly.

Once the instructor has collected and labeled a sufficient number of individual items for reading, he or she can begin to incorporate extensive reading as a regular part of instruction while continuing to build up his or her lending collection. Ideally, the instructor would have enough reading materials that the students have some choice in what they read at any given level of L2 proficiency for the course. Adding extensive reading to a course may include requiring a certain amount of extensive reading each week as part of the course grade (measured in time-on-task, number of pages read, or word count), giving students time in class to read to themselves, and/or periodically reading a story with them in class. The instructor could also develop a comprehension quiz for each item in the library, providing motivation and another scorable item for course grades. This extensive reading program will increase the amount of comprehensible input the students receive and will provide more opportunities for developing L2 proficiency, particularly in reading.

Conclusion

Because comprehensible input is considered essential for language acquisition and proficiency, it stands to reason that an exchange student

---

[27] See chapter 9 for more on promoting reading fluency and chapter 12 for motivation.

will learn more L2 in a shorter amount of time than a student whose only exposure to the language is in a classroom. In other words, large quantities of comprehensible input should promote greater gains in proficiency, and SLA research confirms this. Given the lack of immersion opportunities for ancient language students, this chapter presented three strategies for increasing the amount of comprehensible input in classroom instruction: immersion in the classroom, TPR with TPR Storytelling, and extensive reading. The goal of each approach is to expose the students to as much comprehensible input as possible. The next chapter will address strategies that maximize the quality of comprehensible input, helping the instructor fine-tune and carefully craft the input that his or her students receive to promote even greater gains in acquisition and proficiency.

For Further Reading

American Council on the Teaching of Foreign Languages. "Facilitate Target Language Use." https://www.actfl.org/resources/guiding-principles-language-learning/target-language.

Asher, James J. *Learning Another Language through Actions*. 6th ed. Los Gatos, CA: Sky Oak Productions, 2000.

Grabe, William. *Reading in a Second Language: Moving from Theory to Practice*. Cambridge: Cambridge University Press, 2008.

McQuinn, Scott. "Toward a Principled Communicative Methodology for Teaching the Biblical Languages." Master's Thesis. Fresno Pacific University, 2017.

Ray, Blaine, and Contee Seely. *Fluency through TPR Storytelling: Achieving Real Language Acquisition in School*. 2nd ed. Berkeley, CA: Command Performance Language Institute, 1998.

Saffire, Paula. "Ancient Greek in Classroom Conversation." Pages 158–89 in *When Dead Tongues Speak: Teaching Beginning Greek and Latin*. Edited by J. Gruber-Miller. Oxford: Oxford University Press, 2006.

Turnbull, Miles, and Katy Arnett. "Teachers' Uses of the Target and First Languages in Second and Foreign Language Classrooms." *Annual Review of Applied Linguistics* 22 (2002): 204–18.

CHAPTER 6: QUALITY OF INPUT: INPUT ENHANCEMENT, INPUT FLOOD, AND STRUCTURED INPUT

Imagine that you are a dinner guest at an annual gala put on by the local mayor and city council. You want to be involved in the many important conversations going on around you, so while you discuss education with the university president, you are also listening to at least two other conversations nearby, trying to catch everything that is being said. Of course, you end up only getting fragments of all the conversations. Like everyone else, you don't have enough attentional resources to be able to process everything at once.

Later in the evening, you look up in time to see a very important and unexpected guest make an entrance. Maybe it is a high-ranking army officer in uniform, or perhaps it is a famous movie actress in a glittering gown. Suddenly, every other conversation fades as you are fixed on the important guest. This person has caught the attention of both eyes and ears, and none of the other conversations seem nearly as important. You shift your attention to this one person and take in everything he or she says and does.

The Principle: Quality of Input

As noted in previous chapters and repeatedly throughout the literature on SLA, comprehensible input is an essential ingredient in language acquisition and the development of language proficiency. The previous chapter presented strategies for increasing the amount of comprehensible input for L2 students. However, like a dinner guest at a gala, the learner has limited attentional resources and can be overwhelmed by a plethora of language data in the input, even if it is comprehensible. The result is that the learner does not acquire language as quickly or as efficiently as he or she might. This chapter, then, presents some strategies for improving the quality of the comprehensible input, helping the learner focus on the most important elements in the input. Like the important guest at the gala, language structures that are more visible and more important will draw the attention of the learner, making acquisition more likely.

Intake

Teachers and researchers have noticed that students do not process everything they encounter in the comprehensible input they receive. This has led to some investigation regarding other factors involved in the language acquisition process, including the quality of the input, the *salience* of the target structures, and the nature of student *processing strategies* and *attentional resources.*

To make sense of this complex issue, it is important to understand the difference between language input and language *intake*. Input is language data that is available to the learner but is outside of the learner and independent of the learner. The problem is that teachers and researchers cannot always predict which part of the language data the learners will notice and process.[1] The language data in the input that the leaner attends to and processes for form and/or meaning is called intake.[2] As a psycholinguistic category, intake cannot be measured directly "but only inferred from a learner's subsequent interlanguage change, which in turn is only indirectly accessible via the learner's output."[3] In other words, teachers and researchers can only infer that a learner has derived intake from the input when he or she produces the new structure in the form of L2 output.

As a subset of input, intake is dependent on several factors, including the salience of the target structure (how important or obvious it is) and the attentional resources of the learner (how well the learner is able to recognize and focus attention on the target structure). In short, "mere exposure to input is often not sufficient to trigger interlanguage development."[4]

---

[1] Karin Madlener, *Frequency Effects in Instructed Second Language Acquisition* (Boston: De Gruyter, 2015), 82.

[2] Bill VanPatten, *Input Processing and Grammar Instruction: Theory and Research* (Norwood, NJ: Ablex, 1996), 10.

[3] Madlener, *Frequency Effects*, 82.

[4] Madlener, *Frequency Effects*, 82. See also Michael Sharwood Smith, "Input Enhancement in Instructed SLA: Theoretical Bases," *Studies in Second Language Acquisition*

Figure 1 below depicts the relationship between input and intake:

Figure 1. Basic Processes in Acquisition[5]

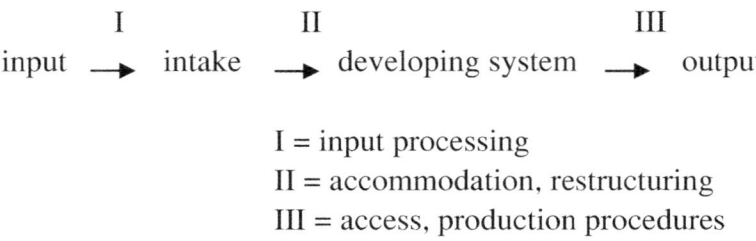

I = input processing
II = accommodation, restructuring
III = access, production procedures

The learner receives input and processes it (I), deriving intake from the input. The intake then causes the learner to accommodate and/or re-structure his or her developing internal language system (II). The learner is then able to access the newly structured language system to produce output that contains the new structure (III).

Krashen and Terrell present a possible solution to the problem of a student's limited intake from comprehensible input. When discussing the Input Hypothesis, Krashen and Terrell note that comprehensible input can be roughly tuned or finely tuned.[6] Roughly tuned comprehensible input is meaningful language input that is just trying to get across a message. Roughly tuned input may include a combination of $i + 1$, $i + 2$, $i + 3$, and/or previously learned material. Students may derive some intake from roughly tuned input, but they are less likely to derive significant quantities of intake.[7] By contrast, finely tuned input is specifically targeted at the next structure the learner will be acquiring. It is carefully crafted so that the number of new structures in the input are limited to the next item(s) the student will be learning, or $i + 1$ only. Students will likely derive more intake from this type of input because

---

15.2 (1993): 167–69; and Swain, "Communicative Competence," 235–53.

[5] Adapted from Bill VanPatten, "Input Processing in Second Language Acquisition," in *Processing Instruction: Theory, Research, and Commentary*, ed. Bill VanPatten (Mahwah, NJ: Erlbaum, 2004), 26.

[6] Krashen and Terrell, *The Natural Approach*, 33–35

[7] Note, however, that roughly tuned input can serve other purposes, such as fluency training, and should not be categorically avoided in language instruction.

it makes the target structure more salient and because it does not drain the attentional resources of the students.

SLA experts have expanded on Krashen and Terrell's ideas and developed several approaches for improving the quality of comprehensible input, the quality of students' process strategies, or both. These approaches focus on "maximizing the learners' chances for incidental learning through increasing the availability and visibility of selected target structures in rich (that is, enriched and structured) input."[8] This chapter covers three of the most common approaches to increasing the quality of the input that students receive with the goal of increasing student intake: *Input Enhancement, Input Flood,* and *Structured Input* as part of an approach called *Processing Instruction* (PI).

Input Enhancement

Input Enhancement is the first approach developed for improving the quality of language input.[9] Input Enhancement is "the process by which language input becomes salient to the learner"[10] or "any pedagogical intervention that is used to make specific features of L2 input more salient as an effort to draw learners' attention to these features."[11] The goal of Input Enhancement is to make the target structure more salient, or more obvious, to the learner. This can be accomplished through a variety of means.

In written input, the target structure can be marked through highlighting, color-coding, bolding, font size, etc. This is also called *Visual Textual Enhancement.*[12] In spoken input, the speaker can highlight the target structure through voice intonation, slowing for emphasis, pauses,

---

[8] Madlener, *Frequency Effects*, 81.

[9] Input Enhancement is also known as "enriched input." See Ellis, *Study of Second Language Acquisition*, 960–61.

[10] Michael Sharwood Smith, "Speaking to Many Minds: On the Relevance of Different Types of Language Information for the L2 Learner," *Second Language Research* 7.2 (1991): 118.

[11] Wynne Wong, *Input Enhancement: From Theory and Research to the Classroom* (Boston: McGraw-Hill, 2005), 32–33.

[12] See Madlener, *Frequency Effects*, 86–88.

etc.[13] This enhancement intentionally draws the learner's attention to the target structure, making the learner more likely to notice and ultimately process the form. While Input Enhancement does not automatically guarantee intake, it does improve the chances of the learner noticing the target structure.[14] This, then, gives the student more opportunity to derive intake from the input, providing more data for the learner's internal developing language system.

Input Flood

Sometimes considered a subcategory of Input Enhancement, Input Flood deserves its own place in the language teacher's toolbox. Input that is flooded "contains massive amounts of exemplars instantiating a selected target construction."[15] For example if the target structure is the third person plural perfect, then the text would be intentionally flooded with examples of the third person plural perfect. This should not be confused with classroom immersion in which the goal is to increase the sheer quantity of input in general. With an Input Flood, the goal is to increase the ratio of target structure occurrences to non-target structure occurrences, intentionally embedding the target structure as frequently as possible within a given text or conversation. The idea is to maximize a learner's exposure to the target structure in the context of meaningful language so that the student will derive more intake from the input.

Structured Input and Processing Instruction

The final approach to improving the quality of language input was first introduced by Bill VanPatten and Teresa Cadierno.[16] Known as *Processing Instruction*, this approach includes three main elements: 1. Explicit grammar explanations, 2. Information about learner processing

---

[13] Madlener, *Frequency Effects*, 86.

[14] Wong, *Input Enhancement*, 33.

[15] Madlener, *Frequency Effects*, 88.

[16] Bill VanPatten and Teresa Cadierno, "Explicit Instruction and Input Processing," *Studies in Second Language Acquisition* 15 (1993): 225–43. See also Bill VanPatten, "Grammar Instruction for the Acquisition Rich Classroom," *Foreign Language Annals* 26 (1993): 435–50.

strategies, and 3. Structured Input Activities,[17] which are the most important of the three elements, based on empirical research.[18]

Recent psycholinguistic research demonstrates that learners have predictable preferences when processing language input.[19] Therefore, VanPatten has developed the following set of principle that describe the typical preferences of language learners when processing input:

Principles of Input Processing[20]

P1. *The Primacy of Meaning Principle.* Learners process input for meaning before they process it for form.

> P1a. *The Primacy of Content Words Principle.* Learners process content words in the input before anything else.
>
> P1b. *The Lexical Preference Principle.* Learners will tend to rely on lexical items as opposed to grammatical form to get meaning when both encode the same semantic information.
>
> P1c. *The Preference for Non-redundancy Principle.* Learners are more likely to process non-redundant meaningful grammatical form before they process redundant meaningful forms.

---

[17] VanPatten, *Input Processing and Grammar Instruction*, 60; Bill VanPatten, "Processing Instruction: An Update," *Language Learning* 52 (2002): 764–65.

[18] See the following studies: Bill VanPatten and Soile Oikkenon. "Explanation Versus Structured Input in Processing Instruction," *Studies in Second Language Acquisition* 18.3 (1996): 495–510; Bill VanPatten, Erin Collopy, Joseph E. Price, Stefanie Borst, Anthony Qualin. "Explicit Information, Grammatical Sensitivity, and the First-Noun Principle: A Cross-Linguistic Study in Processing Instruction," *Modern Language Journal* 97.2 (2013): 504–25.

[19] These principles apply to any language being learned. For a review and discussion of this research, see VanPatten, *Input Processing and Grammar Instruction*, 1–53.

[20] VanPatten, "Input Processing in Second Language Acquisition," 14, 18. Earlier versions of these principles, with discussion, can be found in VanPatten, *Input Processing and Grammar Instruction*, 14–15, 32; Bill VanPatten, "Thirty Years of Input (or Intake, the Neglected Sibling)," in *Social and Cognitive Factors in Second Language Acquisition*, ed. B. Swierzbin, F. Morris, M. Anderson, C. Klee, and E. Tarone (Somerville, MA: Cascadilla, 2000) 299–300; Bill VanPatten, "Processing Instruction," 758.

P1d. *The Meaning Before Non-meaning Principle.* Learners are more likely to process meaningful grammatical forms before non-meaningful forms irrespective of redundancy.

P1e. *The Availability of Resources Principle.* For learners to process either redundant meaningful grammatical forms or non-meaningful forms, the processing of overall sentential meaning must not drain available processing resources.

P1f. *The Sentence Location Principle.* Learners tend to process items in sentence initial position before those in final position and those in medial position.

P2. *The First Noun Principle.* Learners tend to process the first noun or pronoun they encounter in a sentence as the subject/agent.

P2a. *The Lexical Semantics Principle.* Learners may rely on lexical semantics, where possible, instead of word order to interpret sentences.

P2b. *The Event Probabilities Principle.* Learners may rely on event probabilities, where possible, instead of word order to interpret sentences.

P2c. *The Contextual Constraint Principle.* Learners may rely less on the First Noun Principle if preceding context constrains the possible interpretation of a clause or sentence.

In other words, some grammatical structures carry more communicative value to learners than others. A structure with higher communicative value is more likely to be processed and made available for acquisition by the learner.

Because many of these default strategies are less efficient and can interfere with language processing and cause confusion, Processing Instruction provides the student with training in language processing strategies (element two above) plus activities that are specifically designed to push the learners away from their less efficient processing strategies. These are known as Structured Input Activities (element three above). Thus, a typical Processing Instruction lesson will begin with a basic presentation of the new grammatical structure, followed by training in processing strategies, with the bulk of the lesson then made up of Structured Input Activities.

While the first two components of Processing Instruction are significant, by far the most important element is the third component, the completion of student exercises, known as Structured Input Activities. Structured Input Activities must follow six rather stringent guidelines in order to be effective.[21]

First, the instructor must present one thing at a time, requiring the student to grapple with only one new form-meaning connection at a time: one new verbal stem, one new portion of a paradigm, one new vocabulary item, etc. Second, the Structured Input Activities should keep meaning in focus. Instructors must ask the question, "Can learners complete this activity without understanding what they hear or read?"[22] If the answer is "yes," then the criterion is not met. Third, the activities must move from sentences to connected discourse, providing input that is increasingly more complex. Fourth, Structured Input Activities need to use both oral and written input, which appeals to different learning preferences, provides variety, and develops both language skills. Fifth, the learners must do something with the input, usually pushing them to make a choice of some kind based on the input. This is what differentiates Structured Input Activities from simply providing the learners with comprehensible input. The sixth and most important guideline requires that the Structured Input Activities keep in mind the learner's processing strategies.

To summarize, in order to help language learners derive more intake from the available comprehensible input, an instructor can make changes to the quality of the input in order to make the target structure more salient and/or help the student make his or her language processing more efficient. Input Enhancement, Input Flood, and Structured Input are three options for improving the quality of L2 input.

---

[21] For a detailed discussion of Structured Input Activities, see Andrew P. Farley, *Structured Input: Grammar Instruction for the Acquisition-Oriented Classroom* (Boston: McGraw-Hill, 2005), 12–16.

[22] Farley, *Structured Input*, 13.

Rationale for Improving the Quality of Input
in Ancient and Biblical Language Classrooms

As noted above, while comprehensible input is essential for language acquisition, it may not be sufficient. Just because comprehensible input is available does not mean that students will learn when exposed to it. To maximize the intake that learners derive from the comprehensible input, SLA researchers and practitioners recommend altering the input in specific ways. These approaches have been studied in carefully controlled experiments, and the data from these studies indicate that students learn languages more quickly and more deeply with these interventions than they would without them.[23] Such evidence should be considered when planning lessons for biblical and ancient language classes.

Another reason to consider these approaches for the teaching of biblical and ancient languages is the mode used for instruction. All the approaches discussed in this chapter focus on modifying input, often written input. Note that it is much easier to manipulate, control, and enhance written input as described above than it is to consistently adjust spoken input for the same purposes. For this reason, many of the empirical studies conducted for these approaches to input modification specifically use written input. Therefore, the gains made in student learning noted by these studies should be transferrable to biblical and ancient language instruction. Because the primary focus of teaching biblical and ancient languages is to help students understand and interpret written language input, these approaches to input should be considered.

Examples for Biblical and Ancient Language Classrooms

The following activities are examples of how an instructor might promote quality of comprehensible input in his or her class.

---

[23] For a review of research on the efficacy of Input Enhancement, see Zahra Fahker Ajabshir, "The Relative Efficacy of Input Enhancement, Input Flooding, and Output-based Instructional Approaches in the Acquisition of L2 Request Modifiers," *Language Teaching Research* (2020): 1–23, esp. 2. For a review of research on the efficacy of Input Flood, see Madlener, *Frequency Effects*, 88–90. For a review of research on the efficacy of Processing Instruction see Benati, "Classroom-Oriented Research."

Input Enhancement (Hebrew)

The following selection from 1 Sam 24:11–12 [Eng. 24:10–11] has been altered (enhanced) to draw attention to the first common singular suffix on a singular noun in Biblical Hebrew. The text is specifically chosen because of the frequent occurrence of this structure. Unfamiliar vocabulary (those lemmas occurring less frequently than three hundred times in the Hebrew Bible) are replaced with English glosses, forming a diglot weave.[24] Two additional English phrases in brackets provide context.

[David said to himself,]

לֹא־אֶשְׁלַח יָדִי בַּאדֹנִי כִּי־ anointed יְהוָה הוּא׃

[Then David said to Saul,]

וְאָבִי רְאֵה גַם רְאֵה אֶת־ the edge of your garment בְּיָדִי

... דַּע וּרְאֵה כִּי אֵין בְּיָדִי רָעָה

Input Flood (Greek)

The following text is a selection from 1 Tim 1:1–2 flooded with examples of the genitive case. The original passage contains a high concentration of the target structure already. However, removing a few non-target items from the passage creates an even higher ratio of target structure occurrences to non-target structure occurrences. The Greek word ἐπιταγήν "command" has been replaced by an English gloss because it occurs less than ten times in the New Testament. The remaining words occur twenty times or more.

ΠΑΥΛΟΣ ἀπόστολος Χριστοῦ Ἰησοῦ κατ᾽ command θεοῦ σωτῆρος ἡμῶν καὶ Χριστοῦ Ἰησοῦ, Τιμοθέῳ· χάρις, ἔλεος, εἰρήνη ἀπὸ θεοῦ πατρὸς καὶ Χριστοῦ Ἰησοῦ τοῦ κυρίου ἡμῶν.

Processing Instruction (Latin)

Because Latin word order is much more flexible than English word order, English speaking students of Latin are likely to (incorrectly)

---

[24] For information on diglot weave, see chapter 5.

identify the first noun in a sentence as the subject of the verb without looking at the case ending. This corresponds with VanPatten's "First Noun Principle" noted above: "Learners tend to process the first noun or pronoun they encounter in a sentence as the subject/agent." To push the students away from this inefficient default strategy, a Processing Instruction lesson would include the following three elements:

Explicit Grammar Information

Instruction to students: "Latin uses case endings to mark grammatical function. You learned what the case endings look like in previous lessons. These endings identify the function of the noun within a sentence: subject, direct object, indirect object, etc."

Information on Inefficient Processing Strategies

Instruction to students: "In English, unlike in Latin, the position of the noun in a sentence indicates its function. For example, 'The dog bites the man' is very different from 'The man bites the dog.' Therefore, we [native English speakers] expect the first noun in the sentence to be the subject. However, this can cause misunderstanding and confusion when applied to a Latin sentence whose word order is much more flexible. The first noun in a Latin sentence could very well be the direct object or indirect object with the subject coming later in the sentence. Therefore, you will need to pay close attention to the case ending of each noun to determine the noun's function in the sentence."

Structured Input Activities

In the following sample exercises, the students must choose the sentence that best describes each photo. Notice that some of the distractors present a potential subject first, based on the photo, but a closer look at the case endings indicate that the option is incorrect. This forces the students to move away from their default processing strategy ("First Noun Principle") and rely on case endings to successfully complete the exercise, making the student more likely to notice and process these endings.

© Jennifer E. Noonan, used by permission

I.   *Mulierēs manducat pānem*
II.   *Pānem mulier manducat*
III. *Mulierem manducat pānem*
IV.   *Pānis mulierem manducat*

© Jennifer E. Noonan, used by permission

I.   *Mulierēs audit virum*
II.   *Mulierem audit virī*
III. *Mulierem vir audit*
IV.   *Virum mulier audit*

Conclusion

While comprehensible input is considered essential for language acquisition, it is not sufficient. Like the guest at the gala whose attention is divided by the many people and conversations, a language learner can get overwhelmed by too many items in the comprehensible input, making it less likely that he or she will derive intake from the input for further processing. Therefore, SLA researchers and practitioners advocate the manipulation of input to make a target structure more salient, like the glittering gown of the special guest at the gala, helping the students notice the structure so that they have a greater chance of processing it and ultimately acquiring it. This chapter presented three specific strategies for improving the quality of comprehensible input for students: Input Enhancement, Input Flood, and Structured Input Activities in the context of a Processing Instruction lesson. With this, we conclude our discussion of input and now turn our attention to the role of output in language acquisition and proficiency development.

For Further Reading

Benati, Alessandro. "Classroom-Oriented Research: Processing Instruction (Findings and Implications)." *Language Teaching* 52.3 (2019): 343–59.

Farley, Andrew P. *Structured Input: Grammar Instruction for the Acquisition-Oriented Classroom*. Boston: McGraw-Hill, 2005.

Madlener, Karin. *Frequency Effects in Instructed Second Language Acquisition*. Boston: De Gruyter, 2015.

Sharwood Smith, Michael. "Input Enhancement in Instructed SLA: Theoretical Bases." *Studies in Second Language Acquisition* 15.2 (1993): 165–79.

Sharwood Smith, Michael. "Speaking to Many Minds: On the Relevance of Different Types of Language Information for the L2 Learner," *Second Language Research* 7.2 (1991): 118–32.

VanPatten, Bill. *Processing Instruction: Theory, Research, and Commentary*. Mahwah, NJ: Erlbaum, 2004.

Wong, Wynne. *Input Enhancement: From Theory and Research to the Classroom*. Boston: McGraw-Hill, 2005.

CHAPTER 7: OUTPUT

Most school children do not enjoy spelling tests. I know they were not my favorite, and my daughter is quite adamantly opposed to them. However, spelling tests serve an important function in language development. Without spelling tests, readers of English could probably recognize enough words on a page to make sense of the text, but most readers would not develop the proficiency they need to recognize words consistently, quickly, and accurately. They certainly would not develop the proficiency needed to write words accurately if they are not being challenged to produce the words themselves. Spelling tests push the students to learn and internalize certain rules of spelling, such as, "I before E except after C" (plus all the many exceptions in English!). In short, without the challenge of spelling tests, students would be sloppy in their language skills, both receptive and productive.

The Principle: Output

The previous three chapters covered the important role that input plays in language acquisition. This chapter will cover the function of output in language acquisition. Output is quite simply "language that learners produce for the purpose of communication,"[1] and it can be either written or oral. While the role of output in the development of language proficiency is a little less clearly understood than the role of input, it does have a part to play. Among other functions, L2 output pushes the learner to further refine his or her understanding of the language, promoting accuracy and the internalization of patterns in the language, not unlike those spelling tests.

In order to understand the role that output plays in language acquisition, it is important to have a grasp of the mechanics involved in language output. This section will cover the basic processes involved in producing output and the *Output Hypothesis*, a theory for explaining the role of output in language acquisition. The last part of this section will

---

[1] VanPatten and Benati, *Key Terms*, 168.

introduce different types of classroom activities that promote the production of output.

The Basic Processes of Output

When producing language output, an individual must control at least three different language skills: *access, monitoring,* and *production strategies.* Access is the "process of connecting words and expressions to their meanings."[2] A language learner can only access or use forms and structures that he or she has already learned and internalized. Access, therefore, entails drawing upon those forms and structures that have been acquired to communicate meaning.

Moreover, learners can access language data from different forms of language knowledge. Chapter two presented two different types of language knowledge, implicit and explicit. Implicit language knowledge is unconscious and intuitive knowledge, while explicit language knowledge is conscious and formalized. An individual can produce language output by accessing either or both types of language knowledge.

Researchers have found that when a communication task is more oriented toward correctness, the learner is more likely to use explicit knowledge to compensate for any lack of implicit knowledge. In other words, if the learner is expected to produce an utterance with accuracy, he or she is more likely to use explicit language knowledge to complete the task, especially if his or her implicit knowledge is incomplete. Conversely, when a communication task is more oriented toward fluency or communicating meaning smoothly and quickly, a learner is more likely to use implicit knowledge.[3] One of the reasons for this is that accessing implicit knowledge takes less time and is more accurate than accessing explicit knowledge (see discussion in chapter 2).

In addition to mastering access of language knowledge when producing output, an individual must also be able to monitor the output that

---

[2] Tracy David Terrell, "Acquisition in the Natural Approach: The Binding/Access Framework," *The Modern Language Journal* 70.3 (1986): 215. "Access" can also be called "access fluidity" or "lexical access." See Norman Segalowitz, "Access Fluidity, Attention Control, and the Acquisition of Fluency in a Second Language," *TESOL Quarterly* 41.1 (2007): 182.

[3] Ellis, *Instructed Second Language Acquisition*, 194–95.

he or she produces. This means that the individual can ensure that the utterance is grammatically correct and socially appropriate before producing it. This also means that he or she can make a quick correction or adjustment if the utterance is incorrect or misunderstood upon production.[4] The learner must have a precise understanding (implicit or explicit) of the grammar of the language to do this well.

Finally, the individual must have control over production strategies. These strategies allow the learner "to string forms together in appropriate ways."[5] The one producing the output must be able to arrange and rearrange forms and structures in countless ways to communicate meaning to the listener or reader.

As depicted in Figure 1 below, access, monitoring, and production strategies allow the learner to draw from the internal developing language system to produce output. Input and intake, covered in chapters four through six, feed this developing system.

Figure 1. Basic Processes in Acquisition[6]

I   II   III

input → intake → developing system → output

I = input processing
II = accommodation, restructuring
III = access, monitoring, and production strategies

With a basic understanding of the processes involved in output production, we now turn to the Output Hypothesis.

The Output Hypothesis

As noted in previous chapters, comprehensible input is considered essential for acquisition to occur, but it is not sufficient. Therefore, language researchers and educators have sought to supplement comprehen-

---

[4] Ellis, *Study of Second Language Acquisition*, 972.
[5] Terrell, "Acquisition in the Natural Approach," 215.
[6] Adapted from VanPatten, "Input Processing in Second Language Acquisition," 26.

sible input with other strategies that help promote language acquisition and proficiency. As presented in the previous two chapters, some researchers and educators seek to promote language proficiency by increasing or improving the input that their students receive through approaches such as immersion and input enhancement. Others look to output as a means of promoting language proficiency. This has led to the development of the Output Hypothesis.

Swain developed the Output Hypothesis after noticing that students did not reach native-level proficiency in immersion classroom settings where the students received plenty of comprehensible input. She, therefore, suggested that the limited gains were due to a lack of L2 output because output pushes the learners to analyze L2 grammar and syntax more carefully. As Swain notes, "learners … can fake it, so to speak, in comprehension, but they cannot do so in the same way in production."[7] Rod Ellis further explains that "production requires learners to process syntactically; they have to pay some attention to form."[8] These observations are the basis of Swain's comprehensible Output Hypothesis, which claims that "the act of producing language (speaking or writing) constitutes, under certain circumstances, part of the process of second language learning."[9]

Since Swain's original formulation of the Output Hypothesis, further research and discussion have helped to fill in the details and suggest that output production can contribute to acquisition and thus proficiency both directly and indirectly. First, output production can enable acquisition directly by engaging "syntactic processing in a way that comprehension does not."[10] Learners must have a stronger grasp of the L2 forms and vocabulary to successfully produce output than they do to

---

[7] Merrill Swain, "Three Functions of Output in Second Language Learning," in *Principle and Practice in Applied Linguistics: Studies in Honour of H. G. Widdowson*, ed. G. Cook and B. Seidlhofer (Oxford: Oxford University Press, 1995), 127.

[8] Ellis, *Study of Second Language Acquisition*, 261.

[9] Merrill Swain, "The Output Hypothesis: Theory and Research," in *Handbook of Research in Second Language Teaching and Learning*, ed. E. Hinkel (Mahwah, NJ: Lawrence Erlbaum, 2005), 471. This is a later version of the hypothesis, modified from its original formulation. For the original, see Swain, "Communicative Competence," 252.

[10] Ellis, *Study of Second Language Acquisition*, 261. See also Peter Skehan, *A Cognitive Approach to Language Learning* (Oxford: Oxford University Press, 1998), 17.

comprehend input of the same level of difficulty. Production also facilitates acquisition directly by giving learners the opportunity to use what they already know, helping them develop automaticity in their discourse and linguistic knowledge.[11]

Output production can also contribute to L2 acquisition indirectly by allowing learners to test out hypotheses about the target-language grammar and by creating opportunities for instructors to provide focused feedback (i.e., correction).[12] Finally, output production provides the learner with his or her own input, also known as "auto-input," another indirect contribution of output.[13] Thus, output often functions in a refining role in the development of language proficiency.

Having covered basic processes of output and the Output Hypothesis, the next section will present several approaches for promoting language output in the classroom, beginning with the least effective and moving to the most effective approach.

Promoting Output in the Classroom

Instructors can promote language output in the classroom in several ways. One approach is the use of *mechanical drills*, although this approach is not widely supported. "Mechanical drills are those during which the student need not attend to meaning and for which there is only one correct response."[14] An example might be the repetition of a paradigm from memory or the recitation of a memorized dialogue. According to James Lee and Bill VanPatten, these do not do much to help the learner develop fluency or accuracy and are "of dubious value"[15] as they are abstracted from a meaningful context.

A second approach to promoting language output is the use of *meaningful drills*. In meaningful drills, "the learner must attend to the

---

[11] Skehan, *Cognitive Approach*, 17–18.

[12] See Skehan, *Cognitive Approach*, 16–17.

[13] Richard W. Schmidt and Sylvia Nagem Frota, "Developing Basic Conversational Ability in a Second Language: A Case Study of an Adult Learner of Portuguese," in *Talking to Learn: Conversation in Second Language Acquisition*, ed. R. Day (Rowley, MA: Newbury House, 1986), 316.

[14] Lee and VanPatten, *Communicative Language Teaching*, 121.

[15] Lee and VanPatten, *Communicative Language Teaching*, 171.

meaning of both the stimulus and her own answer in order to complete the meaningful drill successfully. Yet there is still only one right answer, and the answer is already known to the participants."[16] An example of a meaningful drill is asking a student to answer a basic question like, "What color is Peter's shirt?" The student must attend to meaning to answer the question, but there is clearly only one right answer, and everyone in the room already knows what that answer is. Meaningful drills are more effective for language learning than mechanical drills, but they are not the most effective approach for promoting language output.

A third, more effective, approach to promoting output is the use of *communicative drills*. "Communicative drills require attention to meaning, and the information contained in the learner's answer is new and unknown to the person asking the question. Thus, the answer cannot be deemed right or wrong in terms of meaning conveyed."[17]

Two types of communicative drills include *information exchange tasks* and *information gap tasks*. In an information exchange task, the interlocutors (teacher-student or student-student) share information that the other does not know. For example, the discussion might center around a favorite movie or family history. In an information gap task, each participant has information that the other participants need to complete the task. The students must seek out, ask, and share information to successfully complete the activity. For example, one student may have one part of a story, while the others have the remaining portions. The students must each inquire of the others to find the rest of the story and put it together in order.

A subset of communicative drills that focuses the learner more precisely on the target structure are known as *structured output activities*. Structured output activities can be used to teach grammar items and/or vocabulary, and they have two defining characteristics. First, like communicative drills, the learners exchange information that was not previously known. Second, they "require learners to access a particular form or structure in order to express meaning."[18] This second characteristic is

---

[16] Lee and VanPatten, *Communicative Language Teaching*, 121.

[17] Lee and VanPatten, *Communicative Language Teaching*, 122.

[18] Lee and VanPatten, *Communicative Language Teaching*, 173.

what differentiates structured output activities from other communicative drills.

Lee and VanPatten suggest the following guidelines for creating structured output activities.[19]

1. Present one thing at a time.
2. Keep meaning in focus.
3. Move from sentences to connected discourse.
4. Use both written and oral output.
5. Others must respond to the content of the output.
6. The learner must have some knowledge of the form or structure.[20]

An example of a structured output activity might be an exercise in which the students share their plans for the upcoming weekend. The target structure would be the first person singular future tense.

This section presented basic skills necessary for L2 output production, including access, monitoring, and production strategies, followed by a discussion of the Output Hypothesis and some different approaches for promoting output in the classroom. The next section provides reasons for incorporating output into the biblical and ancient language classroom.

The Rationale: Output in Biblical
and Ancient Language Classrooms

Many instructors have said, "My students will never need to speak Hebrew/Greek/Latin outside of the classroom, so why should I spend time making them produce it in the classroom?" It is a valid question that needs full consideration. The following explanation provides the basis for promoting L2 output in the biblical and ancient language curriculum.

First, output is also a form of input, which is essential for acquisition. One person's output can be another person's input. Not only that,

---

[19] Lee and VanPatten, *Communicative Language Teaching*, 173.

[20] As with other approaches to promote output, the learner must have some previous knowledge of the structure. Output practice cannot be the starting point for learning a new form or structure. See Lee and VanPatten, *Communicative Language Teaching*, 175.

but the output can also provide a form of input to the one producing it, also known as auto-input.[21] As Michael Sharwood Smith explains, the output a learner produces by means of explicit knowledge can provide feedback and a form of input that helps develop the same learner's implicit knowledge.[22]

Second, output is an important component of meaningful interaction. As noted in chapter three, meaning-focused instruction with its emphasis on input and interaction is a primary means of promoting L2 proficiency. Interaction in L2 requires both input and output to operate. A monologue or one-sided conversation will not suffice. Both discussion partners must participate in the give and take of the conversation, and this requires output.

A third reason for incorporating output into the biblical and ancient language classroom is that output provides the opportunity for the learner to reinforce and fine-tune his or her understanding of grammar. "While input processing is linked to acquiring form and structure, access [as part of producing output] is linked to *accuracy* (correctness) and *fluency* (ease and speed) in output."[23] When the learner is pushed to produce output that is correct and sociolinguistically acceptable, this stretches the limits of his or her competence, providing the opportunity for the learner to "achieve higher levels of linguistic and sociolinguistic competence."[24] Like the spelling tests described at the beginning of this chapter, output forces the learner to process the nuances of the linguistic information he or she is learning on a deeper level.

Relatedly, student output also provides the instructor with valuable information regarding what the student knows, especially what he or she knows implicitly. Because a student can only produce what he or she has internalized (see Figure 1 above), a student's output can be a good indication of the state of the learner's developing internal system. In fact, a learner's performance may be the only way to gauge the level of proficiency in his or her implicit internal system.[25] According to

---

[21] Schmidt and Frota, "Developing Basic Conversational Ability," 316.

[22] Sharwood Smith, "Consciousness-Raising," 166.

[23] Lee and VanPatten, *Communicative Language Teaching*, 169, emphasis original.

[24] Ellis, "A Theory of Instructed Second Language Acquisition," 104.

[25] Ellis, *Study of Second Language Acquisition*, 585.

McQuinn, "It is only by output—whether speaking or writing—that one is able to find out what he *really* knows of the language."[26] With this information, an instructor can help the learner review and reinforce items that are weak or move on to new structures if the current structures are solidly internalized. This, then, leads to the last reason for encouraging output in the classroom.

Student output also provides the instructor with opportunities for focused *feedback*.[27] In the simplest terms, feedback is error correction.[28] Without student output, the instructor would lose this important opportunity to further promote and refine the learner's understanding of the language and its structures. Feedback is advantageous for a couple reasons. First, instruction that comes in the form of feedback is tailored to the needs of the individual student because it is given in response to the student's output. Second, during a live classroom discussion, the potential exists for the instructor to provide feedback immediately, which is usually more effective than delayed feedback.

With these reasons for incorporating output into the biblical and ancient language classroom, we now turn to some specific examples of activities that promote output for Hebrew, Greek, and Latin.

Examples of Output Activities for Biblical and Ancient Language Classrooms

The following activities sample a few ideas for promoting output in biblical and ancient language teaching. As described above, output practice can come in the form of mechanical drills, meaningful drills, communicative drills, and structured output activities. Because mechanical drills are less valuable for language acquisition, this section will focus on the other three approaches for promoting L2 output. Keep in mind that

---

[26] McQuinn, "Principled Communicative Methodology," 56, emphasis original.

[27] Feedback may also be called "negative feedback" or "corrective feedback."

[28] For an overview of the role of feedback in language acquisition, see Hind Talal Mashrah, "The Role of Implicit Negative Feedback in Language Development—Some Reflections," *International Journal of English Language and Translation Studies* 5.1 (2017): 1–7. For an overview of research related to feedback, see Ellis, *Study of Second Language Acquisition*, 803–6.

output activities should not introduce a new form. Rather, output activities review and reinforce structures that the students have already seen.

Meaningful Drill: Oral (Hebrew)

Describe the person:

This activity is intended for beginning Hebrew students. The instructor presents photographs of individuals to the students, one at a time. Students take turns in class describing the person in one sentence. While not necessary, the instructor might also provide a list of previously encountered nouns and adjectives that could potentially be used to describe those individuals. The following are some possible descriptions the students could use:

אִישׁ הוּא

גְּדוֹלָה הִיא

הוּא מֶלֶךְ

הוּא אָב

אֵם הִיא

טוֹבָה הִיא

Communicative Drill: Written Information Exchange (Greek)

An essay in Greek:

This activity is intended for more advanced Greek students. The instructor directs the students to write a short essay of one or two paragraphs in Greek. Potential topics might include "Describe your favorite Mediterranean vacation destination" or "Describe the New Testament Corinthian church." While not necessary, it could be helpful for the instructor to provide a list of vocabulary and grammatical items the students might want to use, based upon their level of language proficiency. The following is a brief sample list:

ἐκκλησία
πόλις
μέγας
μερισθεῖσα (μερίζω)
ἁμαρτωλός

Structured Output: Oral Interactive Activity (Latin)

Going to the market:

This activity is designed for first-year students with some experience. The target structure for this activity will be food vocabulary while reinforcing imperatives. In preparation for this activity, the instructor should ensure that students have solidly acquired the two or three imperatives needed ahead of time so the activity is reinforcing one thing at a time (the food vocabulary) in compliance with Lee and VanPatten's guidelines (above). Have students work in pairs. One will play the role of master or mistress, and the other will play the role of servant. The master or mistress must command the servant to go to the market and get various food items for the household. Have the students change roles after a few trips to the "market." The activity can be more realistic and engaging if the instructor can provide props (food items or plastic food, play money, signs for a market area, etc.). Below is a sample of the vocabulary needed for the activity:

> *exī (eō)*
> *sūme (sūmō)*
> *pānis*
> *fructus*
> *carō*
> *uva*

Conclusion

Like English spelling tests, producing L2 output is important for developing accuracy and helping learners internalize language structures more solidly. This chapter covered the mechanics of language output, including access, monitoring, and production strategies, and the role of output in language acquisition as articulated in the Output Hypothesis. This chapter also discussed some of the reasons for incorporating output into a language classroom, followed by examples for Hebrew, Greek, and Latin. The next section of the book will address language skill development, beginning with an overview the four language skills: listening, speaking, reading, and writing.

For Further Reading

Mashrah, Hind Talal. "The Role of Implicit Negative Feedback in Language Development—Some Reflections." *International Journal of English Language and Translation Studies* 5.1 (2017): 1–7.

Skehan, Peter. *A Cognitive Approach to Language Learning*. Oxford: Oxford University Press, 1998.

Swain, Merrill. "The Output Hypothesis: Theory and Research." Pages 471–83 in *Handbook of Research in Second Language Teaching and Learning*. Edited by E. Hinkel. Mahwah, NJ: Lawrence Erlbaum, 2005.

VanPatten, Bill. *From Input to Output: A Teacher's Guide to Second Language Acquisition*. Boston: McGraw-Hill, 2003.

CHAPTER 8: THE FOUR LANGUAGE SKILLS: LISTENING, SPEAKING, READING, AND WRITING

By the time I started studying music in college, I had been playing the piano for at least ten years. I could play well enough, but I knew I had more to learn, so I thought I was ready to start the process. However, the skills I had to learn were more involved than what I originally thought.

In addition to my weekly private piano lessons, I also took music history, piano pedagogy, and almost two years of music theory. The music theory class was divided into four parts: ear training, sight singing, written music, and keyboard skills. The written portion of the class significantly improved my ability to read music. Suddenly, I was seeing chords and patterns where I had once only seen individual notes on the page. Similarly, the keyboard skills dramatically improved my ability to play by shoring up some of my lower-level processes, so I was freed up to concentrate on higher-level skills like expression and communicating emotions through the music.

As for the other two components of the class, well, I could appreciate the value of ear training and sight singing for the other musicians in the class, but I didn't really see how they applied to me, a piano player. Unlike vocalists or those who play other instruments, pianists cannot change the pitch of their instrument. Instead, pianists rely on professional piano tuners to set the pitch, and then they just play the right keys at the right time, or so I thought. It seemed that the ear training and sight singing were marginal skills for me at best.

A few years later, I developed an ear infection that ruptured my left eardrum and left me temporarily deaf on that side. I was surprised to find that I was disoriented and unable to practice piano as I had before. In fact, I suddenly felt like I had no idea what my left hand was doing because I couldn't hear on that side, even though I could see and feel what my hand was doing. Through that experience, I saw how wrong I was in assuming that pianists do not have to pay attention to pitch when playing. When I lost my hearing, I realized how important my processing of pitch was for being able to play the piano and how much I relied on it to guide me. In the end, all facets of that music theory class directly affected how I played the piano, even the auditory skills that I had once thought to be of marginal value.

The previous section of this book addressed the raw materials of language learning, including types of language knowledge, input, and output. This chapter opens the second main section of the book on the development of language skills and will provide an overview of the four language skills—listening, speaking, reading, and writing—with the next chapter going into greater depth on the skill of reading. In addition to introducing these basic skills, this chapter will address how the four skills relate to the concept of language proficiency and how these seemingly unrelated skills work together, just as I discovered how the different music skills affected my piano playing, even though some of them seemed to be unnecessary at first.[1]

The Principle: The Four Language Skills

Learning a language involves the development of a myriad of skills and competencies usually grouped under one of the four basic language skills: listening, speaking, reading, and writing.[2] Listening and reading are receptive skills while speaking and writing are productive skills. However, learners must be active participants, even for those skills labeled "receptive."[3]

In children, the four skills are learned in a predictable order: listening first, followed by speaking, and then reading, followed by writing. However, the order is more flexible for adult learners who have fully developed cognitive and motor skills and who understand how symbols,

---

[1] Moreover, the four music theory skills correspond quite well with the four language skills. Ear training corresponds to listening, sight singing to speaking, written theory to reading, and keyboard skills to writing. Literacy experts note the similarity between music and language learning processes and even suggest that improved literacy in one will improve literacy in the other. See, e.g., Dee Hansen, Elain Bernstorf, and Gayle M. Stuber, *The Music and Literacy Connection*, 2nd ed. (Lanham, MD: Rowman & Littlefield, 2014).

[2] The role of cultural competence in language learning has become a topic of increasing interest. See Michael Byram and Anwei Feng, "Culture and Language Learning: Teaching, Research and Scholarship," *Language Teaching* 37. 3 (2004): 149–68. While some would add cultural competence as a fifth skill, this chapter will only address the four skills of listening, speaking, reading, and writing.

[3] Lee and VanPatten, *Communicative Language Teaching*, 195.

such as spoken words and letters on a page, can represent real ideas and events.[4] Moreover, the four skills are interdependent and mutually reinforcing with improvement in one skill bringing improvement in the others.[5] Therefore, while the teaching of the four skills may be separated for logistical reasons, SLA researchers and teachers recommend that they be taught together.[6]

The four language skills themselves are comprised of multiple processes and subskills. These subskills are often grouped by the complexity involved in the task. Lower-level processes are those that are basic or foundational and usually simpler, such as letter and word recognition. Higher-level processes are those that are more complex and require more of the learner's attention, such as inferencing and discourse analysis.

Language learners can process language, then, from a bottom-up approach, starting with lower-level processes and moving to higher-lever processes, or from a top-down approach, starting with the higher-level processes. In a bottom-up approach, the learner constructs meaning "by accretion, gradually combining increasingly larger units of meaning from the phoneme-level up to discourse-level features."[7] For example, a reader may start by decoding each word of a text and then stringing the words together. Eventually, he or she will have a full sentence or paragraph and be able to assign meaning to it. Then, finally, he or she can interpret the entire text.

In a top-down approach, the learner uses "context and prior knowledge ... to build a conceptual framework for comprehension."[8] For example, a learner may have the opportunity to listen to a lecture on archaeology in L2. Because the learner knows the topic in advance, he or she will come to the lecture with certain expectations, having activated some specific information stored in long-term memory about

---

[4] McQuinn, "Principled Communicative Methodology," 59.

[5] See, e.g., Joan Carson Eisterhold, "Reading-Writing Connections: Toward a Description for Second Language Learners," in *Second Language Writing: Research Insights for the Classroom*, ed. B. Kroll (Cambridge: Cambridge University Press, 1990), 88.

[6] Eli Hinkel, "Current Perspectives on Teaching the Four Skills," *TESOL Quarterly* 40 (2006): 113.

[7] Larry Vandergrift, "Listening to Learn or Learning to Listen?" *Annual Review of Applied Linguistics* 24 (2004): 4.

[8] Vandergrift, "Listening," 4.

archaeology, and thus the learner will be able to interpret and make inferences along the way as he or she listens. However, during the lecture, the listener may need to seek out the meaning of some specific vocabulary items that are unfamiliar or certain grammatical structures that he or she has never encountered before.

Because each of the four skills has its own set of subskills and approaches to instruction, the next section will briefly cover each of the four skills in turn, starting with the first skill that children acquire, listening.

Listening

The skill of listening is essential for L1 acquisition because it is a child's entry point into the language. For L2 acquisition, listening does not carry the same weight, but it still provides a significant source of comprehensible input for the language learner, making it foundational for language learning.

Listening Skills and Processes

Listening is comprised of several subskills. At the most basic level, listening requires perception and attention.[9] This begins with the physical perception of sound waves by the eardrum which travel to the brain. From this point, the listener must select what to pay attention to and what to disregard, separating language stimuli from non-language stimuli. Attending to language stimuli also involves *phonetic processing*, that is, discerning sounds and discriminating various sounds from one another. A listener must also engage *cross-modal processing*, which involves the listener attending to "information that appears across or in conjunction with other modalities, for example, vision and touch."[10]

At the next level of listening subskills, the listener must organize the aural stimuli and assign meaning to it.[11] "Assigning meaning to

---

[9] Margarete Imhof, "What is Going on in the Mind of a Listener? The Cognitive Psychology of Listening," in *Listening and Human Communication in the 21st Century*, ed. A. D. Wolvin (Malden, MA: Blackwell, 2010), 101–3.

[10] Imhof, "What is Going on in the Mind of a Listener?" 103.

[11] Imhof, "What is Going on in the Mind of a Listener?" 103–7.

perceived and attended stimuli is an interpretative act that involves personal, cultural, and linguistic matters interacting in complex ways."[12] This level of processing aural stimuli includes word recognition, sentence processing, and text representation, which is the collection of interconnected ideas expressed in a message. At this level of processing, the amount of available working memory becomes a significant factor in the learner's ability to comprehend the input he or she is receiving. A learner who struggles to process aural stimuli at the word level, for example, will have very little working memory left to use for the remaining higher-level processes.

The final level of subskills involved in listening is that of integration of information, which is the listener's creation of the big picture from what he or she has heard.[13] At this level, the listener will be able to make inferences, supplementing the aural text and filling in gaps, as necessary. The listener at this level is also involved in structure building, which is the ability to combine the incoming information with information already stored in long-term memory. The integration of information at this level will also form the basis for anything the listener may generate in response to what he or she has heard.

With a basic understanding of the various skills and processes involved in listening, the next section will present some strategies for teaching listening in the L2 classroom.

Teaching the Skill of Listening

Teaching the skill of listening should address its various processes and subskills, keeping in mind that different approaches may be necessary to target different subskills. Below are a few general suggestions for helping students develop listening skills.[14] The last section of this chapter will present a specific example for teaching listening in Hebrew.

First, the instructor should use L2 in the classroom as much as possible to conduct business. For example, make announcements, take roll, assign homework, and describe what is on an upcoming exam in L2.

---

[12] Lee and VanPatten, Communicative Language Teaching, 196.

[13] Imhof, "What is Going on in the Mind of a Listener?" 107–9.

[14] Some are adapted from Lee and VanPatten, *Communicative Language Teaching*, 204.

Because learners have a vested interest in this information, they will be motivated to pay close attention to what is being said and will be more likely to signal nonunderstanding when needed. Student may also find it helpful to have available some L2 phrases that indicate nonunderstanding. Such phrases might include, "Could you speak more slowly?" "I didn't catch that," "What is…?" or "I don't understand…"

Another strategy to increase opportunities and motivation for listening is to allow the learners to take turns suggesting topics and structure discussion in L2. In these situations, the teacher should be a participatory listener, responding as a listener, not an instructor. In this way, the instructor can model how to be a good listener in L2.

For a monologue or other noncollaborative listening practice such as listening to a recording, the instructor should ideally provide student activities in three phases to encourage and promote listening skills: pre-listening, while-listening, and post-listening.[15] Pre-listening activities help orient learners and have been shown to increase comprehension.[16] Such activities might present new vocabulary needed for the task, review existing knowledge of the topic or situation, and help the learners anticipate or predict what a speaker might say about a given topic or situation.

Activities for the while-listening phase should encourage the learners to remain focused on the message, perhaps giving them a list of ideas, words, or phrases to listen for. Post-listening activities could include a summary or review of the message, a comprehension quiz, and/or the opportunity for a personal response to the content of the message.[17]

Speaking

In young children, speaking follows listening but precedes reading and writing. However, as noted above, the order of language skill

---

[15] Alicia Martínez-Flor, and Esther Usó-Juan, "Towards Acquiring Communicative Competence through Listening," in *Current Trends in the Development and Teaching of the Four Language Skills*, ed. E. Usó-Juan and A. Martínez-Flor (Berlin: De Gruyter, 2006), 42.

[16] Lee and VanPatten, *Communicative Language Teaching*, 209.

[17] Martínez-Flor, and Usó-Juan, "Towards Acquiring Communicative Competence through Listening," 41–42.

development can be somewhat different for adult L2 learners, although speaking cannot come first. Since speaking is a form of output, a student can only begin to develop this skill after starting to learn at least one of the receptive skills, listening or reading.

Speaking Skills and Processes

Some consider the skill of speaking to be the most challenging of the four skills because of its complexity and the mental resources it requires. Speaking is "an interactive, social and contextualized communicative event. Therefore, the key role of the speaking skill in developing leaners' communicative competence has also become evident, since this skill requires learners to be in possession of knowledge about how to produce not only linguistically correct but also pragmatically appropriate utterances."[18]

Speaking involves four major processes or skills.[19] The first process is conceptualization, that is, deciding what to say based on context and intended purpose. The second process in speaking is choosing the appropriate words and phrases for the intended message and audience. The third process or skill is articulation. This is the physical act of speaking that involves motor control of the speech organs to execute the message. The final process is monitoring, which is the identification and correction of mistakes as needed. Paying attention to all four processes at once places a significant mental load on the speaker. Add to this mental load the pressure of performing in the time constraints of an ongoing conversation, and one can see why this skill is the most challenging of the four.

Teaching the Skill of Speaking

To teach the skill of speaking, the instructor should provide opportunities for students to use L2 in a range of contexts, carrying out a range of functions, particularly those that would likely be encountered in the

---

[18] Alicia Martínez-Flor, Esther Usó-Juan, and Eva Alcón Soler, "Towards Acquiring Communicative Competence through Speaking," in *Current Trends in the Development and Teaching of the Four Language Skills*, ed. E. Usó-Juan and A. Martínez-Flor (Berlin: De Gruyter, 2006), 139.

[19] Adapted from Willem J. M. Levelt, *Speaking: From Intention to Articulation* (Cambridge, MA: MIT Press, 1989), 9–14.

target culture.[20] The last section of this chapter includes a specific example of an activity for speaking Greek.

One strategy for the elicitation of spoken L2 from the students would be role playing, where each student is assigned a character to portray in a situation that is typical of the target culture.[21] An instructor could also invite a conversation about a given topic or invite the students to participate in completing a particular goal, such as putting together a puzzle or creating a daily schedule. Another option is for the instructor to describe a typical situation in the target culture and ask the learner to explain how he or she would respond to that situation.

Making good use of questions is another option for eliciting spoken language from the students. However, care must be given to the types and variety of questions the instructor uses. An instructor needs to carefully consider the type, length, and quality of answers he or she wants from the students. Many questions fall under the category of initiation ("What is X?"), response ("X is…"), feedback ("Right").[22] While these can be used, classroom discussions should not be limited to these. Other options include referential questions, for which the questioner does not know the answer, closed (yes/no) questions, open (*wh-*) questions, questions for facts, questions for opinions, and questions for reasons or explanations.[23] Using a variety of questions will elicit a variety of responses from the students, providing a richer communicative learning experience.

Reading

Reading typically follows listening and speaking in the natural order of L1 acquisition. However, because it is a receptive skill and because adult learners already understand how letters on a page function as

---

[20] Hadley, *Teaching Language*, 236–37.

[21] The various strategies presented are adapted from Ellis, *Study of Second Language Acquisition*, 167–68.

[22] Christiane Dalton-Puffer, "Questions as Strategies to Encourage Speaking in Content-and-Language-Integrated Classrooms," in *Current Trends in the Development and Teaching of the Four Language Skills*, ed. E. Usó-Juan and A. Martínez-Flor (Berlin: De Gruyter, 2006), 191.

[23] Dalton-Puffer, "Questions as Strategies," 192–93.

language, for adult L2 learners, reading can be learned at the same time as other skills. Because the next chapter addresses the skill of reading in greater detail, this section will only provide a basic overview.

Reading Skills and Processes

Like the other language skills, reading is comprised of several other processes and subskills. Grabe identifies several lower-level processes that must be developed for a learner to become a fluent reader.[24] These lower-level processes include word recognition, *syntactic parsing*, which involves recognizing the significance of word order, determiners, tense, etc., and *meaning proposition encoding*, by which meaning is extracted from words and structures as words and syntax are being parsed. These three processes can be further divided into even more basic subskills, which will be addressed in the next chapter.

Reading also involves several higher-level processes, assuming the learner has enough attentional resources remaining while also performing the lower-level processes.[25] These higher-level processes include comprehension, interpretation, and the control of other attentional resources and processes such as goals, strategies, and the activation of background knowledge.[26]

Teaching the Skill of Reading

While the processes and subskills of reading can be taught using different approaches, the overarching recurring strategy recommended is extensive reading, that is, reading large quantities for long periods of time. According to Grabe, "The need to integrate many processing skills, along with considerable linguistic knowledge, indicates that reading an extensive amount of material over a long period of time is the only way to build mastery of the required skills for reading comprehension."[27] The

---

[24] Grabe, *Reading*, 23–31.
[25] Grabe, *Reading*, 39.
[26] Grabe, *Reading*, 40–55.
[27] Grabe, *Reading*, 57.

next chapter will address some guidelines and suggestions for encouraging extensive reading in L2 classrooms.

Writing

Once a young learner can read, he or she may begin the process of learning to write. The same is also true for most adult learners unless the orthography of L2 is very familiar, in which case, writing can precede reading. Like speaking, writing is a productive skill, but it usually does not carry the same time constraints and pressures that speaking does, making it a little less challenging. However, discourse features become more important to the composition process as written texts are usually longer and more complicated than spoken messages.

Writing Skills and Processes

Writing, like the previous three skills, is a complex process that can be broken down into several subskills and processes. According to Esther Usó-Juan, Alicia Martínez-Flor, and Juan Carlos Palmer-Silveira, "linguistic, cognitive and sociocultural factors have to interact with one another for effective writing."[28] In addition to using linguistic knowledge of L2, good writers also use strategic knowledge of at least three processes to compose a text: planning, evaluation, and revision.[29] They must also use discourse processing at different levels to work and rework the material, making it coherent, grammatically correct, and culturally appropriate. Global discourse processing is more useful at the planning stage of writing while local discourse processing is more useful at the evaluation and revision stages.[30]

---

[28] Esther Usó-Juan, Alicia Martínez-Flor, and Juan Carlos Palmer-Silveira, "Towards Acquiring Communicative Competence through Writing," in *Current Trends in the Development and Teaching of the Four Language Skills*, ed. E. Usó-Juan and A. Martínez-Flor (Berlin: De Gruyter, 2006), 394.

[29] Karen Whalen and Nathan Ménard, "L1 and L2 Writers' Strategic and Linguistic Knowledge: A Model of Multiple-Level Discourse Processing," *Language Learning* 45.3 (1995): 403.

[30] Whalen and Ménard, "L1 and L2 Writers' Strategic and Linguistic Knowledge," 404.

Teaching the Skill of Writing

Instructors can create a wide variety of writing assignments for their students. However, the completion of a writing assignment usually involves the following six steps with the instructor providing support, instruction, and feedback along the way.[31] The last section of the chapter presents a specific example for Latin using these six steps.

First, the instructor creates the assignment and communicates the requirements to the students. Second, the students engage in preparatory work. At this stage, the instructor will likely need to assist by introducing any necessary vocabulary, grammar, and information about the genre that the students will be using. Relevant cultural information will also be helpful. The students then prepare to write by gathering information, taking notes, and writing any reflections needed to help in the writing process.

For the third step, students each write a draft of the assignment. In step four, the students receive feedback on their writing, which is critical to the learning process. Feedback can come from themselves, peers, and/or teachers. For the fifth step, students revise their work based on the feedback they receive. At this point, they may need to return to steps two through four before moving to step six. The last step is submitting the final draft for evaluation by the instructor.

Having covered the four basic language skills, including their component processes and subskills along with some suggestions for instruction, we now turn to evidence that supports and encourages the inclusion of all four skills in any L2 curriculum.

The Rationale: Why Teach the Four Skills

For biblical and ancient languages, the primary goal of language acquisition is the interpretation of ancient texts. Therefore, reading is necessarily the primary goal of instruction and the skill that receives the most

---

[31] Adapted from Barbara Kroll, "Techniques for Shaping Writing Course Curricula: Strategies in Designing Assignments," in *Current Trends in the Development and Teaching of the Four Language Skills*, ed. E. Usó-Juan and A. Martínez-Flor (Berlin: De Gruyter, 2006), 435.

attention. However, the other three skills should not be neglected in biblical and ancient language classrooms. This section explains why.

As discussed in chapter three, meaning-based instruction is the preferred approach for promoting language proficiency regardless of the skill being developed. This type of instruction has two main components: input and interaction. Input can come in the form of listening or reading, so the minimum number of language skills needed for this component of meaning-based instruction is one receptive skill. However, for interaction to take place, at least two interlocutors need to be able to use at least two different language skills, one productive and one receptive. Therefore, at the very minimum, two of the four language skills must be taught to make use of this effective approach to instruction. Limiting instruction to reading skills only will limit one's approach to teaching and thereby restrict the fuller development of proficiency in the language.

The productive skills (speaking and writing) come into play when producing output. As discussed in chapter seven, output also has a role to play in promoting language proficiency. Output sharpens accuracy and deepens acquisition. Therefore, instructors are wise to incorporate these language skills in the curriculum. Students miss out on the opportunity to develop accuracy and further proficiency when they only focus on reading skills.

Additionally, there is strong evidence that the four language skills are "interrelated and mutually reinforcing."[32] Eli Hinkel notes that "commonly accepted perspectives on language teaching and learning recognize that, in meaningful communication, people employ incremental language skills not in isolation but in tandem."[33] Moreover, learning one skill can bring about "cognitive and communicative associates with others."[34] Therefore, an improvement in speaking skills will help improve reading skills and vice versa. For this reason, researchers strongly urge instructors to teach all four skills in the language classroom. According to B. Kumaravadivelu, "all available empirical, theoretical, and pedagogical information points to the need to integrate language skills

---

[32] Kumaravadivelu, "Postmethod," 39.

[33] Hinkel, "Current Perspectives," 113.

[34] Kumaravadivelu, "Postmethod," 39.

for effective language teaching."[35] Atomizing and isolating individual language skills in instruction can limit the development of language proficiency, even when the goal of instruction is only one of the four skills.

As a specific example, one can see the importance of auditory and phonological competence even for the seemingly silent skill of reading. Research in working memory indicates that "all language information used in working memory is stored and rehearsed phonologically."[36] This includes silent reading. Even the visual language information that a person receives in the form of written words is stored phonologically in working memory. Therefore, proficiency in the auditory skills of listening and speaking can directly affect and promote proficiency in the skills of reading and writing. Without competence in listening and speaking, a student's phonological processing can be similarly stunted, resulting in an unnecessary limitation on what he or she can read fluently.

Examples for Biblical and Ancient Language Classrooms

The following examples will cover teaching ideas for strengthening the skills of listening, speaking, and writing. The next chapter will cover reading in greater depth with specific teaching examples to aid in the development of reading skills. Notice that each activity below also fosters cultural awareness, or what some call the "fifth" skill of language learning.

Listening Activity (Hebrew)

This activity uses a short passage of Scripture (Ezekiel 37:11–12) as the basis for developing listening skills in Hebrew. While this activity assumes that the students are at least at the end of their first year of Hebrew, the details can be adapted for students at other levels. The activity is divided into three segments: pre-listening, while-listening, and post-listening.

The pre-listening portion of the activity focuses on preparing the students for the passage and combines two sets of approaches. Bottom-up approaches help develop the lower-level processes involved in

---

[35] Kumaravadivelu, "Postmethod," 39.
[36] Grabe, *Reading*, 34.

listening, especially vocabulary and grammar preparation, while top-down approaches focus on helping the students engage in higher-level processes through what are called *advance organizers*. The purpose of these advance organizers is to prime the students' prior knowledge to help them connect the information in the text with information they already have stored in long-term memory, promoting such processes as interpretation and making inferences.

The bottom-up approaches to pre-listening involve introducing and reviewing vocabulary and grammar items the students will encounter in the passage, especially those that are new or unfamiliar. For example, the students may need to learn all vocabulary items in this passage that occur less frequently than 100 times in the Hebrew Bible, including the following words: יָבֵשׁ "be dry," תִּקְוָה "be cut off," נִגְזַר "grave," and קֶבֶר "hope." Students may also need a review of the form and function of the Hiphil verb or a review of the perfect consecutive used as an imperative. Auditory approaches to learning these words and forms will be especially useful, such as learning to recognize the vocabulary by sound rather than just by sight.

Pre-listening should also include some top-down approaches to prepare the students for listening to the text. As noted above, these advance organizers will help the students engage with the text using higher-level listening processes. One way to do this is to discuss with the class the historical and literary context of Ezekiel 37. For example, recognizing the sociocultural situation of the author and intended audience (i.e., people of Judah in exile who are likely discouraged) will help the students understand and appreciate the hope communicated by these verses. A discussion of the vision that precedes the chosen text will also help the students interpret the message. Finally, the students should understand that what they are going to hear is Ezekiel's recounting of a speech from God, who is explaining the significance of the vision. If these discussions can be done in Hebrew, so much the better.

Another advance organizer to prepare the students for higher-level processing is to discuss the symbolism of death, which is used figuratively in this passage. The instructor could lead a discussion covering the types of situations or events that death can symbolize. Another approach is to discuss the words and ideas that are associated with death and dying, guiding the students to Hebrew words and ideas as much as possible. Particularly relevant for this passage would be words like עֶצֶם "bone" and קֶבֶר "grave."

After the pre-listening phase, the instructor can move into the listening phase of the activity. The instructor should plan to have the students listen to the text at least twice and should also give the students some specific instructions for each time through the text to help them focus their attention. For example, the students might listen for each occurrence of the verb אמר "say" the first time through the text, noting that this often signals a change in speaker. The students might listen for other verbs the second time through or listen for familiar collocations such as כֹּה אָמַר אֲדֹנָי יהוה "Thus says the Sovereign Lord."

After listening to the text several times, the instructor can move onto the post-listening phase of the activity. One option for this phase is to administer a brief comprehension quiz on the text, written in Hebrew if possible. A comprehension quiz also presents the opportunity for an optional follow-up activity in which the students listen to the text one final time, correcting their quizzes as they listen.

A second option for the post-listening phase would be to compose a conclusion or a response to the story. This could be something the class discusses together as a group. However, it could also turn into a writing assignment in which each student pretends to be someone hearing Ezekiel speak this for the first time. The student would then write a brief personal response to the message in Hebrew.

Speaking Activity (Greek)

This activity encourages the development of spoken Greek through a discussion on a particular topic that is relevant to ancient Greco-Roman culture.[37] The activity can be adapted for various levels of Greek language proficiency.

The students and the instructor should gather culture-related materials for various cultural topics. These materials should include passages from the New Testament and other ancient Greek writings but should

---

[37] Adapted from Martínez-Flor, Usó-Juan, and Soler, "Towards Acquiring Communicative Competence through Speaking," 153.

not be limited to these. Topics might include family, law and order, power and politics, or religious practices.[38] Reading materials should be relatively short, appropriate for the level of the students, and in Greek when possible.

After gathering the materials, the class should review any vocabulary and grammar the students might need for the discussion, again, appropriate for the students' proficiency level. The instructor then puts the students into groups of three or four. Each group will select materials that address a topic that interests them. After reading or listening to the culture-related materials, the group will discuss the topic. Each group member should present his or her personal view of the topic in addition to any other ideas related to the topic.

The discussions can be recorded, which gives the instructor the opportunity to review and evaluate each group. However, the recordings can also be used to address the topic together with the entire class or analyze the discussion with the class for language features, such as repetition, pronunciation, vocabulary, etc.

Writing Activity (Latin)

This activity promotes the development of writing in Latin and follows the six-step pattern proposed by Barbara Kroll presented above.[39]

In step one, the instructor creates the assignment and communicates the requirements to the students. Here is a sample assignment idea that can be adapted and used at different stages of language proficiency: "Pretend you are an ancient Roman citizen from Pompei visiting the city of Rome for the first time. Write a letter in Latin describing ancient Rome to a family member or friend back home." Instructors should also provide a few other parameters for the assignment, such as length, making it appropriate for the proficiency level of the students.

The second step is preparatory work. At this stage, the instructor will likely need to assist by introducing any necessary vocabulary, grammar,

---

[38] Bible backgrounds commentaries could be helpful resources for this activity along with works like David A. deSilva, *Honor, Patronage, Kinship, and Purity: Unlocking New Testament Culture*, 2nd ed. (Downers Grove, IL: Intervarsity, 2022).

[39] Kroll, "Techniques for Shaping Writing Course Curricula," 435.

and information about the genre that the students will be using.[40] A sampling of ancient letters in Latin and ancient descriptions of Rome in Latin would also be useful. The students then prepare to write by gathering information, taking notes, and writing any reflections needed to help in the writing process. Instructors may choose to make appointments with individual students or use some class time to provide direction and assistance at this stage.

Once the students have collected information, each one writes a draft of the letter, which is step three. In step four, the students receive feedback on their draft. As noted above, this stage can involve the teacher, other instructors, and/or other students, perhaps exchanging papers in class for review.

After receiving feedback, the students then move on to step five, which involves making changes to their drafts based on the comments they receive. Depending on the types of changes to be made, some students may need to return to steps two through four before submitting. The sixth step is submitting the final draft for evaluation by the instructor.

Conclusion

This chapter introduced the four basic language skills—listening, speaking, reading, and writing—noting how each skill is comprised of many distinct processes or subskills. Much like the four music skills described at the beginning of the chapter, these four language skills are interrelated and mutually reinforcing. Therefore, SLA researchers encourage the teaching of all four skills together in a well-rounded language curriculum. The last section of the chapter presented sample activities that would promote three of the skills, namely listening, speaking, and writing. The next chapter will address the skill of reading in greater depth because it is of particular interest and importance for those who learn biblical and ancient languages.

---

[40] Two potential resources for this activity are Stanley Kent Stowers, *Letter Writing in Greco-Roman Antiquity* (Philadelphia: Westminster, 1986) and Pauline Allen and Bronwen Neil, *Greek and Latin Letters in Late Antiquity: The Christianisation of a Literary Form* (Cambridge: Cambridge University Press, 2020).

For Further Reading

Hinkel, Eli. "Current Perspectives on Teaching the Four Skills." *TESOL Quarterly* 40 (2006): 109–31.

Kumaravadivelu, B. "The Postmethod Condition: (E)merging Strategies for Second/Foreign Language Teaching." *TESOL Quarterly, 28* (1994): 27–48.

Usó-Juan, Esther, and Alicia Martínez-Flor. *Current Trends in the Development and Teaching of the Four Language Skills*. Berlin: De Gruyter, 2006.

Chapter 9: Reading Fluency: Developing Skills that Promote Comprehension and Interpretation

During my second year of seminary, I encountered two related surprises that challenged my thinking about language learning. The first surprise came during the first week of my very first biblical language class. I was surprised to find that the professor wanted us to learn the sounds of the letters, not just their names. I had naively assumed that, since we would only be reading the language (silently), we would not have to learn what the language sounded like. I thought we would only need to learn the language visually, associating groups of new symbols (i.e., words) with their meanings. Over the next few weeks and months, I realized how important the sounds of the language were to my learning and understanding of the language.

I encountered the second surprise a little later in the same class. As I observed my fellow classmates, I noticed that those who could pronounce the language more accurately and could read out loud more fluently were also the ones who were also doing better overall and getting better grades. Although I did not understand the relationship at the time, I could recognize the correlation between reading skills and auditory skills (also called phonological awareness or phonological sensitivity), and I found it fascinating.[1]

The last chapter addressed the four language skills: listening, speaking, reading, and writing. As noted in that chapter, all four language skills play a role in language proficiency, even for those learners whose primary goals are reading and interpreting ancient texts. However, because reading comprehension and interpretation *are* the main goals of those studying the biblical and ancient languages, this chapter addresses the skill of reading in greater depth.

The four language skills are each a collection of many subskills and processes that a learner must master to become proficient in that skill. The skill of reading is no different. To become a fluent reader, a student

---

[1] The correlation between reading skills and phonological awareness is firmly established by research. See Alan Beaton, *Dyslexia, Reading and the Brain: A Sourcebook of Psychological and Biological Research* (Hove, East Sussex: Psychology Press, 2004), 51.

must master many subskills and develop some specific mental processes that contribute to this skill. This chapter will cover these subskills and processes, which will highlight the complexity of the reading task and bring to light various points at which a student may need assistance and training.

The Principle: Reading Fluency

Those who study biblical and ancient languages usually do so to comprehend and interpret ancient written texts, two skills which are an integral part of exegesis. The ability to read the texts fluently, that is, "to read rapidly with ease and accuracy,"[2] is an important prerequisite to achieving text comprehension. Grabe explains this in more detail:

> Effective L1 reading comprehension generally assumes reading fluency—a person reading at a reasonable reading rate, between 250-300 WPM, using very efficient and fast word recognition skills, and combining information from various sources while reading under fairly intense time constraints. This is a realistic explanation of what people do when they are skilled readers, whether in the L1 or the L2. Moreover, reading fluency has been associated with reading comprehension in a wide range of research studies over the past 20 years.[3]

Because fluent reading is a complex mental exercise, this section will start by addressing cognition and memory issues as they relate to reading. The remainder of the section covers the various subskills and processes of reading that must be mastered to achieve fluency and ultimately comprehension, moving from the lower-level processes to the higher-level processes. The last part of this section will address implications for instruction in reading fluency.

---

[2] Grabe, *Reading*, 291.
[3] William Grabe, "Fluency in Reading—Thirty-five Years Later," *Reading in a Foreign Language* 22 (2010): 72.

Working Memory

To better understand how reading processes work, an introduction to human memory in general and working memory in particular is in order. Individuals have a complex memory system that can hold a significant amount of information for different lengths of time. This memory system is represented by a continuum with sensory memory at one end and long-term memory at the other. As its name suggests, sensory memory is information gathered by the senses that is usually forgotten very quickly unless rehearsed. On the other end of the spectrum, long-term memory is the set of records that are processed more deeply and stored in our brains much longer to be retrieved as needed.[4] Long-term memory can be an important resource for readers, being a storehouse for vocabulary and grammar information to be retrieved as needed while reading. However, long-term memory is not the most important form of memory for reading fluency.

Functioning in between the two ends of the continuum is working memory, a set of processes and skills that plays a significant role in memory development in general and in reading fluency and comprehension in particular.[5] Unlike long-term memory, working memory oversees active storage (moving items into and out of long-term memory) and performs processing functions, such as taking in, sorting, rehearsing, using, and evaluating new information.[6] It also interacts with and holds in conscious awareness aspects of long-term memory that are activated at any given moment. This occurs when an individual makes use

---

[4] John R. Anderson, *Learning and Memory: An Integrated Approach*, 2nd ed. (New York: Wiley, 2000), 166. Older theories of memory speak of long-term versus short-term memory, also called working memory. See Henry L. Roediger and Lyn M. Goff, "Memory," in *A Companion to Cognitive Science*, ed. W. Bechtel & G. Graham (Malden, MA: Blackwell, 1998), 250–51.

[5] Grabe, *Reading*, 32.

[6] See Alan Baddeley, "Working Memory: An Overview," in *Working Memory and Education*, ed. S. Pickering (Burlington, MA: Academic Press, 2006), 1–31; Alan Baddeley, *Working Memory, Thought, and Action* (New York: Oxford University Press, 2007), 6–7; Nick C. Ellis, "Memory for Language," in *Cognition and Second Language Instruction*, ed. P. Robinson (Cambridge: Cambridge University Press, 2001), 33–68.

of a skill that has not been practiced in a while, for example, or retrieves the meaning of a word not recently accessed.

However, working memory also has limitations. It is limited in capacity, limited in storage, limited in its links to long-term memory, and limited in its ability to carry out multiple processes simultaneously. More specifically, working memory can only actively maintain information for about one or two seconds, although rehearsal and reactivation can lengthen that time.[7] Additionally, only some of the information that is active in working memory will be transferred to long-term memory. These strengths and weaknesses of working memory affect the way individuals read and comprehend texts as we will see below.

The standard theory of the structure of working memory comes from Alan Baddeley and Graham Hitch.[8] According to this theory, working memory has three components: the central executive, the phonological (or articulatory loop), and the visuo-spatial sketchpad. The central executive is a limited capacity attentional control system that regulates information flow among the other two components of working memory, not unlike the way air traffic control oversees traffic flow at an airport. The phonological loop holds and rehearses sounds and speech-based information, while the visuo-spatial sketchpad holds and rehearses visual images and spatial relations.

Even though the phonological loop is the auditory component of working memory, it is the most important of the three elements of working memory for understanding reading, including silent reading.[9] This is because the phonological loop decodes and stores written words in phonological form for future storage and rehearsal.[10] When a student reads a word silently, the phonological loop converts it and stores it as a memory of sound, as if it had been heard in the ears. Said differently,

---

[7] Baddeley, "Working Memory," 6. See also Baddeley, *Working Memory, Thought, and Action*, 189–209.

[8] Alan Baddeley and Graham Hitch, "Working Memory," in *Recent Advances in Learning and Motivation*, ed. G. H. Bower (New York: Academic Press, 1974), 8:47–89.

[9] Research on working memory indicates that even though written language is received in visual form, the visuo-spatial sketchpad is only minimally involved in reading because it is primarily a linguistic activity. See Baddeley, "Working Memory," 6.

[10] Baddeley, "Working Memory," 6–7. See also Baddeley, *Working Memory, Thought, and Action*, 8–10.

"all language information used in working memory is stored and re-hearsed phonologically," even if it enters working memory via written language.[11] Additionally, the phonological loop is directly connected with the "storage, rehearsal, and reinforced memory of new words in phonological form in working memory" and as such, it is "the foundation of all vocabulary learning."[12] Therefore, reading fluency is highly dependent on the phonological loop in working memory.

However, as with all working memory, the phonological loop is limited. It only stores phonological information for a few seconds unless the information is refreshed with subvocalization or inner speech. This means that when a student stops to look up an unknown word or analyze an unusual phrase while reading, he or she loses from working memory what was just read. After identifying the unknown item, the student must then go back and reread and reconstruct the meaning he or she had been building in working memory. This is one reason rapid word recognition and rapid reading rate as part of reading fluency are important for comprehension. Put differently, "Fluency, and especially automaticity, allows readers to attend to the meaning of the text, the textual context, and required background knowledge without being slowed down by attentional word-recognition demand."[13]

With a basic understanding of working memory, the next section will address the various skills and processes of reading. These processes are dependent on working memory, particularly the phonological loop, to be effective.

Lower-Level Reading Subskills

Reading involves three sets of lower-level skills and processes that must be mastered before a student is able to comprehend and interpret a written text. These skills form the foundation for the higher-level skills, particularly those needed for comprehension and interpretation. According to Grabe, lower-level skills "form a group of skills that have the

---

[11] Grabe, *Reading*, 34.

[12] Grabe, *Reading*, 34. See also Baddeley, "Working Memory," 11, and Ellis, "Memory for Language," 41.

[13] Grabe, *Reading*, 291.

potential to become strongly automatized, and this automatizing of lower-level skills is a requirement for fluent reading."[14] In other words, once the lower-level skills are mastered and automatized, a reader frees up enough working memory to engage in the higher-level skills. The lower-level reading skills are word recognition, syntactic parsing or *word integration*, and meaning proposition encoding.[15]

The most important and involved lower-level skill is word recognition, with there being a high correlation between word recognition and reading comprehension. Grabe notes that "fluent reading comprehension is not possible without rapid and automatic word recognition of a large vocabulary."[16]

The skill of word recognition can be further subdivided into other subskills or processes.[17] These include orthographic processing, which is the ability to recognize letters and visual word shapes; semantic and syntactic processing, which is the ability to process the relationship between words and their neighboring words; lexical access, which is the ability to process and choose the appropriate meaning of a word in its context; morphological processing, which is the ability to recognize and assign meaning to prefixes, suffixes, and derived forms.

One final subskill involved in word recognition should be highlighted: phonological processing, which is the ability to process the sound of the word. Research has demonstrated that "for a very large majority of words that are processed while reading, phonological activation of the form plays a major role."[18] This is a universal phenomenon

---

[14] Grabe, *Reading*, 21. See also Anderson, *Learning and Memory*, 396–397; Jan H. Hulstijn, "Intentional and Incidental Second Language Vocabulary Learning: A Reappraisal of Elaboration, Rehearsal and Automaticity," in *Cognition and Second Language Instruction*, ed. P. Robinson (Cambridge: Cambridge University Press, 2001), 258–86; Keiko Koda, *Insights into Second Language Reading* (Cambridge: Cambridge University Press, 2005).

[15] Martin J. Pickering and Matthew J. Traxler, "Parsing and Incremental Understanding During Reading," in *Architectures and Mechanisms for Language Processing*, ed. M. Crocker, M. Pickering, and C. Clifton (Cambridge: Cambridge University Press, 2000), 238.

[16] Grabe, *Reading*, 23.

[17] Adapted from Grabe, *Reading*, 23–27.

[18] Grabe, *Reading*, 24. See also Charles Hulme et al., "Phonological Skills Are (Probably) One Cause of Success in Learning to Read: A Comment on Castles and Coltheart,"

and is true even for languages like Chinese where the writing is done with symbols that have little or no phonological significance.[19] This provides further rationale for the incorporation of auditory input in a language reading course (see chapters 4, 5, and 6).

These word-recognition subskills—orthographic processing, semantic and syntactic processing, lexical access, morphological processing, and phonological processing—must be automatized before a reader is able to move up to some of the more complex processes involved in reading, but word-recognition is only one of the three lower-level processing skills that a reader needs to master.

A second lower-level skill that contributes to reading fluency is syntactic parsing or word integration. This is the ability to recognize and assign meaning to sentence-level, rather than word-level, markers such as word order, determiners (the, a, this, those, etc.), subordinate clauses, and tense. At this level of processing, the reader must be able to fluently and automatically recognize such structures as marked and unmarked word order, while assigning an appropriate meaning to the different constructions.

The last lower-level process that a fluent reader needs to master is meaning proposition encoding, which builds on the previous two lower-level skills. Words are combined into syntactical structures, which are in turn combined into semantic propositions which a reader must understand to read fluently. A semantic proposition is "a network of small packets of information linked together in a meaning unit"[20] and is approximately equivalent to a phrase or clause units. These packets of meaning are built, activated, or "lit up" in the brain as structures are combined. "As immediate networks are lit up and then added to the bigger network of activated information, the propositions are connected and the textual meaning of what we read is created."[21] Like the previous

---

Scientific Studies of Reading 9 (2005): 351–65.

[19] See, e.g., Bonnie Wing-Yin Chow and Catherine McBride-Chang, "Phonological Processing Skills and Early Reading Abilities in Hong Kong Chinese Kindergarteners Learning to Read English as a Second Language," *Journal of Educational Psychology* 97.1 (2005): 81–87.

[20] Grabe, *Reading*, 31.

[21] Grabe, *Reading*, 31.

two subskills, meaning proposition encoding helps the reader derive meaning from the text being read.

Again, these three lower-level processes—word recognition, syntactic parsing, and meaning proposition encoding—must be developed and automatized before a reader can engage in the higher-level reading processes, which are introduced in the next section.

Higher-Level Reading Subskills

The goal of reading is to go beyond the lower-level reading skills that focus on understanding individual words and phrases. The reader is usually most interested in comprehension of the text as a whole, which "involves the construction of a mental representation of the content of the text."[22] In fact, in most cases, the syntax and semantics of the text itself are quickly forgotten, replaced by this mental representation of what has been read.[23] This process requires that the reader build mental links between words, phrases, sentences, and even paragraphs, all the while transforming the symbols on the page into his or her mental representation of the text. He or she must also be able to draw on general knowledge about the world to supplement the information he or she is processing in the text and make inferences. This also means that the reader must hold in working memory the recently read material while processing the next sentence. Altogether, this puts significant demands on working memory.[24]

As already discussed, each reader is limited in his or her working memory capacity. Therefore, "higher-level processes generally assume that the reader can direct attentional resources to these component

---

[22] Kate Cain, "Children's Reading Comprehension: The Role of Working Memory in Normal and Impaired Development," in *Working Memory and Education*, ed. S. Pickering (Burlington, MA: Academic Press, 2006), 62.

[23] Alan Garnham and Jane Oakhill, "The Mental Models Theory of Language Comprehension," in *Models of Understanding Text*, ed. B. Britton and A. Graesser (Mahwah, NJ: Erlbaum, 1996), 315.

[24] For a detailed discussion of the role of working memory in comprehension, including its limitations, see Walter Kintsch, *Comprehension: A Paradigm for Cognition* (Cambridge: Cambridge University Press, 1998), 217–235.

skills."[25] If a reader is unable to perform or automatize one of the lower-level skills, such as word recognition, he or she will direct all available working memory to decoding words with little or no mental reserve left for the higher-level skills required for comprehension. This also slows the reader down, which interferes with the phonological loop's ability to retain what is read, and ultimately contributes to the breakdown of comprehension.

Assuming, then, that the reader has enough working memory available, he or she will direct attention to the higher-level skills of comprehension and interpretation. There are three main component abilities that a fluent reader uses in higher-order comprehension processing: a *text model of reader comprehension*,[26] a *situation model of reader interpretation*,[27] and "a set of reading skills and resources under the command of the executive control mechanism in working memory."[28] Different text types may require one comprehension processing model (text model or situation model) more than the other, but both models generally come into play while reading.

Using a text model of reader comprehension, a reader derives meaning only as it is represented in the text.[29] In other words, the reader begins to extract information from the text with the first word, and comprehension develops over the course of the text with associations and mental activation (and reactivation) of important elements of that text as the reader continues through the selection.[30] Reading a technical operation manual would require more of a text model of comprehension as the reader moves methodically through the manual, learning new details and

---

[25] Grabe, *Reading*, 39.

[26] The text model can also be called the textbase. See Kintsch, *Comprehension*, 103.

[27] The situation model can also be called the mental model. See Cain, "Children's Reading Comprehension," 62.

[28] Grabe, *Reading*, 39.

[29] Kintsch, *Comprehension*, 105–6, and Walter Kintsch and Katherine A. Rawson, "Comprehension," in *The Science of Reading*, ed. M. Snowling and C. Hulme (Malden, MA: Blackwell, 2005), 211.

[30] Adapted from Grabe, *Reading*, 40–43. See also Walter Kintsch, Walter, Vimla L. Patel, and K. Anders Ericsson, "The Role of Long-Term Working Memory in Text Comprehension," *Psychologia* 42 (1999): 195 and Garnham and Oakhill, "The Mental Models Theory," 317.

associating the new details with those already read. This model draws information from the text rather than from the reader's prior knowledge, although as noted above, both models are usually used together.

The second higher-level reading skill is the situation model of reader interpretation. A situation model is the reader's construction of the situation described in the text.[31] Situation models make extensive use of the reader's prior knowledge of the topic and usually involve spatial, visual, and even personal and emotional information, helping the reader make inferences and interpret what is being read.[32] Moreover, the reader's situation model of the text will ultimately determine what is internalized and retained in long-term memory.[33] Reading poetry would require more of a situation model of interpretation as the reader associates personal experiences and feelings with the words of the poet to interpret and appreciate the text. However, as noted above, the text model would also come into play.

The last element of the higher-level reading processes involves a complex set of components under the direction of the central executive in the reader's working memory.[34] One important job of the central executive is the controlling of attentional resources and attentional processes.[35] Therefore, while reading, the reader's central executive will oversee processes like goal setting ("What am I ultimately trying to get

---

[31] Kintsch and Rawson, "Comprehension," 211; Rolf A. Zwaan and Gabriel A. Radvansky, "Situation Models in Language Comprehension and Memory," *Psychological Bulletin* 123 (1998): 162; Rolf A. Zwaan and David N. Rapp, "Discourse Comprehension," in *Handbook of Psycholinguistics*, 2nd ed., ed. M. Traxler and M. A. Gernsbacher (Burlington, MA: Academic Press, 2006), 726.

[32] Kintsch and Rawson, "Comprehension," 211; Susan R. Goldman, Richard M. Golden, and Paul van den Broek, "Why are Computational Models of Text Comprehension Useful?" in *Higher Level Language Processes in the Brain*, ed. F. Schmalhofer and C. Perfetti (Mahwah, NJ: Erlbaum, 2007), 32; Murray Singer and Jose Leon, "Psychological Studies of Higher Language Processes: Behavioral and Empirical Approaches," in *Higher Level Language Processes in the Brain*, ed. F. Schmalhofer and C. Perfetti (Mahwah, NJ: Erlbaum, 2007), 13–15; and Garnham and Oakhill, "The Mental Models Theory," 317.

[33] Grabe, *Reading*, 43–44. See also David N. Rapp et al., "Higher-Order Comprehension Processes in Struggling Readers: A Perspective for Research and Intervention," *Scientific Studies of Reading* 11 (2007): 289–312.

[34] Grabe, *Reading*, 50.

[35] Baddeley, "Working Memory," 17.

out of this text?"), strategy use ("How do I figure out what this word means?"), and comprehension monitoring ("Do I really understand this sentence?").[36] The central executive may also use metacognitive awareness to monitor whether comprehension is occurring, whether reading goals are being met, or whether a different reading strategy could be more beneficial in that moment. Finally, the central executive may draw on metalinguistic knowledge or conscious knowledge of L2 stored in long-term memory to assist as needed in comprehending the text.

The three higher-level reading skills, then, are the text model of comprehension, the situation model of interpretation, and the central executive control of reading processes. These skills work together to help the reader comprehend and interpret the text being read, which is the foundation of good exegesis. A fluent reader will automatically use the lower-level processes with enough working memory left to devote attention to these higher-level reading skills, deriving more meaning from the text. The next section addresses some instructional strategies to help promote reading fluency and ultimately comprehension.

Promoting Reading Fluency: Implications for Instruction

Reading fluency involves rapid word recognition and a rapid reading rate, both of which ultimately lead to accuracy in comprehension.[37] Because reading fluency is a skill that can be taught, this section addresses some ways to help students move beyond the word-by-word stage through which every reader must pass. Reading fluency skills develop incrementally over time and can benefit from some specific instructional strategies, including the following: promotion of vocabulary learning, extensive reading, reading rate practice, and rereading and recycling of texts.[38]

---

[36] Grabe, *Reading*, 50–56; Cain, "Children's Reading Comprehension," 80.

[37] For a discussion of the connection between reading fluency and accuracy in reading comprehension, see Grabe, "Fluency in Reading," 76.

[38] Grabe, "Fluency in Reading," 72–73; Grabe, *Reading*, 37. See also I. S. P. Nation, *Teaching ESL/EFL Reading and Writing* (New York: Routledge, 2009); Timothy V. Rasinski, *The Fluent Reader: Oral Reading Strategies for Building Word Recognition, Fluency, and Comprehension* (New York: Scholastic Books, 2003); and William Grabe, "Research on Teaching Reading," *Annual Review of Applied Linguistics 24* (2004): 44–69.

Rapid word recognition is by far the most important lower-level reading skill, so it stands to reason that vocabulary learning will be of great significance for reading fluency. A language course that promotes the learning of large quantities of vocabulary will also promote reading fluency and comprehension. The next chapter presents in greater detail the importance of vocabulary learning for developing language proficiency and reading fluency; it also provides suggestions and examples for effectively teaching L2 vocabulary.

Extensive reading is a second strategy for promoting reading fluency. This strategy, also presented in chapter 5, encourages students to read large quantities of text. Because reading skills develop incrementally, an increase in practice and exposure to the language results in further growth, development, and automaticity in reading skills. However, to develop fluency, the reading materials must be at or below the learner's current level of proficiency "so that slow readers can shift from analytical identification to automatic word recognition."[39] Therefore, encouraging students to read large quantities of easy reading materials helps promote reading fluency and ultimately comprehension.

A third strategy that promotes reading fluency is reading rate practice. This type of instruction pushes learners to read at an increasingly faster rate. Although it may seem counter-intuitive at first, an increase in reading rate actually improves reading fluency and comprehension. This is because the student is learning to not fixate unnecessarily on words or word parts, a process which usually results in draining working memory capacity.[40] Instead, the learner is developing faster and more efficient word recognition skills and is further reinforcing known vocabulary, both of which promote reading fluency. In other words, this type of training helps students learn how to "make the best use of what they already know."[41]

---

[39] Mihwa Chung, "The Effect of a Speed Reading Course: A Replication," *Asian Journal of English Language Teaching* 20 (2010): 95.

[40] Paul Nation, "Reading Faster," *International Journal of English Studies* 9.2 (2009): 134.

[41] Chung, "The Effect of a Speed Reading Course," 112.

Finally, encouraging students to reread and recycle texts that have been previously read also promotes reading fluency.[42] As a student reads a text again and again, he or she is likely able to recognize words and phrases more quickly and eventually automatize some of those lower-level reading skills. Doing this frequently with a large quantity of different texts provides even greater opportunity to automatize more words and structures. Instructors can incorporate variety into this task by encouraging the students to read the same text in a different way each time (see below for examples). The instructor could also ask the students to complete different tasks each time they read the same text. Examples of such tasks include completing a summary, filling in an outline, looking for structure signals, or developing a position on a particular issue.[43]

For the development of reading fluency, targeted repetition is the key. Therefore, instructional strategies should include vocabulary development, extensive reading, reading rate practice, and rereading of texts. The development of fluency requires persistence and patience on the part of instructors and students alike. On this point, Grabe succinctly reminds us that "implicit learning is gradual, initially very fragile, and strongly based in repetition of form and process over a long period of time."[44]

Having covered in this section the topics of working memory, reading subskills and processes, and some suggestions for reading instruction, the next section addresses some reasons for incorporating fluency practice in biblical and ancient language classrooms.

The Rationale: Teaching Reading Fluency

Most instructors of Hebrew, Greek, and Latin do not need to be told that reading skills are essential for their students' language development and proficiency. However, as this chapter has demonstrated, a fluent reader needs much more than basic word recognition skills. Word recognition skills are necessarily the focus of early language courses, but reading

---

[42] Grabe, *Reading*, 304–5.

[43] For more suggestions and examples of activities that promote fluency, see Grabe, *Reading*, 304–10 and Rasinski, *The Fluent Reader*.

[44] Grabe, "Fluency in Reading," 73.

comprehension and text interpretation require a hierarchy of skills that only begin with the automatization of word recognition skills. It is not unusual for biblical language classes to cover word recognition skills in the first year and then skip directly to exegesis (comprehension and interpretation) in the second year, assuming that students will somehow develop automaticity and other intermediate reading skills on their own. Instructors should consider including instruction and reading practices that promote the many skills required for reading fluency and accurate comprehension. The previous section introduced approaches to instruction that promote fluency, and the last section of this chapter presents some examples of instructional intervention that would promote fluency.

Instructors should also consider another important aspect of teaching reading: implicit instruction. While implicit instruction was covered in detail in chapter 2, it is worth revisiting here. The development of reading fluency depends more on time spent reading texts, that is, implicit learning, than on discussion of the finer points of grammar, or explicit learning. Grabe makes a strong case for implicit learning in the development of reading skills:

> In fact, many reading skills—automatic word recognition, a large recognition vocabulary, skilled grammatical processing, and the formation of basic meaning proposition units for reading comprehension—only emerge as an outcome of implicit learning (rather than explicit learning of aspects of language knowledge). And implicit learning can only come about through extended periods of exposure and meaningful time on task.[45]

The next section presents some examples of activities that help students develop skills that lead to reading fluency through targeted repetition and implicit learning.

---

[45] Grabe, "Fluency in Reading," 73. See also Ellis, "At the Interface."

Examples for Biblical and Ancient Language Classrooms

As noted above, certain types of instruction are recommended for teaching reading fluency: vocabulary development, extensive reading, reading rate practice, and rereading and recycling of texts. Because examples of vocabulary development and extensive reading are included in other chapters (10 and 5 respectively), the examples in this chapter will focus on activities that involve reading rate practice and rereading and recycling texts.

These fluency activities should be included regularly (even weekly) throughout the students' course of study, beginning as early as the first week or two of language learning.[46] The examples below can be adapted for different levels of language ability by adjusting the difficulty and length of the texts used in the activity.

Reading Rate Practice Activity (Hebrew)

One approach to developing reading fluency is reading rate practice. Paul Nation provides several guidelines for this type of activity.[47] First, the texts should be easy enough that the reader is not interrupted by unknown words, phrases, or discourse markers. The lack of simplified texts and graded readers for Hebrew and other ancient languages presents a significant challenge for implementing this type of activity. Therefore, finding or creating a text that is simple enough for the students to read without interruption is the first goal in creating this activity. Instructors can create their own simple texts. However, if the instructor wants to use an authentic, original text, he or she could create a diglot weave (see chapters 5 and 6 for discussion and examples) or simplify an authentic text through the removal and/or replacement of unknown words and constructions.

---

[46] See Paul Nation, "The Four Strands," *International Journal of Innovation in Language Learning and Teaching* 1.1 (2007): 2–13. Nation recommends that any language course include four strands, each occupying about the same amount of time and attention in the course. One of these four strands is fluency training, which includes activities such as those described in this section. The four strands will be covered in greater detail in chapter 11.

[47] Paul Nation, "Reading Faster," 136.

For the purposes of this example, the text is 2 Kings 4:8–37, Elisha raising the Shunammite's son. This activity assumes that the instructor will make adjustments to the text to match the level of his or her students. This text is a little longer, which will allow for the gains in reading rate to be more noticeable.

According to Nation's second guideline for reading rate practice, the students should be focused on the meaning of the text since comprehension is the ultimate goal. Therefore, once the text has been adapted for the appropriate level of the students, the instructor should also prepare a brief, general comprehension quiz and inform students that they will be quizzed on the content of what they read, which will encourage them focus on the meaning. Quiz questions, preferably in L2, could include items such as the following: "What did the Shunammite provide for Elisha?" "Where did the Shunammite lay her dead son?" "What is the name of Elisha's servant?" The students might also take turns reading out loud to a teacher or fellow student to help maintain a focus on meaning.

Third, the students should receive some pressure to read faster than normal. The process looks like this: the students read the text multiple times; each reading attempt is timed; and the results of each attempt are recorded in a chart, thus providing some incentive to improve each time. The instructor might also hand out rewards for increasing reading rate over multiple attempts. An instructor can time each student reading the entire text, or the instructor can give the students a time limit, perhaps 1 or 2 minutes, and count the number of words they read in that amount of time. If multiple texts at a similar level are available, the instructor can time the students' attempts at reading different texts and record the number of words per minute the students are able to read over several different texts, again motivating the students to read faster each time.

Finally, the speed-reading practice should be done frequently, providing large amounts of reading with texts of reasonable length spread over the length of the term of study. This type of practice promotes an increase in reading rate and a shift from word analysis to automatic word recognition. It also results in a corresponding decrease in the drain of available working memory, which leads to an improvement in reading fluency, and ultimately better comprehension.[48]

Text Rereading Activity 1 (Greek)

Requiring students to reread texts multiple times also provides the opportunity to develop reading fluency. Because the following rereading activity employs an audio recording of the Greek text of Matthew 5:3–10 (with verses 11–12 optional),[49] the passage will not be simplified in any way. Therefore, the student should be familiar with all the vocabulary and grammatical structures in this passage before participating in the rereading activity for optimal fluency development. Note, however, that this passage includes repetition and relatively short clauses, which make listening and reading a little easier. The repetition should also encourage quicker automatization of word recognition.

This activity may be assigned to individual students or to small groups of students. The students begin by listening to the passage while following along silently on their printed text. The students then listen to the passage two more times, reading out loud along with the recording both times. Next, the students read out loud without the recording (one at a time if in a small group). The students then listen to the recording again while following along, paying attention to places where they struggled to read fluently. The students again read the passage solo, working toward greater fluency and increased speed. The last two steps may be repeated as necessary until the students are able to comfortably read the passage by themselves without hesitation or error.

Text Rereading Activity 2 (Latin)

The following set of activities demonstrate another set of options for rereading a text. Consider Matthew 19:16–22 (Vulgate), the story of the rich young man. For this passage, the instructor needs to be sure that the

---

[48] Grabe, *Reading*, 105. See also, e.g., the studies by Mihwa Chung and Paul Nation. "The Effect of a Speed Reading Course." *English Teaching* 61 (2006): 181–204, and Chung, "The Effect of a Speed Reading Course," 95–116.

[49] Recordings of the Greek New Testament are available online, many for free. See, e.g., https://www.koinegreek.com/audio.

students understand most of the words and structures, making any adjustments to the text as needed. These adjustments may involve altering the text in some way (removing/replacing unknown words, creating a diglot weave, etc.) or teaching the unknown words and structures in advance.

Once the students are comfortable with the vocabulary and grammar, the class can move on to the repeated reading activities. This example presents a set of four potential activities for rereading the same text, introducing some variety and interest to the repetition. The first time through the text, the teacher reads the passage out loud while the students follow along.

For the second activity in the set, the students work in pairs. The first person reads the story out loud to the partner at least three times. The partner listens attentively and offers encouragement and correction if necessary. Then, the students switch roles with the second person reading the story at least three times and the first person listening and providing feedback. This type of repetition could also be used in conjunction with reading rate practice (see above). After reading the passage several times, the instructor gives the students a brief comprehension quiz, preferably in L2, with basic questions like the following: "Who are the people speaking in this story?" "Does the rich young man keep the commandments?" "What must the rich young man give up, according to Jesus?"

For the third activity, have the students work in pairs again, this time to act out the story. One student takes the role of Jesus, and the other takes the role of the rich young man. Perhaps one or two groups could perform their rendition for the class.

Finally, the instructor can assign a brief written analysis or devotional thought based on the passage, giving the student an opportunity to read the text yet again. This assignment could be written in L1 or L2.

Conclusion

Proficiency in reading comprehension and interpretation, and thus proficiency in exegesis, depends heavily on the reading skills and reading fluency of the learner. Reading skills include more basic lower-level skills that must be automatized if the reader is to have enough working memory capacity to engage in the higher-level skills required for comprehension. Noteworthy is the fact that some of the important reading skills involve phonological awareness, something that surprised me in my first ancient language courses. Therefore, instructional strategies should encourage reading skills and fluency development through targeted repetition (reading rate practice and rereading texts), extensive reading, and vocabulary training. The next chapter provides a more indepth look at the role of vocabulary learning in developing language proficiency in general and reading fluency in particular.

For Further Reading

Baddeley, Alan. *Working Memory, Thought, and Action.* New York: Oxford University Press, 2007.

Grabe, William. *Reading in a Second Language: Moving from Theory to Practice.* Cambridge: Cambridge University Press, 2009.

Grabe, William. "Research on Teaching Reading." *Annual Review of Applied Linguistics 24* (2004): 44–69.

Kintsch, Walter. *Comprehension: A Paradigm for Cognition.* Cambridge: Cambridge University Press, 1998.

Kintsch, Walter, and Katherine A. Rawson. "Comprehension." Pages 209–26 in *The Science of Reading.* Edited by M. Snowling and C. Hulme. Malden, MA: Blackwell, 2005.

Nation, Paul. "Reading Faster." *International Journal of English Studies* 9.2 (2009): 131–44.

Rasinski, Timothy V. *The Fluent Reader: Oral Reading Strategies for Building Word Recognition, Fluency, and Comprehension.* New York: Scholastic Books, 2003.

CHAPTER 10: VOCABULARY ACQUISITION

Imagine the following hypothetical situation: two different language students are looking at the same sentence. The first student knows all the relevant grammar for understanding the sentence and can parse the verbal forms, noun forms, prefixes, suffixes, etc. However, the first learner does not know any of the vocabulary items in the sentence. The second learner knows all the vocabulary but does not know or recognize any of the grammatical forms. The first learner would not be able to comprehend the intended meaning of the sentence. The second learner, however, could probably understand at least the general idea that sentence is trying to communicate. He or she may not have a precise translation but could at least demonstrate a basic comprehension of the sentence. When it comes down to it, students who have only strong vocabulary knowledge can achieve at least a basic comprehension of a text, but the same cannot be said for students with only strong grammar knowledge.

As demonstrated in the hypothetical situation above, one of the most essential parts of language fluency in general, and reading fluency in particular, is vocabulary acquisition. Grabe notes that a student with limited vocabulary knowledge cannot create a coherent situation model, one important cognitive process that contributes to text comprehension.[1] Therefore, this chapter presents some relevant research for understanding successful vocabulary acquisition, including aspects of knowing a word, factors that affect vocabulary learning, and useful approaches for instruction.

The Principle: Vocabulary Acquisition

As noted in the previous chapter, vocabulary acquisition is one important component of language proficiency and reading fluency. A student who can quickly and automatically recognize a large quantity of vocabulary items is more likely able to read and comprehend texts quickly and accurately. Several studies indicate that readers need to

---

[1] Grabe, *Reading*, 49. See chapter 9 for a discussion of the situation model.

know 95–98 percent of the running words in a text to be able to adequately but perhaps not perfectly comprehend that text.[2] Not only is quantity important, but so is quality or depth of vocabulary knowledge. As with many of the language skills discussed so far, vocabulary learning is a complex process. This section discusses the multi-faceted nature of knowing a word, factors that affect vocabulary learning and retention, and implications for vocabulary instruction.

Aspects of Knowing a Word

Many language students learn vocabulary by using flashcards, much like learning multiplication facts.[3] The good news is that SLA research confirms the effectiveness of this learning technique.[4] However, the use of flashcards is only one of many effective approaches to learning vocabulary. This is because knowing a word is more complex than knowing a multiplication fact. According to I. S. P. Nation, to fully know a word, the learner needs to have a solid understanding of the following aspects of that word: the form of the word, its meaning, and its use.[5] Each aspect has several subcomponents.

As a student learns the form of the word, he or she may learn the spoken form of the word and have phonological knowledge of the word. The student may also learn the written form of the word and have orthographic knowledge of the word, including its spelling and any spelling variants. A student may also learn a word by its word parts. This includes recognizing its base or stem, any affixes, and perhaps the word family from which it comes.

The student also needs to understand the meaning of the word, including its concepts and referents. Some words, especially common words, have a wide range of meanings, and the student must

---

[2] See, e.g., Batia Laufer and Geke C. Ravenhorst-Kalovski, "Lexical Threshold Revisited: Lexical Text Coverage, Learners' Vocabulary Size and Reading Comprehension," *Reading in a Foreign Language* 22.1 (2010): 15–30; and Marcella Hu Hsueh-chao and Paul Nation, "Unknown Vocabulary Density and Reading Comprehension," *Reading in a Foreign Language* 13.1 (2000): 403–30.

[3] See below for more information on the use of flashcards for learning vocabulary.

[4] Nation, *Learning Vocabulary*, 437.

[5] The following discussion is adapted from Nation, *Learning Vocabulary*, 65–85.

differentiate between meanings in a variety of contexts. In addition to knowing the concepts and referents of a given word, the student must also learn associations between words. This would include such associations as synonyms, antonyms, and hierarchical relationships in categories, for example: plant > tree > deciduous > oak > white oak. When a student learns a word, he or she must also connect the meaning of the word with its form. This process usually develops over the course of multiple encounters with the word (see below).

Finally, it is important that the student understand the use of the word. This type of knowledge starts with the basic grammatical function of the word. However, the learner also needs to know any relevant collocations or words that are typically associated with that vocabulary item. For example, certain verbs only take certain prepositions or cases. In addition, the student needs to understand any constraints on the usage of certain words, knowing where a word should not be used. This is particularly relevant for terms that refer to people. Relatedly, a student should understand the register of a word. In other words, he or she should know when to use a particular word given the sociocultural context, whether speaking to a superior, an inferior, or an equal.

Because knowing a word is a multi-faceted process and because human memory is complex, there are several factors that can affect how well a student learns a word and how long or how well he or she will retain it. The next section addresses these issues.

Factors Affecting Vocabulary Learning and Retention

Gaining full knowledge of any given vocabulary item involves many aspects of learning that word, as noted above. However, individual learners and the cognitive process itself are also complex. The following factors affect how a given student will learn and retain L2 vocabulary: motivation, noticing, retrieval, creative use, and interference.[6]

As with other aspects of language learning, student motivation, both internal and external, is a significant factor in the vocabulary learning process.[7] Students are more motivated to learn when the topic is

---

[6] Adapted from Nation, *Learning Vocabulary*, 102–14.

[7] Chapter 12 addresses student motivation in greater detail.

interesting and engaging.[8] Choosing texts and activities that are enjoyable for the students can increase the likelihood that the students learn from them because they are paying more attention to them. For vocabulary learning in particular, an increase in a word's salience in a text will also increase a student's external motivation to learn that word.[9] For example, if the target vocabulary item is necessary or critical for understanding the plot of a story, a student will be more motivated to learn it.

Noticing also plays a significant role in vocabulary learning. When a student consciously or subconsciously notices a word while reading and recognizes it as a useful language item, he or she is more likely to learn it.[10] A student is more likely to notice a word if he or she has had previous contact with the word, if the student realizes that this word fills a gap in his or her knowledge, or if it is more salient (see above).[11] Noticing may also involve removing the word from context for further processing by looking up the word in a dictionary, deliberately studying the word, guessing its meaning from context, or having the word explained by a knowledgeable teacher or classmate.[12]

A student's ability to retrieve a vocabulary item from memory is also a factor in his or her vocabulary acquisition, and retrieval is strongly linked to repetition. When a student makes a form-meaning connection for a particular word, he or she creates a memory trace in the brain. However, this trace will disappear quickly or be displaced in working memory if it is not used or not repeated.[13] When a student has repeated opportunity for retrieving an item, each successful retrieval strengthens the path linking form and meaning, making the memory trace stronger and retrieval more likely in the future.[14] For reading, the greatest

---

[8] Warwick B. Elley, "Vocabulary Acquisition from Listening to Stories," *Reading Research Quarterly* 24.2 (1989): 185.

[9] Joseph R. Jenkins and Robert Dixon, "Vocabulary Learning," *Contemporary Educational Psychology* 8 (1983): 250.

[10] See, e.g., Richard W. Schmidt, "The Role of Consciousness in Second Language Learning," *Applied Linguistics* 11.2 (1990): 129–58; and Ellis, *Instructed Second Language Acquisition*, 190, 195.

[11] Schmidt and Frota, "Developing Basic Conversational Ability," 311–13.

[12] Nation, *Learning Vocabulary*, 103.

[13] Baddeley, *Working Memory, Thought, and Action*, 39.

[14] Note, however, that simple repetition does not guarantee learning. Other factors,

increase in learning a vocabulary item occurs after the learner is exposed to the new word between two and three times.[15] However, data indicates that twenty to fifty repetitions are needed for substantial learning. Ten repetitions are not sufficient to develop full knowledge of a word.[16]

Along with simple repeated retrieval, creative processing of the word is another factor that affects vocabulary acquisition, deepening and enriching vocabulary knowledge. "Creative processing occurs when previously met words are subsequently met or used in ways that differ from the previous meeting with the word. At its most striking, the new meeting with the word forces learners to reconceptualise their knowledge of that word."[17] Creative processing might involve looking at a word from a new perspective, using a picture or object to learn the word, hearing the word instead of reading it, or looking at a different aspect of the word, such as a different inflection, collocation, grammatical context, reference, or meaning. Creative processing can improve the likelihood of retrieval because the brain creates multiple memory cues for that particular word as it is conceptualized in different ways. In other words, the memory trace is more richly encoded because it has more memory cues attached to it.[18] Therefore, if one memory cue is lost or blocked, the learner can use one of the other available memory cues, which ultimately increases the likelihood of retrieval. Creative processing may also lead to mental or semantic elaboration, which deepens and enriches the level of processing of the word and also makes retention and retrieval more likely.[19]

Another issue that affects the acquisition of vocabulary is retention. Words can be easily "lost" or forgotten over time. Therefore, improving word retention can significantly improve a student's vocabulary

---

including the way in which the information is processed, also have a significant effect on learning and memory. See Alan Baddeley, *Essentials of Human Memory*, Classic Edition (London: Psychology Press, 2014), 76–78.

[15] Karina Vidal, "A Comparison of the Effects of Reading and Listening on Incidental Vocabulary Acquisition," *Language Learning* 61.1 (2011): 247.

[16] Nation, *Learning Vocabulary*, 107–8. See also Stuart Webb, "The Effects of Repetition on Vocabulary Knowledge," *Applied Linguistics* 28.1 (2007): 46–65.

[17] Nation, *Learning Vocabulary*, 110.

[18] Baddeley, *Human Memory*, 162.

[19] Baddeley, *Human Memory*, 282.

acquisition. Two approaches can intentionally improve retention: *instantiation* and *imaging*. With instantiation, the learner recalls a specific experience, instance, or example of the meaning of the word to help improve recall. This can be the item itself, a picture or other representation of the item, or some real-life experience or interaction.[20] When a student uses imaging, he or she creates a "deliberate visual image" to help in the learning process, including retrieval.[21]

In addition to the factors that improve vocabulary learning, instructors should be aware of one factor that inhibits vocabulary learning: interference. Learning certain related words at the same time can have a negative effect on retrieval and retention. When learning near synonyms or opposites at the same time, the fragile memory traces can be easily confused, especially at first. Instructors should also try to avoid teaching members of the same lexical set at the same time because these can also cause interference.[22] An example might be learning a group of words for body parts, such as "eye," "nose," "ear," all at the same time. As the student develops a deeper knowledge of these words, the words will necessarily need to be compared and differentiated, perhaps after meeting the words ten times each. However, in the early stages of vocabulary development, learning these words together can cause interference. Note, however, that learning vocabulary in thematic rather than semantic groups can facilitate learning.[23] One example of a thematic group would be words related to the temple, such as "sacrifice," "priest," and "holy."

This section presented several factors that can affect the learning and retention of vocabulary in an L2 course of study, including motivation, noticing, retrieval, creative processing, factors related to retention, and interference. The next section addresses what this information means for vocabulary instruction.

---

[20] Nation, *Learning Vocabulary*, 113; for further discussion of instantiation, see Richard C. Anderson, et al., "Instantiation of Word Meanings in Children," *Journal of Reading Behavior* 10.2 (1978): 147–57.

[21] Nation, *Learning Vocabulary*, 113.

[22] Thomas Tinkham, "The Effects of Semantic and Thematic Clustering on the Learning of Second Language Vocabulary," *Second Language Research* 13.2 (1997): 138–63.

[23] Tinkham, "Semantic and Thematic Clustering," 138.

Vocabulary Learning: Implications for Instruction

One can draw several implications for vocabulary instruction from the information presented above. The overarching strategy is to create the opportunity for repeated retrieval of words in a variety of contexts and the opportunity to process words from different perspectives. These implications can be divided into two basic approaches to vocabulary instruction: direct teaching and indirect teaching. Direct teaching involves a conscious and intentional focus on learning vocabulary items, while indirect teaching involves the incidental learning of vocabulary from context while the reader's primary focus is on the message of the text.[24] These two approaches are complementary, each with its own strengths.

Research indicates that direct teaching of vocabulary can be very effective and efficient in promoting vocabulary acquisition, especially when paired with indirect vocabulary learning from context.[25] Direct instruction of vocabulary can range from an instructor simply inserting a brief definition while reading with students to providing elaborate attention to a specific, usually high-frequency, word. The latter, also called rich instruction, might involve looking at the word in a range of contexts and uses, as in a word study in biblical exegesis, exploring the etymology of the word, or researching other aspects of knowing and understanding the word, such as grammatical use, collocations, or word parts. Using flashcards or word cards is another approach to direct instruction of vocabulary. The last section of this chapter presents examples of direct vocabulary instruction.

Direct instruction has both strengths and weaknesses. As discussed in chapter 2, it is generally true that direct and deliberate language instruction tends to promote explicit learning, which is not as effective for developing language proficiency. However, this rule does not apply to vocabulary learning. Vocabulary that has been learned deliberately and

---

[24] Nation, *Learning Vocabulary*, 348.

[25] Hui-Tzu Min, "EFL Vocabulary Acquisition and Retention: Reading Plus Vocabulary Enhancement Activities and Narrow Reading," *Language Learning* 58.1 (2008): 73–115; Suhad Sonbul and Norbert Schmitt, "Direct Teaching of Vocabulary after Reading: Is It worth the Effort?" *ELT Journal* 64.3 (2010): 253–60; Batia Laufer and Belaa Rozovski-Roitblat, "Incidental Vocabulary Acquisition: The Effects of Task Type, Word Occurrence and Their Combination," *Language Teaching Research* 15.4 (2011): 391–411.

out of context "is stored and accessed in a manner that is similar to existing L1 and L2 lexical knowledge,"[26] making it accessible implicitly as well as explicitly. The narrow focus on individual words promotes storage of the words in long-term memory, making them accessible for working memory during the act of reading and in other types of language use. In this way, direct vocabulary instruction is more efficient than indirect instruction. However, direct instruction can only deal with certain aspects of knowing a word. Aspects of knowing a word that rely on quantity of experience or with some aspects of implicit knowledge of a word, for example, do not benefit much from direct instruction.[27]

Indirect instruction is the other broad approach to teaching vocabulary. With indirect instruction, the learner picks up unknown vocabulary and reinforces previously met vocabulary incidentally through meaning-focused exposure to and use of L2. In a language course that emphasizes reading, this would primarily be in the form of extensive reading of texts in L2. As discussed in the previous chapter, extensive reading promotes reading fluency. It is important to understand that extensive reading also promotes the incidental learning of vocabulary.[28] However, for this incidental learning to occur, the student must know at least 95 to 98 percent of the other words in the text, that is, one unknown word for every twenty to fifty words, the same percentage needed for comprehension.[29] Studies have demonstrated that if the student does not know one word in ten of a given text (90% vocabulary coverage), then successful guessing from context is unlikely and incidental vocabulary learning does not occur.[30] The last section of this chapter includes examples of indirect vocabulary instruction.

While indirect vocabulary instruction may not be as efficient as direct vocabulary instruction, it does offer some benefits. Indirect vocabulary learning provides the opportunity for repetition and the learning

---

[26] Irina Elgort, "Deliberate Learning and Vocabulary Acquisition in Second Language," *Language Learning* 61.2 (2011): 399.

[27] Nation, *Learning Vocabulary*, 94.

[28] For a description and discussion of extensive reading, see chapters 5 and 9.

[29] Nation, *Learning Vocabulary*, 352–54.

[30] Nation, *Learning Vocabulary*, 352–54. See, e.g., Na Liu and I. S. P. Nation, "Factors Affecting Guessing Vocabulary in Context," *RELC Journal* 16.1 (1985): 33–42.

of words in context, which can deepen a student's understanding of the word. Moreover, indirect learning is better for helping students learn the different forms of each word as well as the various collocations of each word.[31]

In sum, learning a word in L2 is a complex process and can be affected by a variety of factors. However, instructional techniques—including direct and indirect approaches—can assist in this process, helping the learner store and retrieve vocabulary more efficiently. The next section addresses issues of vocabulary learning specific to biblical and ancient languages.

The Rationale: Vocabulary Acquisition

As noted above, vocabulary learning is a very important component of language proficiency, reading fluency, and comprehension. The good news is that, on the whole, biblical and ancient language teachers actively teach vocabulary and promote vocabulary learning in their classrooms, usually through direct instruction, which is helpful and efficient. Therefore, this section will address issues of fine-tuning this instruction.

First, in relation to direct instruction, instructors of biblical and ancient languages might consider adding greater variety to their direct vocabulary instruction. Speaking in very general terms, instructors of biblical and ancient languages tend to limit their vocabulary instruction to a basic introduction to the vocabulary list ("Repeat each word after me..."), regular vocabulary quizzes ("Provide the best L1 definition for..."), and encouraging their students to use flashcards at home to study. While these approaches do promote learning, more can be done.

Adding greater instructional variety promotes greater creativity in processing the words. As noted above, this variety provides the opportunity for students to develop more memory cues for words with an associated improvement in retrieval and retention. Space does not allow a complete list here, but instructors might consider adding some of the following direct approaches to vocabulary instruction: using pictures, objects, and/or actions to promote vocabulary learning; creating a

---

[31] Nation, *Learning Vocabulary*, 60.

semantic map of various related words; and intentionally integrating relevant cultural information into vocabulary learning.[32]

In addition to adding variety into the direct teaching of vocabulary, instructors of biblical and ancient languages can also add some indirect vocabulary instruction. This is primarily done through extensive reading of texts that are at or below the students' reading ability with students knowing 95–98 percent of the running words in the text. Listening and interactive activities can also provide sources for indirect vocabulary learning. Indirect vocabulary instruction may seem to be less precise than direct instruction, but teachers can add some intentionality and focus.

First, students can be taught to infer the meaning of words they read in context. This involves strategy training, which is intentionally teaching students to identify such things as grammatical function, word parts, word order, and word choices that will help them narrow the possible meanings of the unknown word. Instructors can also design activities that encourage the processing and use of newly encountered vocabulary in context. For example, students could retell a story they just read (with or without the text in front of them) or do a role play of the text.[33] Instructors can also design texts that strategically place a few carefully chosen vocabulary items more frequently in the text, as in an input flood.[34] Not only does implicit vocabulary instruction provide greater opportunities for repeated encounters with the words, but it also provides students with the opportunity to meet the words in context with their relevant collocations, promoting experience with the word and greater implicit understanding of how the word is used.

Having addressed some reasons for incorporating a wider variety of vocabulary acquisition activities in biblical and ancient language classrooms, the next section presents a few specific examples of vocabulary learning activities.

---

[32] For more ideas and examples, see Paul Nation, ed., *New Ways in Teaching Vocabulary* (TESOL, 1994) and I.S.P. Nation, *Teaching and Learning Vocabulary* (Boston: Heinle and Heinle, 1990).

[33] For more ideas and examples, see Nation, *Learning Vocabulary*, 190–94.

[34] See chapter 6 for discussion and an example of input flood.

Examples for Biblical and Ancient Language Classrooms

The following sample activities are intended to promote vocabulary acquisition in the context of biblical and ancient language learning. The first example, for Hebrew, presents a procedure, which is a set of direct and indirect activities intended to provide a more thorough approach to learning vocabulary. The second example, for Greek, presents flashcards and the keyword technique, two effective direct approaches to learning vocabulary. The last example, for Latin, presents a story retelling activity to promote indirect learning of vocabulary. Each of these activities is drawn from the experience of and research by experts in SLA.

Vocabulary Teaching Procedure: Recycled Words (Hebrew)

One approach to teaching vocabulary is to use a procedure, or a series of steps involving different teaching activities. The procedure ensures that the new vocabulary words are repeated and that different aspects of knowing the words are covered. According to Nation, vocabulary activities must meet the following conditions to result in learning: "interest, understanding, repetition, deliberate attention, and generative use (the use of a word in a new context)."[35] The following procedure, called Recycled Words, is adapted from a strategy developed by Mary E. Blake and Patricia L. Majors and meets all of Nation's criteria.[36]

This instructional strategy is composed of a series of five interrelated stages for teaching vocabulary, some direct and some indirect. The five stages included in Recycled Words are pre-reading activities, oral reading strategies and responses, vocabulary building through focused word study activities, evaluating word knowledge through quizzes or tests, and a collaborative writing workshop. This procedure assumes at least a basic level of language proficiency and would work best with

---

[35] I. S. P. Nation, "Teaching and Learning Vocabulary," in *Handbook of Research on Second Language Teaching and Learning*, ed. E. Hinkel (Mahwah, NJ: Erlbaum, 2005), 585.

[36] Mary E. Blake and Patricia L. Majors, "Recycled Words: Holistic Instruction for LEP Students," *Journal of Adolescent and Adult Literacy* 39.2 (1995): 132–37.

intermediate or advanced students, although the instructor can adjust the procedure and chosen text to accommodate beginners.

The first step in the procedure is pre-teaching the vocabulary. The instructor chooses a target text and then selects words necessary for understanding the text. For the purposes of this example, the chosen text is Jeremiah 26. This text is dense with high-frequency vocabulary, making it accessible for a less experienced group of students.[37] However, it also includes some words, significant for understanding the plot, that are less frequent and might not be as familiar to the students, such as חָצֵר "courtyard," גרע "to reduce, omit," אוּלַי "perhaps," נחם "to comfort, relent," חשׁב "to think, account," מַעֲלָל "deed," שׁכם "to rise early," קְלָלָה "curse," מַדּוּעַ "why?," חרב "to be dry, waste," and קהל "to assemble." These words will be the target items for this activity. Notice that the list does not include near synonyms, opposites, or words from the same semantic category, as these should not be taught at the same time (see above).

In the first stage, pre-teaching, first the instructor reads through the list of words with the students reading each word together, echoing the instructor and practicing correct pronunciation. In another pre-teaching activity, the instructor provides the students with a multiple-choice practice sheet. The sheet lists each of the target words with four possible definitions or synonyms. Students are encouraged to guess the meaning of each word, using their current state of knowledge. This activity serves to heighten the students' awareness of the new vocabulary and provide practice guessing word meanings. As the students read the text (next stage), they can make corrections to this sheet. One question on the sheet might look like the following:

Choose the word that you think is most similar in meaning to the given word.

מַעֲלָל

א: עֵץ

ב: מַעֲשֶׂה

ג: בַּיִת

ד: קָלָל

---

[37] For suggestions of other similar texts, see Bullard, "100 'Simplest' Chapters." Note, however, that "simple" in terms of vocabulary does not always mean "simple" in terms of grammar and syntax.

The second step is oral reading of a text. For this stage, Blake and Majors recommend "jump in" reading. In this activity, one reader begins to read out loud and continues as long as he or she is comfortable. The student is not permitted to read more than one long paragraph and may not read less than a single word that is a complete phrase or idea, such as הִנֵּנִי "Here I am." Students may stop at phrase breaks, using disjunctive Masoretic accents if they are able. When the first reader stops reading, another student jumps in. The students can spontaneously start reading in any order as they are comfortable, or the instructor can predetermine the order of reading. The instructor actively monitors the reading and intervenes as necessary, correcting students, encouraging them, speeding them up, or slowing them down. As students read the selection, they can make changes to their multiple-choice sheet from stage one, using the context of the story to inform their guesses.

The third stage of the procedure is focused word study. Students can practice the target words with basic flashcards for this stage (see below), or they can enhance the basic flashcards by writing the Hebrew word on one side along with its part of speech and the target word used in a sentence. The reverse side, then, has the L1 translation or a picture.[38] Students can also play games with word cards. To do this, the L2 words are written on one set of cards with a separate set of cards for the L1 translations and/or pictures. Students can play matching games like "Memory" or even "Go Fish" with the object of the game being to match each L2 word with its translation and collect as many matches as possible.

The fourth stage of the procedure is evaluating word knowledge. At this stage, the instructor tests the students on their knowledge of the target vocabulary. The instructor can use a variety of formats from formal (provide a translation for each word or match an L2 word to an L1 gloss) to informal (crossword puzzle). Another option is a cloze test, which presents students with a story that includes blanks for target vocabulary items. The student must complete the story using the target words.

---

[38] For a set of Hebrew vocabulary items with pictures, see Scheumann and Scheumann, *According to Their Kinds*. For a similar resource for Greek, see T. Michael W. Halcomb, *800 Words and Images: A New Testament Greek Vocabulary Builder* (Wilmore, KY: GlossaHouse, 2013).

The final stage in the procedure is a writing workshop in which the students create a simple story using the target vocabulary items. This process begins with the instructor presenting his or her own composition. The instructor's composition provides further exposure to the vocabulary and an example to follow. The students then each write a composition, making use of the target items.

The goal of the Recycled Words strategy is to encourage long-term, deeper learning of the vocabulary rather than superficial short-term retention. By covering the new vocabulary items using a variety of modes and activities, the students reinforce memory traces for the unfamiliar words and add memory cues to assist in future retrieval.

Direct Vocabulary Teaching Activity: Flashcards and the Keyword Technique (Greek)

While many students use flashcards, and many teachers recommend them, not everyone knows how or why they should be used. Therefore, at the risk of being redundant, this section will introduce a recommended approach to using flashcards with some of the relevant research that supports their effectiveness for learning vocabulary. The *keyword technique*, which supplements the use of flashcards, will be introduced at the end of this section.[39]

To create a set of flashcards, the student should select a set of L2 words to study, beginning with high-frequency words and words that fulfill the specific needs of the learner. For a student of New Testament Greek, the high-frequency words would be those that occur most frequently in the New Testament.[40] The learner would begin to add less frequent words as learning progresses through the course. Therefore, this activity can be used from the first day of class and continued all the way through the course of study. In the process of choosing words to study, the student can avoid interference and confusion by separating words that should not be learned together, such as words that are formally

---

[39] Adapted from Nation, *Learning Vocabulary*, 445–68.

[40] A Bible software program can generate a list of all New Testament Greek words in order of frequency. For a more robust resource for Greek vocabulary learning, see Warren C. Trenchard, *The Complete Vocabulary Guide to the Greek New Testament*, rev. ed. (Grand Rapids: Zondervan, 1998).

similar (those that look or sound alike), words that belong to the same lexical set, near synonyms, and antonyms. For example, the words ἀγαπάω "I love (unconditionally)" and φιλέω "I love (as a friend)" should not be learned at the same time because they are near synonyms.

Next, the student writes the L2 word on one side of an index card with the L1 meaning on the other side of the card, keeping in mind that there is not a one-to-one correspondence between the L2 word and the L1 gloss. In addition to the L2 word on the first side, the student can also write relevant grammatical information such as part of speech, gender, principal parts, etc. Color-coding can also be used to indicate grammatical information such as gender of nouns or parts of speech. For example, a word written in pink indicates a feminine noun while a word written in yellow indicates a preposition. The student could also include the word in a sentence and put that on the front of the card for context and collocates.

Another variation is to use a picture or a diagram instead of the L1 meaning on the opposite side of the card. Research indicates that some students learn and retain vocabulary better with the use of pictures, which bypasses the L1 and more directly connects form and meaning.[41] The act of drawing on the card may also help improve memory by encouraging deeper focus on the word and its meaning.[42] Writing one's own flashcards instead of using flashcards made by someone else or using a computer program can give the student one more encounter with the word. However, repeated writing does not add significantly to vocabulary learning.[43] Therefore, purchased cards or computer programs[44]

---

[41] See, e.g., Nancy E. Webber, "Pictures and Words as Stimuli in Learning Foreign Language Responses," *Journal of Psychology* 98 (1978): 57–63.

[42] Nation, *Learning Vocabulary*, 449.

[43] Writing can have a small effect on strengthening the form-meaning connection for each word, but it is not as significant as other approaches to vocabulary learning. See, e.g., Susan Jane Gershman, "Foreign Language Vocabulary Learning under Seven Conditions" (PhD diss., Columbia University, 1970); and Margaret Hanratty Thomas and John N. Dieter, "The Positive Effects of Writing Practice on Integration of Foreign Words in Memory," *Journal of Educational Psychology* 79.3 (1987): 249–53.

[44] For example, see flashcards generated by Quizlet (quizlet.com).

can be just as effective as handmade cards, minus one encounter with the target word.[45]

As the student begins to practice with the cards, he or she should adjust the number of words in the stack to be learned based on the difficulty of the words.[46] If the words are more difficult, the stack of active words should be smaller. Practice begins by looking at the L2 word on the first card, saying it out loud to assist the phonological loop, and trying to retrieve the L1 meaning. If he or she is unable to retrieve the meaning, the learner flips the card over for the answer. In this way, the learner moves through the stack of cards one-by-one until the he or she has reviewed all the words. After a few times through the stack, the learner may want to set aside in a separate stack those words that are easier, that is, those whose meaning can be retrieved quickly before turning over the card. This leaves the more difficult words for more frequent repetition and practice. The cards in the stack of easier words should still be reviewed but with longer spacing between repetitions than those that are more difficult (see below).

Two factors are important in the learning of the word: repetition and spaced retrieval. More repetitions are necessary for understanding the many facets of the word and for reinforcing the form-meaning connection for the word. Most researchers find that five to seven repetitions are necessary for learning a word solidly although not completely. This would require at least twenty to fifty encounters as discussed above.

Spaced retrieval is also important because "spaced presentation enhances memory"[47] and results in "more secure learning than massed repetition."[48] Spacing can be achieved in two different ways: by incorporating time between study sessions (hours or days) and by adjusting the number of cards studied in a single pack (space between meetings of the word in a single study session). One critical spacing factor is the time

---

[45] See Nation, *Learning Vocabulary*, 468–69.

[46] See, e.g., the study by Thompson, "Word-List Size."

[47] Baddeley, *Human Memory*, 70.

[48] Nation, *Learning Vocabulary*, 452. See, e.g., the study by Kristine C. Bloom and Thomas J. Shuell, "Effects of Massed and Distributed Practice on the Learning and Retention of Second-Language Vocabulary," *Journal of Educational Research* 74.4 (1981): 245–48.

between the first presentation of the word and the first retrieval attempt. This is something that should be delayed to allow for some mental adjustment. In other words, a student should not go through the stack immediately after making the cards.

Continued spacing of flashcard practice is also important with increasing intervals between meetings of each word. Most forgetting occurs after initial learning. As time passes, the rate of forgetting becomes slower.[49] Also, the human brain needs some time (and perhaps sleep) to adjust to the new lexical knowledge and to change the way the word is stored. "Until this change in storage occurs, newly learned words are functionally separate from the established lexicon."[50] The ideal pattern of spaced of retrievals is not agreed upon, but "the general principle is that successful but difficult retrievals are better for memory than successful but easy retrievals" for establishing a secure memory of the word.[51] Therefore, if the student fails to recall a word, the interval should be shortened between meetings, but if the student recalls correctly, then the delay should be increased.

After many repetitions with spaced intervals, the student should then move to productive recall. To do this, the student flips the cards over, revealing the L1 side of the card. From this side, he or she should try to retrieve the L2 word on the other side, starting with small stacks of cards and working up to larger stacks as the process becomes easier. Additionally, the student should be saying the L2 words out loud to further stimulate the phonological loop of working memory and ultimately encourage storage in long-term memory.[52] For deeper learning, the student can practice putting the L2 word in a phrase or sentence or with some collocates as part of the recall process.

One approach to supplementing vocabulary learning by flashcards is the keyword technique. This mnemonic device uses a student's

---

[49] Henry L. Roediger III, Yana Weinstein, and Pooja K. Agarwal, "Forgetting: Preliminary Considerations," in *Forgetting*, ed. S. Della Sala (Hove, East Sussex: Psychology Press, 2010), 6.

[50] Nation, *Learning Vocabulary*, 453.

[51] Nation, *Learning Vocabulary*, 454; see also Baddeley, *Human Memory*, 70.

[52] See Nick C. Ellis, "Vocabulary Acquisition, Word Structure, Collocation, Word-Class, and Meaning," in *Vocabulary: Description, Acquisition and Pedagogy*, ed. N. Schmitt and M. McCarthy (Cambridge: Cambridge University Press, 1997), 133.

creativity to learn words that may be more difficult to retrieve, and it is surprisingly effective.[53] For each L2 vocabulary item, the student thinks of an L1 word that sounds like the beginning of the word or all the word. The learner then creates a visual image, often fanciful or imaginative, that combines both words. For example, when learning the word καρπός "fruit," the student might connect the initial sound of the word with the English word for a type of fish, the carp. The student would then create a mental picture of a fish that is eating fruit to help remember that καρπός, which sounds like "carp," means "fruit." The more imaginative the image, the more memorable it is.[54]

This technique does have a few limitations. First, it is most effective when the learner, not the teacher, identifies the keyword and creates the image because the student needs the opportunity for extended focus and reflection on the word for deeper learning. Second, some words are more suitable for the technique than others. For example, L2 words with concrete definitions work better than words with more abstract meanings.[55] Another limitation noted by some studies is that the keyword technique is more effective for initial learning and should be supplemented with other strategies for long-term retention.[56] However, the

---

[53] The effectiveness of this technique is supported by studies such as the following: Joel R. Levin, et al., "Mnemonic Versus Nonmnemonic Vocabulary-Learning Strategies for Children," *American Educational Research Journal* 19.1 (1982): 121–36; Mark A. McDaniel and Michael Pressley, "Putting the Keyword Method in Context," *Journal of Educational Psychology* 76.4 (1984): 598–609; Michael Pressley et al., "Mnemonic Versus Nonmenemonic Vocabulary-Learning Strategies: Additional Comparisons," *Journal of Educational Psychology* 74 (1982): 693–707.

[54] This technique can be particularly effective when combined with memory palaces or method of loci, which is a memory enhancing technique that intentionally encodes information to be remembered along an internal mental visuospatial route to promote greater retrieval. See Martin Dresler et al., "Mnemonic Training Reshapes Brain Networks to Support Superior Memory," *Neuron* 93 (2017): 1227–35. I am indebted to Andrew Coutras for suggesting this idea.

[55] James W. Hall, "On the Utility of the Keyword Mnemonic for Vocabulary Learning," *Journal of Educational Psychology* 80.4 (1988): 555.

[56] Alvin Y. Wang and Margaret H. Thomas, "Effect of Keywords on Long-Term Retention: Help or Hindrance?" *Journal of Educational Psychology* 87.3 (1995): 468–75; Alvin Y. Wang, et al., "Long-Term Retention under Conditions of Intentional Learning and the Keyword Mnemonic," *Bulletin of the Psychonomic Society* 31.6 (1993): 545–47.

overwhelming evidence is that the technique is effective and works in a variety of contexts.

Using flashcards supplemented by the keyword technique to learn L2 vocabulary is effective and efficient, as supported by empirical research cited above. These two complementary approaches are also simple, inexpensive, and available to anyone with a pencil, a few index cards, and a little imagination.

Indirect Vocabulary Teaching Activity: Retelling a Story (Latin)

This last vocabulary acquisition example makes use of indirect instruction. Retelling a story provides learners with an opportunity to indirectly learn vocabulary in a meaningful context.[57] Nation explains the rationale behind this type of activity: "From a vocabulary-learning point of view, the text provides new vocabulary and a context to help understand the vocabulary, and the retelling gives learners the chance to productively retrieve the vocabulary and ideally make creative use of it."[58]

To design the activity, the instructor chooses or prepares a carefully selected text, making sure the students know at least 95 to 98 percent of the running words. As noted elsewhere, this can be the most challenging part of the activity for the ancient language instructor. Ideally, this activity would be carried out in a second semester course or after, sometime after the students have acquired a modest vocabulary and some experience with the language. Even so, the chosen text will likely need some modification (simplification, diglot weave, etc.). For the purposes of this activity, the chosen text is Acts 27 (Vulgate). The instructor should modify the text as necessary to achieve 95 to 98 percent vocabulary coverage for the level of his or her students.

Additionally, the instructor may want to intentionally embed some specific vocabulary items into the text, words that he or she wants the students to learn or to process more deeply through this activity. Remember that words in the same semantic field should not be learned together, but words clustered around a similar theme can be grouped together for effective learning. Therefore, in this lesson, the instructor

---

[57] Adapted from Nation, *Learning Vocabulary*, 191–92.
[58] Nation, *Learning Vocabulary*, 191.

may want to choose words related to the theme of sailing, including such vocabulary items as *navigo* "I sail," *ventus* "wind" *onus* "cargo," and *gubernator* "navigator, captain."

Once the text has been prepared, the students read the text and then retell it in L2. The retelling can be done in a variety of ways. One of the less threatening approaches is to have the students work in pairs, where one student retells the story to the other, and then they switch roles. However, a student could retell the story to the instructor or to a group of students. In another variation, the activity could be more interesting if each student has a different story to read and retell.

The instructor can also place parameters on the retelling of the story by giving students a time limit. A variation on this is the 4/3/2 activity.[59] For this variation, a student retells the story a total of three times, each time to a different student. He or she gets four minutes to talk to the first student, three minutes to talk to the second, and two minutes for the third talk. The repetition and push to speak more quickly each time offers the student opportunity for more fluent retrieval of vocabulary items.

Another variation is to provide the listening student in each pair with a set of guiding questions, preferably in L2.[60] In this way, the retelling is more like an interview and can be a little less intimidating. Moreover, the instructor can design the questions in such a way as to elicit target vocabulary items from the student retelling the story.

Conclusion

This chapter addressed vocabulary acquisition, which is essential for language proficiency and reading fluency. As the opening scenario suggests, a student with only grammar knowledge cannot comprehend a text, but one with only vocabulary knowledge can. The chapter began

---

[59] This activity has received some attention in research and instruction. See, e.g., Nel de Jong and Charles A. Perfetti, "Fluency Training in the ESL Classroom: An Experimental Study of Fluency Development and Proceduralization," *Language Learning* 61.2 (2011): 533–68; Supot Arevart and Paul Nation, "Fluency Improvement in a Second Language," *RELC Journal* 22 (1991): 84–94; Paul Nation, "Improving Speaking Fluency," *System* 17.3 (1989): 377–84.

[60] Adapted from Moina Simcock, "Developing Productive Vocabulary Using the 'Ask and Answer' Technique," *Guidelines* 15.2 (1993): 1–7.

with what we know about the various aspects of knowing a word and factors that affect vocabulary learning, retrieval, and retention, followed by implications for instruction. The last two sections addressed vocabulary learning in biblical and ancient language classes and some specific examples of how to design activities for vocabulary acquisition. The next chapter discusses various approaches to syllabus design for language courses.

For Further Reading

Baddeley, Alan. *Essentials of Human Memory*. Classic Edition. London: Psychology Press, 2014.

Bloom, Kristine C., and Thomas J. Shuell. "Effects of Massed and Distributed Practice on the Learning and Retention of Second-Language Vocabulary." *Journal of Educational Research* 74.4 (1981): 245–48.

Laufer, Batia, and Geke C. Ravenhorst-Kalovski. "Lexical Threshold Revisited: Lexical Text Coverage, Learners' Vocabulary Size and Reading Comprehension." *Reading in a Foreign Language* 22.1 (2010): 15–30.

Hulstijn, Jan H. "Intentional and Incidental Second Language Vocabulary Learning: A Reappraisal of Elaboration, Rehearsal and Automaticity." Pages 258–86 in *Cognition and Second Language Instruction*. Edited by P. Robinson. Cambridge: Cambridge University Press, 2001.

Nation, I. S. P. *Learning Vocabulary in Another Language*. 2nd ed. Cambridge: Cambridge University Press, 2013.

Nation, I. S. P. *Teaching and Learning Vocabulary*. Boston: Heinle & Heinle, 1990.

Nation, Paul, ed. *New Ways in Teaching Vocabulary*. TESOL, 1994.

Chapter 11: Course Design and Syllabus Structure

Maria sat down for her first class of English as a second language and was surprised to find her instructor talking about how to pass the TOEFL (Test of English as a Foreign Language), an exam usually required for admission into an English-speaking university. She just wanted to be able to travel in the United States as a tourist and was not sure if this course was really what she needed. Peter, a third semester Latin student, found himself with a new instructor who was apparently unaware of what he had learned the previous semester. Peter was overwhelmed and mostly lost for several weeks until he got caught up. John entered his first semester Greek class with some apprehension. He hadn't studied a language in years. However, as the instructor began, John recognized that he was learning a familiar phrase from the New Testament—in Greek. John began to relax. He thought he might be able to do this after all.

The Principle: Course Design and Syllabus Structure

A well-designed course is critical to the success of the students and requires thought and intentionality. A good course not only presents the required course material, but it also considers the needs of the student. The good news is that there are many good syllabus options available. In fact, one could argue that there are as many syllabus variations as there are instructors when it comes to language teaching. In many ways, this is a good thing. An instructor must create and adapt a course that fits his or her unique situation, taking into consideration the needs of the students and the environmental constraints of the teaching locale. However, teachers and textbook authors for ancient languages often use the same basic syllabus structure—usually the grammar-based syllabus—without awareness of other options, let alone serious consideration of them.

Creating a good course can be a challenging process. It begins with an analysis of student needs and environmental factors, which the instructor uses to define the scope and content of the course. Once the instructor has defined the content of the course, he or she needs to decide what will be the unit of progression and how to sequence the units of the course. However, to be most effective, the instructor should also be aware of the relevant pedagogical principles that undergird effective course design. Therefore, this section will begin with a discussion of these important pedagogical principles and then move on to the steps for planning a syllabus, including some of the more common types of language syllabus options.

Pedagogical Principles for Course Design

When designing a course, an instructor needs to consider many important pedagogical principles. I. S. P. Nation and John Macalister list no less than twenty such principles, drawn from the fields of SLA, first language pedagogy, and general pedagogy.[1] These can be grouped into three general categories: content and sequencing, format and presentation, and monitoring and assessment.

Content and Sequencing

The first category of pedagogical principles for course design is content and sequencing. The discussion below will address each of the following principles in turn: frequency, learning strategies and learner autonomy, spaced retrieval, interference, forward motion, language system, teachability, and learning burden.

In terms of frequency, the course should focus on the high-frequency items in the language because these will cover a large proportion of the text(s) to be learned. However, once these are acquired, it takes many low-frequency items to be able to access the language fully. Therefore, learning strategies should also be an important part of the language curriculum, teaching learners how to learn and promoting

---

[1] The following discussion is adapted from I. S. P. Nation and John Macalister, *Language Curriculum Design* (New York: Routledge, 2010), 37–69. Other similar lists can be found in Rod Ellis, "Principles of Instructed Language Learning," *System* 33 (2005): 209–24; H. Douglas Brown, "Requiem for Methods," *Journal of Intensive English Studies* 7 (1993): 1–12; and Karl J. Krahnke and Mary Ann Christison, "Recent Language Research and Some Language Teaching Principles," *TESOL Quarterly* 17.4 (1983): 625–49.

autonomy, which leads to the development of independent life-long learners of the language.

The previous chapter addressed the importance of using spaced retrieval and avoiding interference when learning vocabulary. The same is true for most types of learning, including grammar and other language components. When designing a language course, the instructor should plan for some spacing between retrievals of any given aspect of language learning. At the same time, he or she should avoid teaching together at the same time language items that are too similar, thus avoiding interference.

Another critical component of course design is forward motion. The course should necessarily keep moving forward, continuing to add language items, skills, and strategies. Therefore, each course should have a concrete set of goals that the instructor wishes to achieve, beyond just "covering the first 10 chapters of the textbook" (see the discussion on needs analysis below). Relatedly, when teaching the language system of the course, an instructor needs to focus on the generalizable features of the language system. In other words, "Does today's work help the learners to deal with tomorrow's task?"[2] Does the instruction move the students closer to achieving the goals of the course? For example, when teaching an unknown word, an instructor should try to focus on the underlying concept of the word, not just the meaning in a particular context.

The course design should also take into account the teachability of certain language items and the order of acquisition. Said differently, certain elements of the language are necessary for learning other elements. For example, students of Hebrew need to learn the inseparable prepositions (ב, כ, ל) and the definite article before they can learn how the prepositions combine with the article. The combination of preposition and article is not teachable until after learning the component parts. Relatedly, learners themselves go through predictable stages in language acquisition. Formal instruction seems to have little influence on these natural acquisition orders, although it can increase the rate of acquisition.[3]

---

[2] Nation and Macalister, *Language Curriculum Design*, 43.

[3] A great deal of research has been done on natural acquisition orders for English. Students of English as a second/foreign language learn certain language items in a

Finally, the instructor should consider the learning burden of each language item. A good course "should help learners make the most effective use of previous knowledge."[4] Each learner brings with him or her a knowledge of language, even if that knowledge is limited to L1. A good example of this prior knowledge is cognate vocabulary, such as the Latin *thronus*, "throne." A well-designed syllabus will help the students make use of this prior knowledge while providing extra time in the syllabus for other items that have a greater learning burden.

Format and Presentation

The second category of pedagogical principles for course design is format and presentation. Many of these principles appear elsewhere in this book, so this section will only address them briefly. As addressed in chapter 12, instructors should deliver material in a way that promotes student interest and motivation and takes into consideration student learning styles. The course should also incorporate the following important elements of language learning: comprehensible input (chapters 4, 5, and 6), output (chapter 7), and fluency practice (chapter 9). In addition, a good syllabus design will include plenty of time in the language (see chapters 3 and 5).

Two other pedagogical principles from this category not addressed elsewhere in this book are deliberate language learning and a balance of instructional elements. First, a good course should include opportunities for deliberate language learning, including explicit information about grammar rules and vocabulary nuances, as well as opportunities for deep processing. Deep processing might include word studies or opportunities for critical analysis of complex syntax, perhaps in the form of intensive reading and/or careful exegesis. An instructor can use a variety

---

predictable sequence. For example, students go through the following stages when learning negation: as negation outside of a sentence ("No you eat") to negation with don't ("He don't can do that") to full and proper negation ("She doesn't do that"). See Pienemann, "Outline of Processability Theory"; and Pienemann, *Language Processing*. Unfortunately, no similar studies exist for acquisition orders in Hebrew, Greek, or Latin, although some of Pienemann's more general principles regarding acquisition orders may apply.

[4] Nation and Macalister, *Language Curriculum Design*, 47.

of approaches to do this, including in-class discussions, activities, or homework assignments.

The last critical factor to consider in this category is the balance of instructional elements in the language syllabus. In other words, ideally, how much time should be spent on each element of language instruction? Nation and Macalister recommend that the course be equally divided between *four strands of language learning*: meaning-focused input, language-focused learning, meaning-focused output, and fluency activities.[5] This means that the instructor spends about 25 percent of class time on each strand, and the students spend about 25 percent of their time outside class on each strand.

The meaning-focused input strand of the course focuses on bringing a large quantity of input to the learners while the learners are focused on the message, with only a small number of unfamiliar language features. Meaning-focused input activities might include listening to stories, listening while reading, extensive reading, and communicative interaction, such as conversation or written exchange.

In language-focused learning, the instructor guides the students in a deliberate focus on the features of the language, including pronunciation, spelling, vocabulary, intensive reading, and grammar study.[6] Feedback to the learner, often in the form of error correction, is also considered part of this strand of language learning.

During the meaning-focused output strand of the course, students create messages in L2 while the focus is on meaning, again with only a small number of unfamiliar language features used. Meaning-focused output activities might include short talks, writing stories and letters in L2, and communicative interaction.

The fourth strand of language learning is fluency development. This portion of the course is often overlooked as being superfluous, but it is a critical component of language development.[7] In fluency development, the focus of the learner is again on the message encoded in the

---

[5] Nation and Macalister, *Language Curriculum Design*, 51. See also Nation, "Four Strands." These should not be confused with the four skills covered in chapter 8.

[6] For an excellent discussion of grammar teaching options, see Rod Ellis, "Teaching and Research: Options in Grammar Teaching," *TESOL Quarterly* 32.1 (1998): 39–60.

[7] See chapter 9 for further discussion of the role of fluency in language learning.

language, not on the language features themselves. In fact, in this strand of language learning, there should be no unfamiliar language features. The instructor should view this as an opportunity for the student to get a large quantity of practice with some pressure to process faster each time, helping the student transition from word-by-word analysis to fluent retrieval. Activities in this strand might include listening to stories, easy extensive reading or repeated reading, speed reading, and short writing assignments.

Monitoring and Assessment

As an instructor develops his or her course, the last category of pedagogical principles to consider involves monitoring and assessment. In this category, the focus is on responding to the needs of the students as the class progresses, which includes monitoring the effectiveness of the course and responding to student errors with feedback.

First, the instructor maintains an ongoing evaluation of the effectiveness of the course in terms of its ability to meet the needs of the learners in the given context (see the next section on needs analysis and environmental analysis). The instructor may need to make changes along the way based on the abilities of the students and any changes in the environment in which the class is delivered.

Second, the instructor needs to consider how he or she will respond to students' work, and specifically, how he or she will correct their errors to help them improve in their study. A great deal of SLA research is dedicated to effective feedback.[8] A few examples of corrective feedback include explicit feedback ("no, the correct answer is..."), recast (repeating the incorrect statement but with the correct word or form), requests for clarification ("did you mean...?"), and restatements emphasizing the incorrect form in a manner that draws attention to the incorrect form.

However, as Karl J. Krahnke and Mary Ann Christison note: "Error produced in the process of acquiring a second language should be viewed as a natural product of the acquisition process, as a source of information on learner strategies, and as a problem best addressed

---

[8] See the summary by Ellis, *Study of Second Language Acquisition*, 227–28.

through more input and interaction rather than through correction and drill."[9] In other words, rather than constantly correcting student errors, the instructor should use the student errors as a guide indicating the specific deficit they have in their language proficiency. To make up for this deficit, the instructor needs to find ways to provide more examples of the correct form (input) and more opportunities to use the item correctly (interaction).

The pedagogical principles outlined above should be taken into consideration when designing a course for language instruction. The next section addresses the steps an instructor should take when developing the structure of a language syllabus.

Steps for Designing a Syllabus

Every course design or syllabus structure has at least three minimum requirements.[10] First, the course must have a rationale for the selection of items to be covered in the course. The instructor must carefully consider what to include and what not to include, usually based on a *needs analysis* and *environment analysis*. Second, the course must have a rationale for the chosen *unit of progression*, also called the *unit of analysis*.[11] The instructor can organize the course by many different units of progression, such as grammatical structures, vocabulary items, topics, and tasks. Finally, the course needs a rationale for the grading or sequencing of the units. The ordering of certain elements is significant for the success of the course, and the sequence of units is necessarily dependent on the unit of analysis chosen. Each of these three requirements for syllabus design is described in greater detail below.

Determine the Scope of the Course

The first step in structuring a syllabus is to determine what the course should cover. The instructor should take time to consider what the learners need from the course, also called a needs analysis. For modern

---

[9] Krahnke and Christison, "Recent Language Research," 642.

[10] Michael H. Long, *Second Language Acquisition and Task-based Language Teaching* (West Sussex, England: Wiley & Sons, 2015), 205–6.

[11] Nation and Macalister, *Language Curriculum Design*, 71.

languages, the results of a needs analysis can vary widely. For example, some students need to learn English to go to college, some students need to learn French to be flight attendants on transatlantic flights, while some other students need Hindi to serve on medical mission trips. For biblical and ancient languages, the range of student needs is much more focused, usually limited to reading, comprehending, and interpreting ancient texts. However, it is still important to perform a needs analysis to fine-tune the goals of the course and to create a course that will best serve the specific students who will be taking the course.

In a needs analysis, the instructor considers where and how the learners will use the language and then what specific language elements and skills the learners will need for that situation. He or she will need to consider what the learners know and what the learners lack, identifying the gap between the learners' present knowledge and the knowledge required to accomplish their goals. This can and often should be a collaborative process in which the instructor consults the students and others, such as professionals who serve in the target situation.[12]

In addition to a needs analysis, the instructor should also consider the results of an environment analysis. In an environment analysis, the instructor considers external factors that can affect the goals of the course, what can be included in the course, and how to teach and assess the course. The environment analysis often focuses on constraints imposed by the learning environment, such as time constraints, the ability or background of the learners, the ability and training of the teacher(s), the physical classroom environment, and the availability of resources.[13] This would also include constraints put on the course by the institution such as wider curriculum developments. An instructor, therefore, will need to ensure that Greek 2 prepares the students for Greek 3, for example, especially if the instructor of Greek 3 uses a very different approach to teaching and course design.

---

[12] For some helpful questions to use when conducting a needs analysis, see Nation and Macalister, *Language Curriculum Design*, 26.

[13] For questions helpful in conducting an environment analysis, see Nation and Macalister, *Language Curriculum Design*, 16–17.

Determine the Unit of Progression

Once the instructor has chosen the material to include in the course, he or she needs to decide what unit of progression or unit of analysis to use. There are many good options. This section will highlight some of the more commonly used units, beginning with those that can be serialized, that is, those that have individual items that can be presented in a series, and moving to those that represent a field of knowledge.

Some units of progression involve items that progress in a definite series, such as vocabulary, grammar, and skill development.[14] A lexical syllabus is organized by vocabulary items. In this type of course, individual L2 words are the unit of progression.[15] A grammar-based syllabus is organized by grammatical constructions, such as nouns, prepositions, and past tense verbs. A syllabus based on component skills uses language skills and subskills, such as writing poetry or giving a speech, as the unit of progression. These skills can then be further divided into their component subskills, such as writing a narrative, comprehending poetry, or composing the introduction to a speech.

Other units of progression fall into the category of field of knowledge. These units of progression are more flexible and can usually be arranged in almost any order.[16] A discourse syllabus uses genres or topic types, such as law and historical narrative, as the unit of progression. A syllabus based on situations and roles would adopt as the unit of progression specific language use situations, such as ordering at a restaurant or purchasing a train ticket. This differs slightly from the component skills approach described above in that it focuses on the situation as a whole rather than building up to a skill through its various subskills.

Among the various syllabus types, the *task-based syllabus* has received a great deal of attention in SLA research and literature.[17] The unit

---

[14] Nation and Macalister, *Language Curriculum Design*, 72.

[15] See John McH. Sinclair and Antoinette Renouf, "A Lexical Syllabus for Language Learning," in *Vocabulary and Language Teaching*, ed. R. Carter and M. McCarthy (London: Longman, 1988), 140–60.

[16] Nation and Macalister, *Language Curriculum Design*, 72.

[17] See, e.g., Michael H. Long, *Second Language Acquisition*; Rod Ellis, *Task-Based Language Learning and Teaching* (Oxford: Oxford University Press, 2003); and Dave Willis and Jane Willis, *Doing Task-Based Teaching* (Oxford: Oxford University Press,

of progression in this type of syllabus is the task, defined as "an activity which requires learners to use language, with emphasis on meaning, to attain an objective."[18] Rod Ellis elaborates: "While a task requires a learner to act *primarily* as a language user and give focal attention to message conveyance, it allows for peripheral attention to be paid to deciding what forms to use."[19] Tasks can range from navigating customs at the airport to completing a geometry exercise to explaining the rules of a board game. Michael Long emphasizes the ordinary nature of the task in a task-based syllabus: "By 'task' is meant the hundred and one things people *do* in everyday life, at work, at play, and in between. Tasks are the things people will tell you they do if you ask them and they are not applied linguists."[20]

The advantage of the task-based syllabus is that the students learn to complete real world tasks with real language, rather than modified or simplified samples. This is also what distinguishes it from the component skills syllabus and the syllabus based on situations and roles. The disadvantage is that the focus of the course can be more on fluency than on accuracy.[21] An instructor needs to have other ways of checking to be sure that all the necessary grammar and vocabulary items are covered by the course.

2007).

[18] Nation and Macalister, *Language Curriculum Design*, 80. For a comprehensive definition of "task," see Long, *Second Language Acquisition*, 108–10. See also the summary of similar definitions collected by Ellis, *Task-Based Language Learning*, 4–5.

[19] Ellis, *Task-Based Language Learning*, 4–5, italics original.

[20] Michael H. Long, "A Role for Instruction in Second Language Acquisition: Task-Based Language Teaching," in *Modelling and Assessing Second Language Acquisition*, ed. by K. Hyltenstam and M. Pienemann (Clevedon, England: Multilingual Matters, 1985), 89, italics original.

[21] Nation and Macalister, *Language Curriculum Design*, 81. However, advocates of the task-based syllabus offer solutions to this perceived disadvantage. For example, Ellis differentiates between focused tasks, those that intentionally elicit a target form, and unfocused tasks, those that just elicit "general samples of learner language" (*Task-Based Language Learning*, 142). He argues that both should be used to promote a balance of fluency and accuracy. Willis and Willis encourage instructors to focus on specific language forms at the end of a task sequence, offering opportunity for the development of accuracy (*Task-Based Teaching*, 25).

The task-based syllabus is also to be differentiated from the task-supported syllabus which usually follows a sequence of grammatical forms, even though it does incorporate tasks as part of the language curriculum.[22] Instead, using a task-based syllabus, the instructor helps the students learn the needed grammar and vocabulary for the task at hand in a more inductive approach to language learning.

While there are many options to choose from when adopting a unit of progression for a course, an instructor does not have to choose one unit of progression to the exclusion of all others. Some units of progression can be combined. For example, a discourse-based syllabus can also use serialized vocabulary at the same time, although one of the two units must be chosen as primary when they present conflicting options for sequencing. The next section addresses issues of sequencing a syllabus, the last step in the design process.

Determine the Sequence of Units

Once the instructor has determined the scope of the course and has chosen a unit (or units) of progression for the course, he or she is ready to sequence those units.[23] Instructors are a little more limited when it comes to sequencing options. Units of progression can be structured using a linear approach or using a modular approach, and each unit of progression lends itself to one or the other.

In linear sequencing, each lesson is dependent on the lesson before, while in modular sequencing, each lesson or module is separate from the others so that the lessons can be completed in any order. Serialized units of progression lend themselves more to the linear approach to sequencing, while the modular approach works better with units of progression that represent a field of knowledge, such as topics or tasks.

Because language learning tends to build on itself, especially in the early stages, and because instructors tend to favor the serialized units of progression, the linear approach is used more frequently than the modular approach, although it does have some disadvantages. For example,

---

[22] Nation and Macalister, *Language Curriculum Design*, 80.

[23] This discussion adapted from Nation and Macalister, *Language Curriculum Design*, 82–85.

the linear approach does not take into account absenteeism, nor does it adapt to different learning styles and learning speeds well. It also does not readily incorporate the need for students to use recycled material, especially for fluency development. According to Nation and Macalister, "The worst kind of linear development assumes that once an item has been presented in a lesson, it has been learned and does not need focused revision."[24]

Two variations of the linear approach to sequencing, the spiral curriculum and the matrix model, help to remedy these disadvantages. With the spiral curriculum, the instructor decides on the major items to cover, and then he or she covers them several times throughout the course at increasing levels of detail.[25] For example, an instructor might cover a high-frequency grammatical pattern early in the course and then present additional elaborations and applications for the pattern each time the course returns to that topic in the spiral. The order of items in the spiral and the span between meetings can be adjusted to suit the complexity of the topic and the amount of time students need to accommodate the new material.

One advantage of the spiral curriculum is that it provides for easily monitored recycling of material. In other words, an instructor can use a story or activity, change it slightly for the next cycle to encourage the students to deepen their processing, and help the students develop fluency at the same time. The spiral syllabus also provides the opportunity for learners who were left behind to catch up at the next cycle, while making sure that the full value of the most important aspects of the language are addressed.

The matrix model is similar to the spiral curriculum in that the course intentionally addresses items repeatedly over time. For example, topics one through three are addressed in the first round of instruction over several weeks, and then those same three topics are covered again in a second round over the next several weeks. However, rather than increasing the complexity of instruction at each meeting like the spiral syllabus does, the matrix model changes the approach and provides

---

[24] Nation and Macalister, *Language Curriculum Design*, 82.

[25] Jerome S. Bruner, *The Process of Education* (Cambridge: Harvard University Press, 1977), 13, 52–54.

diversity in the repeated instruction. In other words, the same material is met in different contexts, perhaps in different genres or in different tasks, rather than at different levels of complexity. The structure might look like this:

> Week 1 = topic 1 in narrative
> Week 2 = topic 2 in narrative
> Week 3 = topic 3 in narrative
> Week 4 = topic 1 in poetry
> Week 5 = topic 2 in poetry
> Week 6 = topic 3 in poetry

As with the spiral syllabus, the matrix approach allows for flexibility in the number of items covered in each cycle and the amount of time between meetings of each item. The matrix model provides advantages that are very similar to the spiral curriculum as discussed in the previous paragraph.

The modular approach is less common than the linear approach, especially for entry-level language courses, although it is recommended for a task-based syllabus and other syllabus designs that use a field of knowledge as the unit of progression.[26] The modular approach assumes that each lesson is self-contained and not dependent on any knowledge or skills gained in the other lessons of the course. The advantage of the modular approach is that the syllabus is much more fluid, and instructors have greater flexibility in the ordering of the course. Students can potentially cover the modules in any order they choose. The disadvantage of the modular approach is that, especially for beginners, learning a language is difficult to separate into discrete, unrelated modules. More advanced courses, however, could be more easily separated into unrelated units, such as "historical narrative" and "poetry" or "going shopping" and "ordering at a restaurant." These, then, could be covered in any order.

Once an instructor chooses to use a modular approach or a linear approach to sequencing, he or she must determine what that sequence will be. For serialized units of progression, the sequencing is usually

---

[26] Rod Ellis, "Designing a Task-Based Syllabus," *RELC Journal* 34.1 (2003): 77–78.

determined by principles such as frequency or difficulty. The units themselves as well as a needs analysis will help determine the sequencing principle. For example, a lexical syllabus will often start with the most frequently occurring words and move to the less frequent ones. A skills-based syllabus will begin with the simpler component subskills and progress to the more complex skills. A modular approach, such as in a task-based syllabus, allows for a little more flexibility, and student needs can help determine what the precise order of presentation will be. Some students necessarily prioritize certain tasks, situations, or genres over others.

In conclusion, the process of course design should be based on sound pedagogical principles. With these principles in mind, the process of developing a syllabus structure then moves through three stages: deciding on the scope and content of a course, based on needs analysis and environment analysis; choosing the unit of progression for the course; and choosing the sequence of units. The next section addresses some issues specific to course design and syllabus structure for biblical and ancient languages.

The Rationale: Syllabus Design for Biblical and Ancient Language Courses

For biblical and ancient languages, the first step in creating a syllabus structure, determining the scope and content of the course, is simpler than for modern languages. For the biblical languages in particular, the canon is fixed and therefore the grammar and vocabulary are clearly limited. Even for Latin, the corpus is much smaller than, say, for French or German. Therefore, the scope and content of these courses will be much more clearly defined and conducting a needs analysis will return a fairly predictable set of goals for the learners.

However, in terms of units of progression and sequencing, those who write biblical and ancient language textbooks have many more options than what they are currently utilizing. For example, a survey of textbooks for Biblical Hebrew reveals that most follow a grammar-based syllabus.[27] Even some of the recent textbooks that are moving

---

[27] Noonan, "Recent Teaching Grammars." Two exceptions follow a more inductive

toward a more communicative approach to teaching Hebrew still organize the lessons primarily by grammar topics.[28]

The downside of using a grammar-based syllabus is that the order of topics is not conducive to communication, and it is the act of communication, both giving and receiving, that promotes language acquisition (see chapter 3). A related downside is that, usually, a grammar-based syllabus introduces grammar topics in the same order as a reference grammar, starting with nouns, prepositions, and adjectives. Without verbs, it is difficult to understand a story, have a conversation, or ask a question. Therefore, the grammar-based syllabus relies more heavily on rote memorization of decontextualized vocabulary and paradigms, which is not as effective as learning language in context through communication. Moreover, the grammar-driven, rote memorization approach can lead to frustration and boredom in the students.

So, what would it look like to choose a different unit of progression for a biblical or ancient language syllabus? One easy option is the lexical syllabus.[29] Hebrew, Greek, and Latin all have frequency lists available to use for structuring a vocabulary-based syllabus.[30] An instructor or textbook author could use these frequency lists as the backbone of a

---

approach, which may bear some similarity to a task-based approach, although not entirely: Kittel, Hoffer, and Wright, *Biblical Hebrew;* and William Sanford LaSor, *Handbook of Biblical Hebrew* (Grand Rapids: Eerdmans, 1978).

[28] See, e.g., Cook and Holmstedt, *Beginning Biblical Hebrew*; Overland, *Learning Biblical Hebrew Interactively*; and Dallaire, *Biblical Hebrew*. Three recent exceptions to the grammar-based syllabus include materials by the Biblical Language Center (https://www.biblicallanguagecenter.com/), Aleph with Beth (https://www.glossahouse.com/aleph-with-beth) and Alpha with Angela (https://www.youtube.com/channel/UCe0ilqwSO8XVnCw4m3UYC1Q).

[29] Jeremy Thompson advocates for the primacy of vocabulary over grammar in the Biblical Hebrew classroom, supporting a more vocabulary-based syllabus. See his "Learning Biblical Hebrew Vocabulary: Insights from Second Language Vocabulary Acquisition" (PhD diss., University of Stellenbosch, 2010), especially pages 184–85.

[30] See, e.g., Larry A. Mitchel, *A Student's Vocabulary for Biblical Hebrew and Aramaic, Updated Edition: Frequency Lists with Definitions, Pronunciation Guide, and Index* (Grand Rapids: Zondervan, 2017); Bruce M. Metzger, *Lexical Aids for Students of New Testament Greek* (Grand Rapids: Baker, 1998); Trenchard, *Complete Vocabulary Guide*; Christopher Francese, *Core Latin and Ancient Greek Vocabularies* (Carlisle, PA: Dickinson College Commentaries, 2020).

syllabus and draw in grammar topics as they become relevant and necessary. Perhaps even better, it is possible to incorporate in the list of vocabulary items some of the more commonly used conjugated forms. For example, in Hebrew, the conjugated form וַיֹּאמֶר "and he said" is in the top 20 most frequently used words in the Hebrew Bible. This word can be taught as a chunk, basically as a vocabulary item, in the first week or two and then analyzed later in the course. The sequencing of the lexical syllabus would necessarily be linear, although grammar topics and complex vocabulary items could be introduced and reviewed in a spiral fashion.

Another approach to syllabus design for ancient languages might be a discourse-based syllabus in which the main units of the course are different types of discourse, such as narrative, poetry, or epistle. Each type of discourse uses grammar, vocabulary, and syntax that is somewhat unique to that genre, so the subtopics would overlap and yet be distinct in many ways, encouraging a mix of new items and review items in each lesson. The sequencing in this type of course could be modular, although a linear matrix model could also work with the grammar topics covered several times, each in a different discourse context.

Instructors might also consider the task-based syllabus in which the "task" is the unit of progression. For modern language instruction, these tasks are real-world activities like going to the grocery store or calling the repairman. However, the ancient texts also describe real-word activities. They are just not as familiar to modern learners. Teaching a "farmer" how to sell his "crop" at a "market" would be a task that teaches not only the language but also the culture of the text. The syllabus could progress in a modular fashion with tasks being interchangeable, although one could conceivably overlay a lexical syllabus that provides a more linear approach to the structure of the tasks.

Another approach to the task-based syllabus may be closer to addressing the needs of biblical and ancient language students. A needs analysis of biblical and ancient language students would reveal that most of them are learning the language to read and interpret the ancient texts, and in the case of the biblical language students, usually for the purpose of teaching the text, ministering to others, and enriching their personal relationship with God. What if these are the tasks of the syllabus, then? The tasks could be broken down further into more specific goals and skills, such as preaching from a narrative text or praying the Psalms for devotional purposes. Even first year students could conduct a word study in L2 or read one simple verse in L2, thus setting them up to complete such tasks. The instructor would then select the grammar and vocabulary needed for each lesson based on the task at hand. However, as noted above, an outside checklist of overall grammar and vocabulary may also be needed to ensure adequate coverage of these items.

The point of this section is that there are many good options available for structuring a syllabus for biblical and ancient languages, but many of these have not been used or even considered. For the sake of creating interesting and pedagogically sound courses, some of these would be worth exploring.

Examples for Biblical and Ancient Language Classrooms

The following examples represent three different options when it comes to syllabus structure. Due to space limitations, the outlines presented below are necessarily not complete or exhaustive. However, they offer a preliminary look at some potential structures for biblical and ancient language courses.

A Serialized Linear Syllabus: The Lexical Syllabus (Hebrew)

The first sample syllabus is a lexical syllabus for a first year Biblical Hebrew course. A needs analysis indicates, as expected, that the students have no prior knowledge of Hebrew and would like to learn how to read the Hebrew Bible for personal study and ministry-related purposes. Based on an environment analysis, the wider curriculum of the institution expects the students to know all the Hebrew words of the Bible that occur more than one hundred times and most of the basic grammar at the end of their first year. This, then, establishes the scope and content of the course.

For the lexical syllabus, each vocabulary item is the unit of progression, and it makes the most sense to progress through the vocabulary items in order of frequency with the most frequent items first. To determine the sequence, the instructor can use an electronic resource like

Logos or Accordance or a print resource like Larry A. Mitchel's *A Student's Vocabulary for Biblical Hebrew and Aramaic*.[31] If the course takes two full semesters of sixteen weeks each, then each week of the course will need to introduce about twenty new words to cover all the Hebrew words that occur more than one hundred times.

One of the challenges of creating a lexical syllabus for beginners is the lack of useable items in the first few lessons. The most frequent vocabulary words in Hebrew do not allow for many useful, meaningful sentences. Therefore, it would be advisable to not strictly follow the frequency list, at least not in the first two or three lessons. Instead, the instructor can mix in vocabulary items that are a little more productive and useful for maintaining simple dialogue, even if they are a little less frequent. For example, the first lesson could include such words as שָׁלוֹם "shalom/peace/greetings" and שְׁמִי "my name is…."

With the unit of progression and sequencing of units established, the instructor can then focus on how to incorporate other aspects of the course, particularly grammar. There are a few possible options. The instructor could supplement the lexical syllabus with a grammar-based syllabus, covering pronouns followed by nouns followed by adjectives, etc. within the overall structure of the vocabulary frequency list. However, this could create a mismatch between vocabulary and grammar since Hebrew is poor in adjectives, which are typically covered early, and rich in verbs, which are typically covered late. The instructor could also selectively choose to study Hebrew texts with a high concentration of the frequent vocabulary items, drawing grammar topics from these texts. Another option, mentioned above, is to treat inflected forms and common colocations as vocabulary items and include them in the list of items to cover.[32] Any grammar instruction would arise from the inflected forms as they appear on the list in order of frequency.

---

[31] Mitchel, *Student's Vocabulary*.

[32] Each week's list of "vocabulary" would necessarily be longer than twenty items with this approach.

A Field of Knowledge Modular Syllabus: The Discourse-Based Syllabus (Greek)

A second option for a syllabus structure is a discourse-based syllabus in which the topics are modular with some flexibility in the order of presentation. A needs and environment analysis highlight a situation like that described above for the Biblical Hebrew course, so the scope and content would also be similar but for New Testament Greek. The unit of progression, however, would be discourse type, limited to genres found in the New Testament. The structure of the course is potentially flexible as the instructor could change the order of the main topics (narrative, epistle, and apocalyptic literature). It would also be possible to change the order of many of the subtopics within each main topic.

The outline below provides a basic idea of how the discourse syllabus might be organized. For each subtopic, the outline provides some ideas for the type of grammar and vocabulary that unit might cover, keeping in mind that a separate exhaustive checklist of grammar and vocabulary items should be maintained to ensure that all the relevant materials are covered in the course. The example below provides more details at the beginning of the outline for the purpose of illustration with only general headings provided at the end. Notice that some grammar topics are covered in multiple places because they occur in different genres (for example, the aorist and prepositions). This provides some natural places for review and the potential for incorporating fluency practice in the course.

I. Main Discourse Type: Narrative
   a. Subtopic: Events in the past (main clauses)
      i. Grammar:
         1. Verbs: aorist active indicative
         2. Nouns: nominative and accusative
         3. Other: basic syntax/word order
      ii. Vocabulary: [Select vocabulary based on chosen texts from the Gospels and Acts that will be used in classroom instruction and practice, beginning with some of the more frequently occurring items.]

      b. Subtopic: Direct speech
        i. Dialogue
          1. Giving commands
            a. Grammar: imperatives and a few prepositions
            b. Vocabulary:
              i. Verbs (imperatives) and auxiliary words for practicing commands in the classroom, such as ἆρον/ἄρετε "pick up!" and θές/θέτε "put!"
              ii. Vocabulary needed to read examples of imperatives from the New Testament
            c. Other: status and respect in the ancient world, especially as expressed in commands
          2. Questions and Answers
            a. Grammar: present active indicative, future active indicative, review aorist
            b. Vocabulary: question words
            c. Other: syntax of questions
          3. Other dialogue…
        ii. Monologue…
      c. Subtopic: Background information and subordinate clauses
        i. Background information
          1. Grammar:
            a. Verbs: perfect, pluperfect
            b. Nouns: genitive and dative
            c. Other: more prepositions
          2. Vocabulary: [from selected Gospels and Acts texts]
        ii. Temporal clauses…
        iii. Relative clauses…
        iv. [Etc.]
  II. Main Discourse Type: Epistle
    a. Subtopic: Opening greeting
    b. Subtopic: Thanksgiving
    c. Subtopic: Body
    d. Subtopic: Greetings to specific individuals
    e. Subtopic: Closing
  III. Main Discourse Type: Apocalyptic Literature

A Task-Based Lesson with a Focus on the Four Strands (Latin)

The final example of syllabus design is a single task-based lesson for Latin that highlights the incorporation of the four strands discussed above. This task would be one of many that make up the entire course. The order of tasks could be flexible, or they could be more fixed as determined by a needs analysis in consultation with the students.

The task chosen for this lesson is the daily assigning of jobs to servants in an ancient Roman estate, using a role-play approach. The assumed setting is a large Roman household that employs many servants, each one specializing in a certain set of jobs on the estate. As the day begins, the master or mistress of the home must direct each servant to his or her assignment for that day.

The task meets the criteria of Dave Willis and Jane Willis for being included in a task-based syllabus:[33]

- *"Does the activity engage learners' interest?"* This task should be interesting and engaging as the students explore ancient home economics and estate management.
- *"Is there a primary focus on meaning?"* Because the focus is on accomplishing the task with the language as a tool in accomplishing the task, the criteria is met.
- *"Is there an outcome?"* The outcome is the successful instruction and dismissal of the servants to their various tasks.
- *"Is success judged in terms of outcome [rather than grammatical accuracy]?"* Success is judged by whether the servants can understand the master/mistress and go out to complete their tasks.
- *"Is completion a priority?"* Yes, the master/mistress must assign jobs to each of the servants to complete the task.
- *"Does the activity relate to real world activities?"* Yes, the task involves real ancient world activities.

To successfully complete this task, the students must make use of certain words and structures of the Latin language, which will be introduced, practiced, and reinforced through the course of the instruction. The required vocabulary should include household words, including

---

[33] Willis and Willis, *Task-Based Teaching*, 13.

indoor and outdoor items and locations as the servants may work inside or outside the house. In terms of grammar, the master/mistress must use many imperatives as he/she directs the servants to their respective jobs. The instructor may also need to provide some cultural background information as an advance organizer for this task, explaining the functions of a typical estate and some of the typical activities of the servants.

Incorporating the four strands is an integral part of this lesson. Therefore, the activities are organized by the four strands below:

1. ***Meaning-Focused Input Activity:*** Instructor gives each student a printed map of an ancient Roman estate with an aerial view of the house divided into rooms, along with any outbuildings, gardens, etc. Each student also receives a pawn from a board game or a small "servant" made of paper or clay. The instructor also has a map and a "servant." The instructor gives a command to his or her "servant," such as *Ambulā ad vineam* "Walk to the vineyard." The instructor then moves the small "servant" to the correct location on the map, modeling for the students where to send their servants. As students catch on, the instructor can stop modeling first and simply give commands while checking the students' accuracy in moving their "servants" around the estate.

2. ***Language-Focused Learning Activity:*** For this part of the learning, the instructor will guide the students in focused vocabulary learning, including flashcards and some rich explanation on a few significant words needed for the task. The instructor will also provide some specific grammar explanation for the imperative forms needed for this task.

3. ***Meaning-Focused Output Activity:*** This will be a written output assignment with the following instructions for the students: "Write a checklist as master/mistress of the house. Who will do what chore? What will you say to each servant?"

4. ***Fluency Activity:*** This activity will require that the instructor label and perhaps decorate the classroom appropriately so the "servants" can go to various locations in the classroom as if they were areas of the "estate." The instructor should model this activity first as master/mistress with some of the more

proficient students as "servants." Then, each student takes a turn being master or mistress and commands classmates as servants, using and reusing the checklist already completed in the Meaning-Focused Output Activity and the examples of previous classmates and the instructor.

Conclusion

Creating a course that meets the needs of the students is of utmost importance. Language students like Maria and Peter in the opening of this chapter would have had a greater chance for a successful outcome if their instructors had considered their needs and priorities when planning the class. To promote better student outcomes, this chapter presented important principles to consider when designing a pedagogically sound course for language acquisition. After these principles, the discussion turned to three steps to follow for good syllabus design, including a discussion of various syllabus options. The chapter concluded by addressing issues unique when designing biblical and ancient language syllabi in with specific examples. Having completed the larger section on skill development, the next section of the book looks at issues related to the learner, beginning with learner differences in language acquisition and how to adjust language instruction to accommodate these differences.

For Further Reading

Ellis, Rod. *Task-Based Language Learning and Teaching*. Oxford: Oxford University Press, 2003.

Long, Michael H. *Second Language Acquisition and Task-based Language Teaching*. West Sussex, England: Wiley & Sons, 2015.

Nation, I.S.P., and John Macalister. *Language Curriculum Design*. New York: Routledge, 2010.

Nation, Paul. "The Four Strands." *International Journal of Innovation in Language Learning and Teaching* 1.1 (2007): 2–13.

Sinclair, John McH., and Antoinette Renouf. "A Lexical Syllabus for Language Learning." Pages 140–60 in *Vocabulary and Language Teaching*. Edited by R. Carter and M. McCarthy. London: Longman, 1988.

CHAPTER 12: LEARNER DIFFERENCES

Jane, a bright student with a great deal of natural language aptitude, enters her first Latin class. She is not excited about the class and is only taking it because it is required for her program of study. She finds the class to be lackluster and the instructor boring and, at times, intimidating, so she only puts in enough work to make a passing grade. Once the class is over, she forgets most of what she learned.

Malcolm, on the other hand, does not have a strong natural aptitude for languages, but he is eager to learn as much about Biblical Greek as he can. The instructor makes the course fun and interesting. She takes a personal interest in Malcolm so that even when he is worried that he isn't going to make it, the instructor's encouragement and belief in him helps him press on and gain an appreciation for the language, a passing grade, and a desire to learn more.

Saint Augustine highlights the contrast succinctly: "Hence it is plain enough that for learning a language free interest has greater power than frightening constraint."[1]

The Principle: Learner Differences

Most language instructors would agree that not all language learners are created equal. While working under similar conditions, some students can acquire native-like language abilities while others struggle to learn a few basic phrases. Researchers in SLA examine the causes and patterns of many of these differences and their implications for language pedagogy. Learner differences can be grouped into cognitive differences, such as working memory, and affective differences, such as foreign language anxiety. While the discussion below is not exhaustive, it will introduce some of the more commonly recognized differences among language learners, followed by some implications for instruction.

---

[1] Augustine, *The Confessions of Saint Augustine*, trans. John K. Ryan (New York: Image Books, 1988), 16.

Cognitive Differences

Language learners exhibit a range of cognitive abilities when it comes to acquiring language. However, this is more complex than just being "bright" or being "slow." One's cognitive ability has many components, including the ability to perceive and encode sound, grammatical sensitivity, and working memory. Moreover, many believe that a learner's age and learning style can affect how well he or she can acquire language from a cognitive perspective.

Aptitude

As most educators are aware, aptitude plays a significant role in a student's ability to learn practically anything, including languages. Research in SLA has focused on various aspects of learner aptitude that promote language acquisition. For example, because phonology plays a significant role in language learning, one's ability to perceive and encode sounds is an important factor in language acquisition.[2] Grammatical sensitivity, including pattern recognition ability, is another aptitude that can impact a student's ability to acquire language.[3]

One's aptitude with respect to working memory, also called working memory span, can also affect the ability to acquire language. The span of one's working memory is "capable of predicting a remarkably wide range of complex cognitive processes," including language learning.[4] Research in working memory has explored such areas as an individual's speed of processing and an individual's ability to inhibit distractions and irrelevant information with important implications for educators.[5]

In addition to examining individual aspects of aptitude, some researchers focus on aptitude complexes or clusters. These are important combinations of cognitive abilities that relate to language learning and

---

[2] VanPatten and Benati, *Key Terms*, 42. In fact, some instructors have observed that musicians are better at hearing and pronouncing language than their non-musician counterparts, likely because their natural phonological aptitude has been fine-tuned through years of musical practice (Brian Schultz, email with author, August 14, 2019).

[3] VanPatten and Benati, *Key Terms*, 42.

[4] Baddeley, *Working Memory*, 189.

[5] For a full discussion, see Baddeley, *Working Memory*, 189–209.

are at least somewhat dependent on context.[6] For example, when completing a complex task, such as reading a text in L2, an individual draws on a cluster of cognitive resources, such as attention, working memory, short-term memory, long-term memory, and basic processing skills. The successful combination of these resources will lead to a successful outcome for the task at hand.

While aptitude can be a significant indicator of one's ability to learn language, some have noticed that aptitude plays more of a role in predicting language learning success after the learner has reached the age of seventeen years.[7] Before puberty, a learner's natural language learning faculty seems to override other aspects of cognitive aptitude. This, then, leads to issues related to a learner's age discussed in the next section.

Age

In first language acquisition studies, researchers have noticed that there is an age, after which human beings are no longer capable of fully learning L1 due to a loss of language learning mechanisms. "If children did not receive sufficient linguistic input prior to a certain age (puberty), then those mechanisms would cease being available and language acquisition would be severely hampered if not be impossible."[8] This period, during which a child can fully learn L1, is called the critical period.

Because many observe that L2 learning seems to become more difficult with age, some suggest that there is also a critical period for second language learning. According to the *Critical Period Hypothesis*, "there is a limited developmental period during which it is possible to acquire a language, be it L1 or L2, to normal, nativelike levels. Once this window of opportunity is passed, however, the ability to learn languages declines."[9] Not everyone agrees that there is a critical period for

---

[6] Peter Robinson, "Individual Differences, Cognitive Abilities, Aptitude Complexes and Learning Conditions in Second Language Acquisition," *Second Language Research* 17 (2001): 372.

[7] See, e.g., Robert M. DeKeyser, "The Robustness of Critical Period Effects in Second Language Learners," *Studies in Second Language Acquisition* 22 (2000): 499–533.

[8] VanPatten and Benati, *Key Terms*, 23.

[9] David Birdsong, "Introduction: Whys and Why Nots of the Critical Period Hypothesis for Second Language Acquisition," in *Second Language Acquisition and the Critical*

second languages, and some propose that there are multiple critical periods for certain dimensions of learning L2 but not for others.[10] Regardless, there is general agreement that language learning becomes more difficult with age.

Researchers suggest various reasons for this decline, such as loss of neural plasticity, atrophy in the language learning faculty from lack of use over time, and loss of access to the language learning faculty at a certain age.[11] One of the more compelling explanations is that the brain is too efficient and therefore the L1 gets in the way of learning L2 for adults.[12] For example, the brain of an English-speaking adult has used the word "house" millions of times to mean a permanent lodging place. As a result of the repeated exposure, the brain has strengthened the neural links to the word "house" to the point that when introduced to the Latin word *domus*, the well-worn mental machinery inhibits the learning of the new word. Thus, the older a person gets, the more repetitions they compile for each L1 word, making it more and more difficult to create neural pathways for the newly learned L2 word.

Learning Styles

Along with aptitude and age, many researchers contend that an individual's learning style can also affect the success of a language learner.[13] Learning styles, also called cognitive styles, refer to "someone's overall

---

Period Hypothesis, ed. D. Birdsong (Mahwah, NJ: Erlbaum, 1999), 1.

[10] See, e.g., David Birdsong, "Interpreting Age Effects in Second Language Acquisition," in *Handbook of Bilingualism: Psycholinguistic Approaches*, ed. J. Kroll and A. M. B. de Groot (Oxford: Oxford University Press, 2005), 109–27; and Lynn Eubank, and Kevin R. Gregg, "Critical Periods and (Second) Language Acquisition: Divide et Impera," in *Second Language Acquisition and the Critical Period Hypothesis*, ed. D. Birdsong (Mahwah, NJ: Lawrence Erlbaum, 1999), 65–99.

[11] Birdsong, "Introduction," 3–8.

[12] Julia Herschensohn, *Language Development and Age* (Cambridge: Cambridge University Press, 2007), 217–27.

[13] However, styles-based instruction has come under scrutiny more recently. See, e.g., Joshua Cuevas, "Is Learning Styles-Based Instruction Effective? A Comprehensive Analysis of Recent Research on Learning Styles," *Theory & Research in Education* 13.3 (2015): 308–33.

preferences for learning and processing information from the environment."[14]

Different researchers identify different categories of learning styles. For example, Howard Gardener promotes the idea of multiple intelligences, such as musical intelligence, bodily-kinesthetic intelligence, and linguistic intelligence.[15] Rod Ellis differentiates between a "studial learner," who may struggle with meaning-focused instruction, and an experiential learner who is predisposed to focus on communication and may struggle with form-focused instruction.[16] Others contrast learning styles such as concrete versus abstract.[17]

Madeline Ehrman and Betty Lou Leaver have developed a cognitive styles construct using the terms ectenic and synoptic to differentiate general learning styles relevant for language acquisition. Their construct is based on ten subscales that measure learning preferences and abilities such as global processing versus particular processing.[18] According to Ehrman and Leaver, "The synoptic-ectenic distinction addresses the degree of conscious control of learning desired or needed."[19] Synoptic learners tend to "trust their guts" and leave more to unconscious processes, while ectenic learners tend to prefer conscious control over their learning.[20]

Research on learning styles yields a variety of possible learning preferences. Regardless of the categories or labels, however, the implication of such research is that students with learning styles that are incompatible with the instructional style of their class may have to deal with greater anxiety, which impacts their affective orientation (see below).[21] Thus, if the instructor uses a more compatible instructional style,

---

[14] VanPatten and Benati, *Key Terms*, 44.

[15] See Howard Gardner, *Multiple Intelligences: New Horizons* (New York: Basic Books, 2006).

[16] Ellis, *Instructed Second Language Acquisition*, 188.

[17] VanPatten and Benati, *Key Terms*, 44.

[18] Madeline Ehrman and Betty Lou Leaver, "Cognitive Styles in the Service of Language Learning," *System* 31 (2003): 391–415.

[19] Ehrman and Lever, "Cognitive Styles," 395.

[20] Ehrman and Lever, "Cognitive Styles," 395.

[21] Ellis, *Instructed Second Language Acquisition*, 188. Again, as noted in footnote 13 above, not all researchers agree that using learning styles as a guide for instruction is

it will positively affect the outcomes for learners with a preference for that learning style.

In sum, there are many cognitive differences can affect the speed of acquisition and ultimate proficiency attainment for language learners. These include differences in aptitude, age, and learning styles. The next section will address affective factors that can affect the language acquisition process.

Affective Differences

In addition to the cognitive differences described above, affective factors can also affect how quickly and how deeply a learner can acquire a new language. Affective factors include such concepts as the affective filter, foreign language anxiety, enjoyment, attitude, emotion, and motivation. The affective factors may, in fact, be more influential than the cognitive factors for instructed language learning. Ellis goes so far as to claim that "only learners with a positive affective orientation to learning the L2 are likely to benefit from the instruction."[22] The good news is that instructors can influence the affective disposition of learners more easily than they can change or influence their cognitive factors.

The Affective Filter and Foreign Language Anxiety

As part of his Monitor Model of language acquisition, Krashen proposed the *Affective Filter Hypothesis*. According to Krashen, "the affective filter is a mental block that prevents acquirers from fully utilizing the comprehensible input they receive for language acquisition."[23] When the filter is "up," the learner may understand what he or she hears and reads, but the input will not be fully processed and thus not ultimately acquired. The affective filter goes up "when the acquirer is unmotivated, lacking in self-confidence, or anxious, when he is 'on the defensive' … when he considers the language class to be a place where his weaknesses will be revealed."[24] By contrast, the filter goes down

---

effective.

[22] Ellis, *Instructed Second Language Acquisition*, 188.

[23] Krashen, *Input Hypothesis*, 3.

[24] Krashen, *Input Hypothesis*, 3.

when the learner is not worried about failure and "considers himself to be a potential member of the group speaking the target language."[25] Moreover, what causes anxiety in one person may not cause anxiety in another. Therefore, the affective filter can account for some of individual variation in the level of L2 attainment for learners.[26]

Related to the affective filter is a condition known as *foreign language anxiety*, which can similarly affect outcomes for language learners. Foreign language anxiety is "the feeling of tension and apprehension specifically associated with second language contexts."[27] This anxiety may be connected with performance anxiety and with the unique challenges the learner faces in the language classroom, especially in terms of self-concept and self-expression.[28] The language ego, a learner's second identity that is intertwined with a new way of expressing himself or herself in L2, is fragile and can be defensive, leading to a raising of inhibitions.[29] Relatedly, an L2 learner may plateau in his or her language learning progress due to a fear of losing his or her L1 identity.

Foreign language anxiety can cause any number of negative outcomes, including an increase in negative self-talk, forgetting, missing class, and procrastination. An anxious student may also exhibit a decrease in his or her ability to take up input, store language, retrieve information, and respond to errors. He or she may also be less likely to volunteer or participate in class.[30]

---

[25] Krashen, *Input Hypothesis*, 3–4.

[26] Krashen, *Input Hypothesis*, 44.

[27] Peter D. MacIntyre and R. C. Gardner, "The Subtle Effects of Language Anxiety on Cognitive Processing in the Second Language," *Language Learning* 44.2 (1994): 284.

[28] Elaine K. Horwitz, Michael B. Horwitz, and Joann Cope, "Foreign Language Classroom Anxiety," *Modern Language Journal* 70.2 (1986): 128.

[29] Tammy Gregersen, "Language Learning Vibes: What, Why and How to Capitalize for Positive Affect," in *The Affective Dimension in Second Language Acquisition*, ed. D. Gabryś-Barker and J. Bielska (Bristol, UK: Multilingual Matters, 2013), 90. See also H. Douglas Brown and Heekyeong Lee, *Teaching by Principles: An Interactive Approach to Language Pedagogy*, 4th edition (White Plains, NY: Pearson Education, 2001), 76–77.

[30] Gregersen, "Language Learning Vibes," 91. See also, Tammy Gregersen and Elaine K. Horwitz, "Language Learning and Perfectionism: Anxious and Non-Anxious Language Learners' Responses to Their Own Oral Performance," *Modern Language Journal* 86.4 (2002): 562–70.

Enjoyment, Attitude, and Emotions

The affective filter and language anxiety are both strongly related to how much the learner is enjoying his or her study of L2, which is a complex interplay between attitude and emotions. While instructors may readily see the connection between student attitude and student outcomes, the role of emotions in learning is often underrated. However, research indicates that "in learning, emotion is pivotal because it drives attention, which in turn drives memory."[31] Antonio R. Damasio explains further that "intuition is simply rapid cognition with the required knowledge partially swept under the carpet, all courtesy of emotion and much past practice."[32] Therefore, if a learner is feeling positive emotions about learning and has a positive attitude, his or her enjoyment of the class will increase, leading to a dropping of the affective filter and greater gains in learning. If, however, the learner perceives or experiences negative emotions or attitudes toward learning, the affective filter will go up, inhibiting learning.

Motivation

Another affective factor that comes into play in language learning is motivation. Related to desire, motivation can be defined as "a willingness to learn or do something."[33] Motivation helps the learner stick with the task of learning. Closely related to affective factors like emotion and attitude covered in the previous section, motivation has to do with the value placed on learning by the learner, including his or her interest and excitement about learning the language, resulting in action. "At the core of motivation is agency: the act of making choices in acts of self-determination."[34]

Researchers study motivation in language learning from a macro approach and from a micro approach. On the macro level, motivation in a

---

[31] Gregersen, "Language Learning Vibes," 90. See also Robert Sylwester, "How Emotions Affect Learning," *Educational Leadership* 52.2 (1994): 60–64.

[32] Antonio R. Damasio, *Descartes' Error: Emotion, Reason, and the Human Brain* (London: Penguin Books, 1994), xiii.

[33] VanPatten and Benati, *Key Terms*, 43.

[34] Brown and Lee, *Teaching by Principles*, 84.

language learner is often associated with interest in the target speakers, the target culture, and issues of intercultural communication.[35] On a micro level, researchers associate motivation with the following: a learner's willingness to communicate, which is a complex interplay of personality and proficiency; a learner's motivation for specific language tasks in the classroom; and a student's willingness to use learning strategies to increase the efficacy of his or her learning, which demonstrates motivation.[36] The most effective form of motivation is intrinsic, or internal, motivation. However, it is possible for intrinsic motivation to develop out of extrinsic, or external, motivation.[37] A student can begin language study out of obligation and ultimately come to love learning the language for its own sake. Unfortunately, the reverse can also be true.

In conclusion, many factors play a role in a language learner's ability to acquire L2. These include cognitive factors, such as aptitude, age, and learning styles, and affective factors, such as enjoyment, motivation, and anxiety. Because each of these factors can vary widely from one person to the next, individual learners exhibit a wide variety of abilities when it comes to learning a new language. To be most effective, language instructors should be prepared to teach a diverse group of students. The next section presents a few considerations for language teaching with learner differences in view.

Implications for Instruction

Only in very small classes do teachers get to work with a homogenous group of students. Therefore, it is nearly impossible to cover every potential teaching scenario when it comes to individual differences among learners. This section, then, will focus on a few big-picture ideas and approaches for working with a diverse classroom of learners, including the concept of flow, some strategies for instructors, and some strategies for students.

---

[35] See R. C. Gardner, Social Psychology and Second Language Learning: The Role of Attitude and Motivation (London: Arnold, 1985).

[36] Zoltán Dörnyei, "Attitudes, Orientations, and Motivations in Language Learning: Advances in Theory, Research, and Applications," *Language Learning* 53 (2003): 12–16.

[37] Nation and Macalister, *Language Curriculum Design*, 50.

Flow

Before discussing strategies, language instructors should understand the idea of *flow*. This is a general concept that can help with goal setting in the classroom, especially when attempting to lower the affective filter. Flow is a psychological construct that refers to "the experience of complete absorption in the present moment," usually while participating in an activity that is self-rewarding.[38] The ideal conditions for flow to occur seem to be when the student is working on a task that is challenging but not overwhelming, in other words, not too easy and not too hard. If the task is too easy, the learner gets bored, but if the task is too challenging, the learner gets frustrated.[39] Tammy Gregersen compares the concept of flow with Krashen's $i + 1$ Input Hypothesis, where the language learner receives input that is just above his or her current level of proficiency for optimal acquisition.[40] When designing assignments and conducting classroom activities and tasks, an instructor will want to aim for those that promote the students' experience of flow, maintaining an awareness that this sweet spot may be different for each student. Fostering flow may also require adjusting learning activities on the fly as the instructor notices either boredom or frustration. The more students can experience flow, the more the affective filter is lowered and the less anxiety they may feel, ultimately promoting more language acquisition. With the concept of flow in mind, we now turn to some instructional strategies for instructors and for learners.

Strategies for Instructors

To reach a variety of students, instructors can employ two broad instructional strategies: creating a positive learning environment and incorporating variety into the classroom. Because the affective factors play such a significant role in language learning, the classroom environment is

---

[38] Jeanne Nakamura and Mihaly Czikszentmihalyi, "The Experience of Flow: Theory and Research," in *Oxford Handbook of Positive Psychology*, 3rd edition, ed. C. R. Synder, S. J. Lopez, L. M. Edwards, and S. C. Marques (Oxford: Oxford University Press, 2021), 279.

[39] Nakamura and Czikszentmihalyi, "Experience of Flow," 280.

[40] Gregerson, "Language Learning Vibes," 94. For discussion of Krashen's Input Hypothesis, see chapter 4.

critical to promoting student success. Instructors should actively work to create a relaxed, friendly, safe, and enjoyable environment for the students. This might include incorporating humor, intentionally celebrating each victory, and encouraging positivity among the students (e.g., "I know this is hard, but look at how much you have learned already!"). Promoting community in the classroom is another way to create a positive learning environment as "building community, social networks and intimate relationships make people happy."[41] The next chapter will address in greater detail the importance of the social dimension of language learning.

A positive learning environment provides several benefits. First, it fosters more positive emotions and attitudes, which usually result in an increase in motivation and enjoyment. Not only is this type of environment more pleasant for all involved—both students and instructors—it also promotes language acquisition. Students are more likely to internalize language data, participate in activities, and exhibit better study habits.

A second strategy for reaching students with a variety of language abilities is to incorporate variety. Because learners are diverse, the regular and intentional use of variety can help reach more learners and can stave off boredom. Variety can come in the form of different teaching techniques (small group activities, direct instruction, singing a song, discussion, etc.), teaching different skills (reading, listening, etc.), different props (photos, videos, stuffed animals, etc.), and perhaps even a different location or time of day.

While this approach may take more time and effort, it has several benefits. First, it allows the instructor to incorporate various instructional styles. In this way, more students are given the opportunity to receive instruction that is compatible with their aptitudes, preferred cognitive styles, and learning preferences. Second, greater variety also has the potential to decrease boredom in the classroom and promote interest through novelty. The instructor will be able to maintain the attention of the students better by changing activities frequently as weariness sets in and interest begins to fade.

---

[41] Gregerson, "Language Learning Vibes," 97.

Strategies for Students

Many of the factors that create differences among language learners are internal, and so external influences from instructors can only go so far when dealing with learner differences. Therefore, another approach to helping learners deal with these factors is to teach them strategies for learning and strategies for maintaining and improving their motivation to learn.

Instructors are not bound to teaching language only; they can also teach students how to learn, which can have far-reaching effects. For example, taking ten minutes of class time from the first week to provide specific instruction on how to use flashcards effectively (see chapter 10) has the potential to set the students on a course for more successful vocabulary acquisition throughout the term. Other similar instruction might cover the importance of large quantities of input (see chapters 5 and 9) or how to use spaced retrieval to maximize study time (see chapters 10 and 11).

Instructors can also equip students to improve their motivation and attitudes to the class through self-regulatory strategies.[42] Students may need help setting realistic goals or preserving the goals they have already. Instructors can also help students learn to monitor and control their concentration and avoid procrastination. Another self-regulatory strategy is learning how to eliminate boredom and add interest to the task at hand, while also eliminating negative environmental influences. Finally, instructors can help students manage their emotional state and encourage emotions that help promote learning.

In conclusion, each individual learner comes with a set of differences when it comes to ability and willingness to learn language. These differences can be cognitive or affective and will have a significant impact on how quickly he or she can progress toward proficiency. However, instructors can address some of these differences through instructional strategies and through training the students how to learn and how to become more self-motivated.

---

[42] Zoltán Dörnyei, *Motivational Strategies in the Language Classroom* (Cambridge: Cambridge University Press, 2001).

The Rationale: Learner Differences
and Biblical and Ancient Language Courses

While all language instructors must deal with a wide range of learner differences, teachers of biblical and ancient languages have at least two notable challenges to surmount when it comes to learner differences: age and motivation.

The first common challenge facing instructors of ancient languages and biblical languages especially is the age of their students. Many Hebrew and Greek students take their first L2 course in a master's level program. Therefore, these students are necessarily older than their modern language counterparts who often enroll in their first L2 class in high school or even earlier. The older students tend to learn language more slowly and often feel greater apprehension about language learning than younger students would. Therefore, biblical language teachers need to be sensitive to the needs of their older students, providing more academic support, such as scaffolding assignments and offering tutoring opportunities, and more emotional support, such as positive reinforcement and creating community in the classroom.

A second challenge for biblical and ancient language instructors is low levels of motivation. Required language classes often have the reputation of being the most feared in some programs of study. Moreover, because the students are learning a language that no longer has any native speakers, they have fewer opportunities for practice and fewer reasons to prioritize the study of L2. Institutional requirements often do not help the situation. When language instructors are expected to teach large quantities of information in a short period of time, or language requirements are cut altogether, students are not motivated to make language learning a priority either. Therefore, instructors of biblical and ancient languages need to be intentional about finding ways to motivate their students and about helping them progress from extrinsic motivation to intrinsic motivation. The next section provides a few specific examples.

Examples for Biblical and Ancient Language Classrooms

The following examples present some specific ideas for motivating language students in their acquisition of Hebrew, Greek, and Latin.[43] These examples primarily target affective factors, although they create some flexibility in the course, which could also accommodate cognitive differences.

Track Learners' Progress (Hebrew)

One strategy for bringing down the affective filter and encouraging students to continue their learning is to help them see their progress in language learning. The basic idea is to keep track of measurable improvements and present the data in a way that allows the student to recognize his or her progress over time with the goal of informing the student and helping generate excitement.[44] This goes beyond just posting grades for assignments. For example, instructors can keep a running tally of verses successfully translated, keep track of how long it takes to learn a stack of vocabulary cards at 80 percent accuracy, or create a graph of each student's reading rate as measured periodically throughout the course.

A specific example of this strategy is to track the number of vocabulary words the student has learned over the course of the term. A tally of vocabulary for Hebrew might look something like this at week twelve of a lexical syllabus (see chapter 11):[45]

Number of Words Learned in this Chapter: 23
Number of Words Learned to Date: 286
Number of Word Occurrences in the Hebrew Bible Learned in this Chapter: 4,510x

---

[43] For other motivational ideas, see Dörnyei, *Motivational Strategies*; Nation, *Learning Vocabulary*, 593–95; and Nation and Macalister, *Language Curriculum Design*, 50–51.

[44] Nation, *Learning Vocabulary*, 593; and Nation and Macalister, *Language Curriculum Design*, 50.

[45] This idea is adapted from William D. Mounce, *Basics of Biblical Greek Grammar*, 4th ed. (Grand Rapids: Zondervan, 2019).

> *Number of Word Occurrences in the Hebrew Bible Learned to Date:*
>   298, 677x
> *Percent of Total Word Count in the Hebrew Bible Learned to Date:*
>   71.42%

When students realize that they have learned over 71 percent of all the running words in the Hebrew Bible by week twelve of their course, they feel a certain pride in the accomplishment and are encouraged to continue their study. Their affective filter comes down a little more, and they get a stronger feeling that they are capable of learning what is needed for reading the Hebrew Bible. In short, they are more motivated to continue learning.

Promote Learner Autonomy (Greek)

Promoting autonomy, or an internal locus of control, is another strategy for contributing to a learner's positive affective disposition toward a course and for giving the student an increased sense of enjoyment. A learner's perception of his or her ability to control a situation is closely related to self-esteem and self-confidence.[46] Therefore, greater autonomy can lead to an increase in self-confidence, a dropping of the affective filter, and an increase in motivation with corresponding improvements in learning. By contrast, feelings of obligation and an external locus of control can lead to frustration and a raising of the affective filter. An instructor can promote learner autonomy in many ways, including teaching learning strategies, explaining the rationale and goals of a unit of study, offering options when it comes to classroom activities, and including learners in the syllabus design process.[47]

One specific way to promote learner autonomy is to give learners a measure of choice when it comes to completing their individual Greek practice for each unit. The practice could be in the form of in-class activities or homework assignments. Rather than assigning all the exercises available or assigning the same set of exercises to everyone (for

---

[46] Zoltán Dörnyei, *Motivational Strategies*, 29.

[47] For a discussion of negotiated syllabus design, see Nation and Macalister, *Language Curriculum Design*, 149–58

example, assigning all the odd numbered exercises at the end of the chapter), the instructor can assign a predetermined fraction of the total exercises for all the students. Each student gets to pick which exercises to use for practice, provided he or she completes the specified number.[48] In this way, interest, aptitude, and autonomy all come together as the student chooses how to practice for that unit, potentially giving the student greater satisfaction in learning. This also moves the locus of control to the student, which can lead to more intrinsic motivation. The remaining exercises from the set that were not completed provide additional optional practice for those who need it or want it.

The challenge for the instructor when utilizing this type of strategy is ensuring that there are enough exercises to choose from for each unit and making sure that all the exercises are at a comparable level of difficulty. Some textbooks include an abundance of exercises for each unit, making this strategy easy for the instructor, but some include only enough to give the students a little practice. Instructors should be prepared to write their own assignments, which may involve searching the New Testament for good examples from the original texts.

Mastery Quizzes (Latin)

Another strategy for motivation is the creation of mastery quizzes.[49] Unlike traditional achievement quizzes for which the student gets only one attempt, mastery quizzes allow a student to retake each quiz multiple times. Some quizzes could even be set up to allow for an unlimited number of retakes in a set timeframe, like a week. Mastery quizzes are

---

[48] For example, John D. Schwandt includes three sets of translation exercises at the end of lesson 31. An instructor might ask students to choose seven exercises of the fourteen listed in the first set (Greek to English exercises), ten of eighteen in the second (English to Greek exercises), and four of the six in the last set (Scripture passages) (*An Introduction to Biblical Greek: A Grammar with Exercises* [Bellingham, WA: Lexham, 2020], 265–67).

[49] For more information about mastery quizzes, see Eunbae Lee and R. Lainie Wilson Harris, "The Effects of Online Glossary Quizzes and Student Autonomy on Domain Vocabulary Learning in Business Law," *Journal of Computing in Higher Education* 30.2 (2018): 326–43; and Richard W. Egan, Jerry Fjermestad, and Davida Scharf, "The Use of Mastery Quizzes to Enhance Student Preparation," *Journal of Higher Education Theory and Practice* 17.8 (2017): 36–42.

usually administered electronically through a learning management system with an algorithm that draws items randomly from a question pool.

A weekly Latin vocabulary quiz is an ideal place to incorporate a mastery quiz. The key is to create a deep question pool from which to draw. For example, the instructor should create a question pool of at least forty to fifty multiple choice or short answer vocabulary questions for each quiz of ten questions. When testing a list of twenty vocabulary items, for example, creating forty to fifty questions may require creativity. An instructor could expand the pool by including inflected forms, short phrases, and both Latin-to-English and English-to-Latin questions. Additional options include questions in which the students must choose a Latin vocabulary item that describes a picture or choose a picture that matches the Latin word. Also, if the instructor wants to make the vocabulary learning cumulative, he or she can add items from previous weeks to the current quiz pool.

Once the question pool is established and the electronic quiz created, the students would receive unlimited opportunities to complete the quiz on their own time before the established deadline. Additionally, a time limit for each attempt would ensure that the students do not have enough time to look up each word while taking the quiz. For a vocabulary quiz, one to two minutes per question should be sufficient. Once the quiz closes, only the highest score is recorded for grading purposes.

There are several advantages to using a mastery quiz, all leading to an increase in student motivation and ultimately student learning. First, this approach gives the students the opportunity for plenty of practice, potentially leading to a significant increase in a student's exposure to input. Students could even conceivably use the mastery quizzes for practice as they would flashcards. Second, the mastery quiz is set up so that the stakes are relatively low. If the student does not perform well, he or she can retake the quiz. This has a significant impact on the student's affective filter. Because the risk of failure is low, the affective filter is also low. Third, this approach is flexible and adaptable for students with varying levels of natural aptitude. A struggling student can get more practice without penalty, and the student who is excelling can practice, or not, at his or her leisure. Finally, a mastery quiz moves the locus of control to the student. He or she must take responsibility for learning. A perfect score is within reach of almost every student should he or she be willing to invest the time.

Conclusion

The subject of this chapter was the language learner, with a focus on learner differences and how these differences affect the speed and depth of learning and ultimately the level of proficiency achieved. Like Jane and Malcolm who were introduced at the beginning of the chapter, each learner has a unique mix of cognitive skills and affective dispositions that contribute to an overall ability and willingness to learn a new language. However, instructors can promote learning through various instructional and motivational strategies. The last section of the chapter presented some specific strategies for motivating students to learn in biblical and ancient language learning situations. As we continue to focus on the learner in this section, we now turn to sociocultural factors that affect language learners.

For Further Reading

Birdsong, David, ed. *Second Language Acquisition and the Critical Period Hypothesis.* Mahwah, NJ: Erlbaum, 1999.

Dörnyei, Zoltán. "Attitudes, Orientations, and Motivations in Language Learning: Advances in Theory, Research, and Applications." *Language Learning* 53 (2003): 3–32.

Gabryś-Barker, Danuta, and Joanna Bielska, eds. *The Affective Dimension in Second Language Acquisition.* Bristol, UK: Multilingual Matters, 2013.

Nakamura, Jeanne, and Mihaly Czikszentmihalyi. "The Experience of Flow: Theory and Research." Pages 279–96 in *Oxford Handbook of Positive Psychology.* 3rd edition. Edited by C. R. Synder, S. J. Lopez, L. M. Edwards, and S. C. Marques. Oxford: Oxford University Press, 2021.

Robinson, Peter. "Individual Differences, Cognitive Abilities, Aptitude Complexes and Learning Conditions in Second Language Acquisition." *Second Language Research* 17 (2001): 368–92.

CHAPTER 13: SOCIOCULTURAL ASPECTS OF SECOND LANGUAGE ACQUISITION

Jonathan is looking forward to his next Hebrew class. He and his small group have been analyzing a passage from the book of Isaiah together, and they will put the finishing touches on their project in the next class session. Jonathan recently met with the mentor/tutor for the class to go over his contribution to the collaborative project. The tutor had pointed him to a few resources that would further strengthen his analysis of both Hebrew language and ancient Near Eastern culture. Jonathan is excited to share with the group what he has learned and to learn from the contributions of the rest of the group as they complete the project.

Carrie, by contrast, is heading to the next meeting of her third-semester Greek class with some apprehension. Even though she spends hours completing her translation and exegetical notes, she never feels fully prepared. She worries that when the professor calls on her to read and translate that she will trip over her pronunciation, forget the meaning of a word, or find out that her exegetical notes do not meet the professor's expectations. Some of the others in the class also seem to feel anxious when it is their turn to read in class, but she doesn't get much opportunity to interact with them or collaborate, so she is not sure what they know or how they feel. The professor is not unkind, but Carrie feels that he has unrealistic expectations of what she can accomplish on her own. She would like to work with a study partner, but he insists that the students do their work independently.

The Principle: Sociocultural Aspects of Second Language Acquisition

Language is inherently a social endeavor. Human beings use language to give and receive messages, which requires, at the very least, two people in a social relationship. It stands to reason, then, that language learning should also incorporate instructional approaches that are sensitive to sociocultural issues, more like Jonathan's Hebrew class, and perhaps not conducted in near isolation, like Carrie's Greek class.

Over the past few decades, research in SLA has seen an increase in studies that address sociocultural aspects of language acquisition. Overall, the consensus is that cultural knowledge and social interaction are significant for, if not essential to, language acquisition. McQuinn summarizes the rationale for this position: "Language learning involves both a biological/cognitive ability that is innate within every human being, and also an intimate social engagement with the world around oneself."[1]

This first section of the chapter will identify and discuss three significant areas in which language learning interacts with sociocultural issues informed by SLA research: culture, community, and sociocultural theory as it relates to L2 acquisition. The section ends with some implications for instruction.

Culture

The first sociocultural aspect of language acquisition instructors should understand is the relationship between language and culture. Language is a powerful tool because it "encodes the culture's theory of experience."[2] A language and its culture, therefore, are intimately connected.[3] Michael Agar coined the term *"languaculture"* to describe this intimate relationship between language and culture. "The *langua* in languaculture is about discourse, not just about words and sentences. And the *culture* in languaculture is about meanings that include, but go well beyond, what the dictionary and grammar offer."[4]

Language acquisition, therefore, encompasses more than just learning word meanings or use of grammar. It necessarily includes learning about L2 culture, discourse, pragmatics, and *sociolinguistic competence* —even if that learning is implicit.[5] As any careful word study will

---

[1] McQuinn, "Principled Communicative Methodology," 73.

[2] Gordon Wells, "The Complementary Contributions of Halliday and Vygotsky to a 'Language-Based Theory of Learning,'" *Linguistics and Education* 6 (1994): 72.

[3] Brown and Lee, *Teaching by Principles*, 81.

[4] Michael Agar, *Language Shock: Understanding the Culture of Conversation* (New York: Morrow, 1994), 96, italics original.

[5] Joan Kelly Hall and Lorrie Stoops Verplaetse, "The Development of Second and Foreign Language Learning Through Classroom Interaction," in *Second and Foreign Language Learning Through Classroom Interaction*, ed. J. K. Hall and L. S. Verplaetse

demonstrate, individual words cannot be fully understood without a cultural context. Therefore, when an instructor teaches a language, he or she also teaches "a complex system of cultural customs, values, and ways of thinking, feeling, and acting."[6] If an instructor understands the culture of the L2 and encourages cultural understanding among his or her students, the students can reach greater levels of language proficiency, both in production and interpretation skills.

Community

Community is another important sociocultural dynamic in second language acquisition that instructors should understand. According to James F. Lee and Bill VanPatten, "The psycho-social purpose of language involves using language to bond socially or psychologically with someone or some group or to engage in social behavior in some way."[7] This clearly requires community.

For most language learners, the goal of language acquisition is to participate in a community of people who speak the L2. For example, someone may learn Japanese for the purpose of conducting business in Japan, thus participating in the Japanese business community. Learning another language at least implies an interest in the community that speaks that language, if not an overt desire to identify with the community in some way.[8] In the absence of an available community of speakers, a learner's identification with the community is often "generalized to the cultural and intellectual values associated with the language, as well as to the actual L2 itself."[9] A situation like this may occur when the language is taught in a classroom far from any community of native speakers or when the language no longer has living native speakers. Thus, the community of the L2 is an important dimension of learning the L2.

(Mahwah, NJ: Erlbaum, 2000), 6.

[6] Brown and Lee, *Teaching by Principles*, 82.

[7] Lee and VanPatten, *Communicative Language Teaching*, 53.

[8] Dörnyei, "Attitudes, Orientations, and Motivations," 5.

[9] Dörnyei, "Attitudes, Orientations, and Motivations," 6. See, e.g., the study by Zoltán Dörnyei, "Conceptualizing Motivation in Foreign Language Learning," *Language Learning* 40 (1990): 46–78.

Community may also be found in the language classroom itself and can play a significant role in the learning process. "Cooperative learning acknowledges the place of affect in education, highlighting the importance of positive interdependence, the feeling among group members that the group sinks or swims together."[10] Participating in a social environment reduces feelings of isolation and feelings of being incompetent.[11] Students who bond with their community of fellow L2 students are more likely to actively engage in learning and tend to feel less anxiety (see chapter 12). Therefore, positive social interaction in the classroom can be a strong motivating factor for students. Moreover, according to sociocultural theory, described below, social interaction is central to the learning process itself.

Sociocultural Theory

Connected with the work of Lev Vygotsky, sociocultural theory is first and foremost a theory of learning.[12] This theory is cognitive in nature and holds that learning comes about primarily through social interaction. In other words, "cognition originates in social interaction and is shaped by cultural and sociopolitical processes. That is, cultural and sociopolitical processes are central, rather than incidental, to cognitive development."[13] Because human language is primarily social in nature, this theory of learning is particularly well suited for SLA research and pedagogy. As already noted in chapter 3, input and social interaction are

---

[10] George M. Jacobs and Thomas S. C. Farell, "Paradigm Shift: Understanding and Implementing Change in Second Language Education," *TESL-EJ* 5.1 (2001): 6. See also David W. Johnson and Roger T. Johnson, *Learning Together and Alone: Cooperative, Competitive, and Individualistic Learning*, 4th ed. (Boston: Allyn and Bacon, 1991).

[11] McQuinn, "Principled Communicative Methodology," 73.

[12] See Lev Vygotsky, *Thought and Language*, trans. newly revised and edited by Alex Kozulin (Cambridge: MIT Press, 1986). For more recent formulations of the theory, see the following introductions: James P. Lantolf, "Second Language Learning as a Mediated Process," *Language Teaching* 33 (2000): 79–96; and James P. Lantolf and Steven L. Thorne, *Sociocultural Theory and the Genesis of Second Language Development* (Oxford: Oxford University Press, 2006).

[13] Karen Ann Watson-Gegeo, "Mind, Language, and Epistemology: Toward a Language Socialization Paradigm for SLA," *The Modern Language Journal* 88 (2004): 332.

the essential components of meaning-focused instruction, which promotes the acquisition of implicit language knowledge.

The following discussion outlines a few of the key constructs of sociocultural theory, especially as they relate to language acquisition. These constructs include mediated learning, the *Zone of Proximal Development*, and internalization.

Mediated Learning

One of the main constructs in sociocultural theory is mediated learning. According to sociocultural theory, "all mental activity is symbolically mediated."[14] Language is the primary tool for mediating mental activity, including learning. "In Vygotskian theory, then, language is viewed as both a means of accomplishing social interaction and of managing mental activity, with the former serving as the basis for the latter."[15] According to this theory, learning, including language learning, is the result of social interaction that is dialogic in nature. This dialogue may be external with an interlocutor, usually a peer or a more advanced mentor, or internal by means of private speech.

External dialogue or social interaction as a mediator of learning can potentially be viewed from two different but related perspectives. In the first view, the interlocutor helps with *scaffolding* by means of affectively and cognitively supporting the learner.[16] This may happen through waiting, prompting, helping to construct a sentence, and explanation.[17] In the second view, the interlocutor mediates learning by successfully adapting interaction to the proficiency level of the learner.[18] In other words, the interlocutor does not talk above or below the learner.

---

[14] James P. Lantolf and Tracy G. Beckett, "Sociocultural Theory and Second Language Acquisition," *Language Teaching* 42.4 (2009): 459.

[15] Ellis, *Study of Second Language Acquisition*, 525.

[16] Pauline Foster and Amy Snyder Ohta "Negotiation for Meaning and Peer Assistance in Second Language Classrooms," *Applied Linguistics* 26 (2005): 413–14.

[17] See study by Amy Snyder Ohta, "A Longitudinal Study of the Development of Expression of Alignment in Japanese as a Foreign Language," in *Pragmatics in Language Teaching*, ed. K. R. Rose and G. Kasper (New York: Cambridge University Press, 2001), 103–20.

[18] See Matthew E. Poehner and James P. Lantolf, "Dynamic Assessment in the Language Classroom," *Language Teaching Research* 9 (2005): 233–65.

When the interaction is reciprocal and the interlocutor can adjust to the learner's level of proficiency, the mediation is usually successful.

Inner dialogue or inner speech can also promote learning, using such forms as imitation, vicarious response (answering internally to a question asked of someone else), and mental rehearsal.[19] This type of inner dialogue is usually used for practicing L2, but it can also be used for self-regulating, such as urging oneself to act. This inner dialogue, like the external dialogue described above, is also a form of mediated learning.

The Zone of Proximal Development

A second important construct for sociocultural theory is the zone of proximal development, or the ZPD. Sociocultural theory sees learner development as progressing through three stages, the middle stage being the ZPD.[20] At the first or lowest stage, the learner is unable to complete the task at hand, even with assistance. As an example, consider a baby learning to walk. At the lowest stage, a newborn baby is unable to crawl, let alone walk, even with assistance. At the other end of the process, the final stage is called development, and it describes what the learner can do independently as demonstrated by his or her activity. At this stage, the baby is walking without holding onto anyone or anything. In between the lowest and the highest stage is the ZPD where learning takes place. At this level, a learner demonstrates what he or she can potentially do, with evidence coming from what he or she can do with assistance from an expert or through collaboration with peers. Returning to the baby learning to walk, when in the ZPD, the baby can walk while holding a caregiver's hand for support until he or she develops the muscles, coordination, and balance to walk alone.

The ZPD assumes that "development has both a social and a psychological dimension," and it is the social aspect that moves the learner from needing assistance to becoming autonomous.[21] Collaborative activity, therefore, plays a significant role in cognitive development, and the collaborator is often an instructor or a more knowledgeable assistant.

---

[19] Amy Synder Ohta, *Second Language Acquisition Processes in the Classroom: Learning Japanese* (Mahwah, NJ: Lawrence Erlbaum, 2001), 30–72.

[20] Adapted from Ellis, *Study of Second Language Acquisition*, 531–33.

[21] Ellis, *Study of Second Language Acquisition*, 532.

Moreover, the ZPD is not an attribute of the learner; rather, it is centered on social activity, is open-ended, and emerges in the process of completing tasks.

Internalization

Internalization is the last construct of sociocultural theory as it relates to language acquisition. Sociocultural theory proposes three forms of regulation: object-regulation, other-regulation, and self-regulation. Internalization is the process of moving from object-regulation, through other-regulation, to self-regulation. In language acquisition, this involves moving the language from the environment to the brain.[22] In the process of internalization, verbal interaction, often with a more knowledgeable assistant or instructor, is the principal means of moving from other- to self-regulation.[23] In language acquisition terms, this means that verbal interaction moves L2 from the environment to the brain as the learner gains increased control over L2 with a corresponding increase in his or her ability to use L2 to regulate thought.

This section presented three important areas of sociocultural interaction that come into play in language learning: culture, community, and sociocultural theory. The next section draws a few important implications for instruction from these principles.

Implications for Instruction

Because cultural knowledge and social interaction play a significant role in the language acquisition process, this section presents a few general suggestions for language instruction. Beginning with the importance of cultural knowledge and connection with a language community, the first suggestion is to intentionally teach L2 culture with the language. The remaining implications for instruction are drawn from research and practice involving sociocultural theory and include social learning, scaffolding, and dynamic assessment.

---

[22] Ohta, *Second Language Acquisition Processes*, 11.
[23] Ellis, *Study of Second Language Acquisition*, 534.

Teach Culture with Language

Because cultural practices and beliefs play a role in understanding what the language is communicating, SLA practitioners recommend that L2 culture be intentionally taught with the language.[24] While language can presumably be taught alone, "it is also socially and culturally bound, which makes language learning a deeply social event that requires the incorporation of a wide range of elements of the L2 culture."[25]

Therefore, instructors should actively seek to promote a deeper understanding of the L2 culture as an integral part of L2 language instruction. This may involve such teaching techniques as a brief explanation of the cultural significance of a vocabulary item, a more complex presentation covering a set of customs from the L2, or an activity that helps students practice nuanced social interaction in L2 and build sociolinguistic competence.

Social Learning

A second suggestion for language instruction that incorporates sociocultural insights is to promote social learning whenever possible. If sociocultural theory is correct, learning takes place in the context of social interaction. Therefore, rather than expecting students to learn independently, an instructor should create opportunities for social interaction as part of the learning process. The social interaction may be among peers, or it may involve groups that include a more advanced mentor or teacher. For peer interaction, the instructor can assign classroom activities that require collaboration, group projects, and study partners. Incorporating a more knowledgeable mentor in the process might involve tutoring sessions, one-on-one meetings with the instructor, or pairing a more advanced student with a beginner for guidance, interaction, or as part of an assigned project.

---

[24] See Kumaravadivelu, "Postmethod," 40–41.
[25] Dörnyei, "Attitudes, Orientations, and Motivations," 4.

Scaffolding

A specific application of social learning is an instructional technique known as scaffolding. The scaffolding metaphor is drawn from the realm of building construction where a scaffold is used to support a wall while it is being built. Once the wall is complete and able to stand on its own, the scaffold can be removed. As it relates to the field of SLA, Richard Donato describes scaffolding in the following manner: "In social interaction a knowledgeable participant can create, by means of speech, supportive conditions in which the novice can participate in, and extend, current skills and knowledge to higher levels of competence."[26] Donato's "knowledgeable participant" is often assumed to be an instructor or more advanced student; however, recent research has addressed the significant role that a peer can play in scaffolding.[27]

Scaffolding is closely related to the ZPD as the partner, whether superior or peer, works with the learner at his or her level (ZPD) to promote and assist with further learning.[28] Scaffolding can occur on a micro level in which learners collaborate on a classroom activity and learn from each other in the process. Scaffolding can also occur on a macro level, such as a large project that is completed in stages, allowing for feedback and collaborative learning at each stage of the process.

Dynamic Assessment

A final instructional strategy that incorporates sociocultural insights is dynamic assessment. This type of assessment "seeks to determine the instructional investment likely required to move individuals beyond

---

[26] Richard Donato, "Collective Scaffolding in Second Language Learning," in *Vygotskian Approaches to Second Language Research*, ed. J. P. Lantolf and G. Appel (Norwood, NJ: Ablex, 1994), 40.

[27] Donato, "Collective Scaffolding," 51. See also Amy Snyder Ohta, "Rethinking Interaction in SLA: Developmentally Appropriate Assistance in the Zone of Proximal Development and the Acquisition of L2 Grammar," in *Sociocultural Theory and Second Language Learning*, ed. J. P. Lantolf (Oxford: Oxford University Press, 2000), 51–78; and Amy Snyder Ohta, *Second Language Acquisition Processes*; and Neomy Storch, "Patterns of Interaction in ESL Pair Work," *Language Learning* 52 (2002): 119–58.

[28] Some researchers understand scaffolding and the ZPD as two distinct concepts. For a summary of these issues, see Lantolf and Thorne, *Sociocultural Theory*, 274–76.

their current level of functioning."[29] In contrast with traditional types of assessment, dynamic assessment "refers to the integration of instruction and assessment processes within a single procedure that looks beyond whether student independent performance at a given moment in time is successful or unsuccessful."[30] A dynamic assessment is interested in "the degree of modifiability" of the student's cognitive processes rather than his or her level of functioning with the goal of identifying the student's learning potential.[31]

Instead of administering a static assessment, which tests the learner's ability to perform at a given level, the assessor, usually a peer or mentor, works with the learner in his or her ZPD to determine more precisely what the learner can do independently, what he or she can do with assistance, and how much more assistance the student will need before functioning independently using the skill or knowledge that is the focus of the assessment. To best accomplish this, the assessor dialogues with the learner rather than presenting an assessment to be completed independently by the learner. The teacher is diagnosing in real time what the learner needs in a manner that is not focused on task completion or performance.[32] The results of the dynamic assessment are used to inform and refine current and future instruction given to the learner. While a dynamic assessment may involve more time and effort than a traditional assessment, the results are more nuanced and detailed, providing deeper insight into the student's ability and more useful information for instructional planning.

To summarize, SLA research and practice indicates that language instruction that is sensitive to sociocultural issues can be effective and

---

[29] Tziona Levi and Matthew E. Poehner, "Employing Dynamic Assessment to Enhance Agency Among L2 Learners," in *The Routledge Handbook of Sociocultural Theory and Second Language Development*, ed. J. P. Lantolf, M. E. Poehner, and M. Swain (New York: Routledge, 2018), 296.

[30] Levi and Poehner, "Employing Dynamic Assessment," 296.

[31] Alex Kozulin and Erica Garb, "Dynamic Assessment of EFL Text Comprehension," *School Psychology International* 23.1 (2002): 114.

[32] Kimberly Buescher, "A Sociocultural Approach to Second Language Literacy Pedagogy," in *The Routledge Handbook of Sociocultural Theory and Second Language Development*, ed. J. P. Lantolf, M. E. Poehner, and M. Swain (New York: Routledge, 2018), 381.

motivating for students. Instructors are thus encouraged to employ instructional strategies developed from sociocultural theory and research, including teaching culture with language, creating opportunities for social learning, scaffolding, and dynamic assessment.

Sociocultural Instruction in Biblical and Ancient Language Courses

Incorporating sociocultural teaching practices in biblical and ancient language classes poses at least two unique challenges the instructor may need to overcome: cultural distance and the general trend in these courses to maintain traditional approaches to language instruction.

The most obvious challenge to teaching sociocultural aspects of ancient languages is that these so-called "dead" languages have no community of living native speakers. The cultures in which these languages originated is now far removed from our modern industrial and technological societies, foreign in almost every sense of the word. Moreover, instructors have no recourse to native speakers or materials from the native culture beyond the available texts and some archeological artifacts. This limits both their knowledge and their pedagogical resources when teaching sociocultural aspects of the L2. In contrast with modern language learning, ancient language instructors cannot assign an interview with a native speaker or tell students to read the news or watch a movie in the L2, giving them the opportunity to pick up both language and culture. Therefore, the intentional teaching of culture, at least what we do know, is even more important for biblical and ancient languages. Students are unlikely to learn this information in any other context.

Another challenge facing biblical and ancient language teachers is that the traditional approach to L2 instruction has promoted independent learning of the languages. For decades and perhaps centuries, students of the biblical and ancient languages have been expected to memorize paradigms and vocabulary on their own and then read and translate the texts independently of their classmates. This approach does not make use of a potentially rich source of learning: dialogue and interaction with other students. As the paradigm shifts away from traditional approaches to L2 instruction, more instructors may be able to reap the benefits of social interaction in biblical and ancient language classrooms.

Examples for Biblical and Ancient Language Classrooms

The following examples present some specific ideas for incorporating sociocultural instructional techniques in Hebrew, Greek, and Latin classrooms. The Hebrew example focuses on teaching culture in the language. The Greek and Latin examples highlight two approaches to teaching reading using sociocultural instructional techniques.

Teach Culture in the Language (Hebrew)

As noted above, instructors should look for ways to incorporate the teaching of culture in their L2 classrooms, but this does not have to be a separate part of the class session. This activity provides an example of teaching ancient Israelite culture using Hebrew. The activity is intended for more advanced students, perhaps second year or beyond.

The activity will require the following preparations: Prior to the activity, the instructor should assign the students to read an article on the archaeological significance of the four-room house in the Levant as it relates to Israelite society.[33] He or she should also pre-teach (or review) relevant vocabulary items, such as בַּיִת "house," קִיר "wall," דֶּלֶת "door," אֶבֶן "stone," etc.[34] This activity also requires a scale model or diagram of an ancient Israelite four-room house and perhaps a photo of the archaeological remains of such a house.[35] The instructor may also want a map of the Levant handy for reference. Finally, the instructor should prepare a handout with a simple drawing of a four-room house for the students to label with a list of vocabulary items to use.

At the beginning of the activity itself, the instructor projects an image of a four-room house on the wall or encourages students to gather

---

[33] A good example is Avraham Faust and Shlomo Bunimovitz, "The Four Room House: Embodying Iron Age Israelite Society," *Near Eastern Archaeology* 66.1/2 (2003): 22–31.

[34] Chapter 10 explains that vocabulary of the same lexical set should not be introduced at the same time to avoid interference. However, because this is a more advanced group, it is assumed that many of the vocabulary items were learned previously. Therefore, this presentation of vocabulary would entail at least some review, and interference would not be a significant issue.

[35] For several such photos and diagrams, see Faust and Bunimovitz, "The Four Room House."

around a model or diagram of the house so that everyone can see. He or she then begins to point out features of the house in Hebrew הִנֵּה הַקִּיר, "Here is the wall," going back to check comprehension using questions like מַה־זֶּה? "What is this?" or אַיֵּה הַדֶּלֶת? "Where is the door?"

Students then break into small groups. The group members begin by working together to label a drawing of a four-room house on the pre-made handout, using the list of vocabulary items included on the sheet. Next, they discuss the article they read, using a few questions prepared by the instructor as prompts, such as: מִי בָּנָה בָּתִּים שֶׁל אַרְבָּעָה חֲדָרִים "Who built four-room houses?" Students should interact in Hebrew as much as possible, but the instructor may also allow for some L1 if necessary, depending on the level of the students.

Division-of-Labor Reading (Greek)

The second example is an activity informed by sociocultural theory called division-of-labor reading or division-of-labor pedagogy.[36] The intent of this activity is to help students move from first-year language-focused courses to more advanced courses with a literary and exegetical focus. Therefore, this activity should be used at the beginning of a second-year course as students shift from decoding words and sentences to interpreting and analyzing longer passages. This activity begins as a group project that moves each learner toward independent reading by working through several stages. The groups will likely take a week or more to complete all the stages for one passage.

The instructor begins the activity by dividing the students into groups of four and assigning the target passage. The passage should be a self-contained narrative and long enough to be divided into four sections. For this example, the target passage is John 5:1–18. The students study the text together, covering three basic concepts of text analysis and interpretation that are divided into four roles each. The concepts and their corresponding roles are summarized below:

---

[36] Adapted from Kimberly D. Buescher, "Developing Second Language Narrative Literacy Using Concept-Based Instruction and a Division-of-Labor Pedagogy" (PhD diss., The Pennsylvania State University, 2015).

CONCEPT/STAGE	CORRESPONDING ROLES
1. Foundation	A. Vocabulary: Research unknown vocabulary. B. Grammar/discourse: Investigate difficulties related to morphosyntactic features. C. Main idea: Summarize the main idea of the text. D. Predication: Predict what will happen next (based on the text itself, not event probabilities).
2. Organization	A. Beginning: Identify the event that initiates the conflict and sets off a complex reaction. B. Complex reaction: Identify the emotional or cognitive response of the character(s) and the goal(s) that he or she wants to achieve. C. Goal path: Identify the action or plan of the character(s) and the consequence of the attempt, including whether the goal is achieved or not. D. Ending: Identify the event or events that bring the narrative to a close.
3. Genre	A. Field: Identify the subject matter or social activity of the passage. B. Tenor: Identify the relationships between the participants. C. Mode: Identify the role that language plays in the interaction of the story. D. Purpose: Identify the reason for the story.

Each group of four students begins with the foundation stage and covers the first section of the text (John 5:1–5). The instructor assigns to each student in the group one of the four roles corresponding to the foundations stage: vocabulary, grammar/discourse, main idea, and predication. Each student then researches his or her respective role and reports back to the group. For the foundations stage, the roles need to report to the group in the order listed above with vocabulary first and predication last as the later roles are dependent on the information provided by the roles that come before.

The first stage also includes opportunities for mediation from an instructor or a more advanced student, such as a tutor or graduate assistant. For example, the student covering the vocabulary role may need assistance with using a lexicon. The student covering the grammar/discourse role may need direction in finding good sources for more advanced morphosyntactic information.

Once all four students have reported to the group and synthesized the first section, they rotate roles for the second section of the passage (John 5:6–9). The process then repeats with the different students researching each role for the second section and reporting to the group. After completing the second section, the students rotate roles again for the third and fourth sections until each student has taken a turn with each foundation role and the entire passage has been successfully covered.

The students then move on to the second stage of analyzing the passage, looking at the organization of the narrative, which necessarily depends on the work completed for the foundations stage. The organization stage focuses on the literary structure of the narrative, including sequence of events, setting(s), reactions, goals, outcomes, etc. From the perspective of biblical exegesis, this corresponds to a literary analysis of the text. Once again, each student will take one of the corresponding roles for this concept (beginning, complex reaction, goal path, ending) and identify the part of the story fulfilled by that role.

At this stage of the process, each student should examine the entire passage rather than individual sections unless the passage is significantly longer than the target passage for this example with subplots that can be analyzed. Again, mediation from an instructor or tutor may be helpful as students work on their assigned roles. The students report back to the group, and the group members work together to create a cohesive representation of the structure of the passage.

The last stage of the process addresses the genre concept and builds on the work the students completed for the previous two stages, the foundation and organization concepts. Once again, each student takes one of the four roles that correspond with the genre concept, applies it to an understanding of the entire passage, and reports back to the group. As with the previous stages, mediation may be needed, especially in helping students identify and use relevant resources. The group members then work together to construct the context and situation of the text. For biblical exegesis, this stage corresponds to historical and cultural background research and could easily be adapted accordingly.

Incorporating a scaffolding approach to the activity, the entire process can then be repeated with a different text and with greater responsibilities given to each student. Instead of one role, the students could each take on two or more roles at a time for each stage of the process. Eventually, as the process is repeated, the students can progress to the point where they have the ability and confidence to complete all four roles for all three stages independently.

Dynamic Assessment as an Instructor-Mediated Reading Strategy (Latin)

One final activity that incorporates a sociocultural approach to language learning is an example of dynamic assessment in a Latin classroom. Dynamic assessment is a means of both assessing student potential and promoting student learning.[37] This activity is intended for more advanced Latin students, perhaps second year or later. While the procedure begins with a static test, the focus of the activity is the mediated learning in the form of dynamic assessment that comes after the initial static test.

The first stage of the process is a multiple-choice comprehension test (the static test) on a passage in Latin. For this example, Julius Caesar's *Gallic War*, book 2, chapter 1 is the target passage (Gallic War 2.1). Possible test questions might include, *Ubi erat Caesar?* "Where was Caesar?", *Quis contra Romam coniuravit?* "Who conspired against Rome?", *Cur contra Romam coniuraverunt?* "Why did they conspire against Rome?" This type of intervention is most effective with static test questions that depend on cognitive reading and test-taking strategies rather than questions that depend on prior knowledge, memory, or automatized skills.[38]

After the student completes the static test, the instructor reviews the test with the student. This is where the dynamic assessment takes place. The purpose of the review is for the instructor to mediate strategies that will help the student focus on using text structure, cohesion devices, and background knowledge to elicit meaning from texts and questions. The instructor and student work together on each test item, talking through the strategies the student used for reading and answering test questions.

---

[37] Adapted from Alex Kozulin and Erica Garb, "Dynamic Assessment of Literacy: English as a Third Language," *European Journal of Psychology of Education* 19.1 (2004): 65–77; and Kozulin and Garb, "Dynamic Assessment of EFL," 112–27.

[38] Kozulin and Garb, "Dynamic Assessment of Literacy," 69.

As a part of the dynamic assessment, the instructor might use questions like the following: "What categories of pre-knowledge [were] required in order to answer the questions (e.g., question words, personal pronouns, negative contractions, sentence structure, use of metaphoric language, etc.)?" "Which strategies and procedures could be employed in order to answer the questions?"[39] Using the answers to these and similar questions, the instructor should then adapt instruction to the student's ability by presenting more useful and efficient strategies, depending on the student's ability, and by demonstrating how various strategies can be transferred from one test question to another.

At the end the dynamic assessment phase, each student receives an information page for study at home with relevant vocabulary, grammar, and strategies noted. After giving each student enough time to review the strategies presented in the dynamic assessment, the instructor administers a second static test like the first but using a different passage. This gives the students opportunity to make use of the new reading and test-taking strategies, practicing and reinforcing the new knowledge and skills.

Conclusion

When language instruction is sensitive to sociocultural issues, like Jonathan's Hebrew class described at the beginning of the chapter, L2 proficiency improves as does student enjoyment. This chapter summarized some of the research and literature in SLA that addresses sociocultural issues as they relate to language acquisition, including culture, community, and sociocultural theory for language learning. After a summary of the research, the chapter discussed how this information relates to language acquisition in general and some of the unique challenges for ancient and biblical language learning. The chapter ended with a few specific classroom examples for Hebrew, Greek, and Latin that incorporate sociocultural instructional practices.

---

[39] Kozulin and Garb, "Dynamic Assessment of Literacy," 72.

For Further Reading

Hall, Joan Kelly and Lorrie Stoops Verplaetse, eds. *Second and Foreign Language Learning Through Classroom Interaction*. Mahwah, NJ: Erlbaum, 2000.

Lantolf, James P. "Sociocultural Theory and L2: State of the Art." *Studies in Second Language Acquisition* 28 (2006): 67–109.

Lantolf, James P. *Sociocultural Theory and Second Language Learning*. Oxford: Oxford University Press, 2000.

Magnan, Sally Sieloff. "The Unqualified Promise of Teaching for Communicative Competence: Insights from Sociocultural Theory." Pages 350–79 in *Sociocultural Theory and the Teaching of Second Language*. Edited by J. P. Lantolf and M. E. Poehner. London: Equinox, 2008.

Vygotsky, Lev. *Thought and Language*. Translation newly revised and edited by Alex Kozulin. Cambridge: MIT Press, 1986.

CHAPTER 14: CONCLUSION

As the field of instructed SLA continues to evolve, it provides us with greater understanding of how language students learn best. This book introduced twelve of the most important principles drawn from the field of SLA research and practice for the purpose of distilling this vast body of knowledge and presenting it succinctly to instructors of biblical and ancient languages. My hope is that these principles will encourage and inform instructors and students as they pursue excellence in the teaching and learning of Hebrew, Greek, and Latin.

After briefly summarizing these principles, this last chapter recommends future directions for the field of ancient language instruction and offers a few suggestions for instructors who want to incorporate SLA principles into their teaching.

Section 1: Types of Language Knowledge and Types of Language Instruction (Chapters 2–3)

The first section of the book lays the foundation for the others by defining language proficiency along with the two types of language knowledge—implicit and explicit—and the two main types of language instruction—meaning-focused and form-focused. By way of review, implicit language knowledge is unconscious and intuitive, while explicit knowledge is conscious and articulated, often in the form of rules. The two different types of language instruction largely correspond to the two different types of language knowledge. Meaning-focused instruction generally promotes the acquisition of implicit language knowledge through the use of input and interaction in the classroom. Form-focused instruction, by contrast, generally promotes the learning of explicit language knowledge using reactive and proactive instruction that focuses on grammatical accuracy.

Section 2: The Raw Materials of Language Acquisition: Input and Output (Chapters 4–7)

With an understanding of implicit and explicit language knowledge and their respective instructional approaches, the second set of chapters moves on to the raw materials of language acquisition: input and output. To achieve proficiency in a language, SLA experts agree that students must have access to comprehensible input, that is, language data a learner receives that he or she can understand. Because comprehensible input is so important for language acquisition, this section also presented strategies for increasing the quantity of comprehensible input in the classroom and strategies for increasing the quality of comprehensible input. After covering input, this section then turned to the important role of language output, the other raw material of language acquisition.

Section 3: Language Skill Development (Chapters 8–11)

The third section of the book shifted the focus to issues concerned with various language skills and skill development in language acquisition, building on the raw materials of language acquisition from the previous section. After introducing and describing the four language skills—listening, speaking, reading, and writing—we looked at the skill of reading in greater depth because it is central to the needs of students who study biblical and ancient languages. Also of particular interest to ancient language study is vocabulary acquisition, which was covered after reading fluency. To bring this section to a close, chapter 11 covered course design and syllabus structure, which integrates the various skills into a cohesive language course.

Section 4: The Role of the Learner (Chapters 12–13)

In the concluding section of the book, learner-related issues were the topic of focus. Specifically, these chapters addressed differences among learners, including cognitive and affective factors, and sociocultural aspects of language acquisition, including culture, community, and sociocultural theory as it relates to SLA.

Where Do We Go from Here?

As we can see from these twelve principles, the growing field of SLA adds to our knowledge of how language learning works. At the same time, the field of ancient language instruction is also growing and changing. Many instructors are learning from the field of SLA, and many are experimenting with changes and improvements in their classes, but there is more work to be done. Potential areas for future development in ancient language instruction include more empirical research focused on biblical and ancient language acquisition, the development of more instructional materials that incorporate SLA principles of language acquisition, and more training in SLA principles for instructors of biblical and ancient languages.

Empirical Studies

The field of SLA contains thousands of published empirical studies that address a myriad of language acquisition issues for modern languages. These empirical studies are language learning experiments conducted in controlled environments with statistical analysis of the results. Most of what we know about second language acquisition comes from these studies. However, the literature contains very few empirical studies that investigate biblical and ancient language acquisition.[1] While we can generally assume that what is true for modern language acquisition should also be true for ancient language acquisition, without empirical studies, we cannot fully affirm this. Therefore, one of the future directions for biblical and ancient language studies should be carefully controlled empirical studies of various language learning phenomena in Hebrew, Greek, Latin, and other ancient languages, using statistical analysis to interpret the results.

Instructional Materials

In addition to empirical studies in ancient languages, a second area with room for future development is that of instructional materials. Throughout this volume, I have noted places where biblical and ancient language instructors lack some of the rich teaching materials that modern language instructors enjoy. Textbooks that are founded on solid principles

---

[1] At the time of this writing, I am aware of only a few empirical studies that investigate biblical and ancient language learning: Quast, "Using Processing Instruction"; Thompson, "Learning Biblical Hebrew Vocabulary"; Thompson, "Word-list Size"; David Weyrick and David Baker, "An Investigation of Biblical Language Study from 1986–1991 at Ashland Theological Seminary," *Bulletin of Higher Hebrew Education* 5–6 (1992–1993): 56–67.

of SLA are absolutely necessary. However, we also need graded readers—and lots of them. We also need to develop more creative and pedagogically sound supplemental materials, such as games in L2, objects and props for classroom use, photos, videos, and other computer-based interactive materials. What I am suggesting here is not a simple increase in quantity, but also an increase in quality and variety.

Teacher Training and Instructional Support

Those who teach biblical and ancient languages need more than just materials as described above, however. They also need training in how to use them. Because approaches and methodologies for biblical and ancient language instruction have lagged behind those used for modern language instruction, many ancient language teachers have not witnessed or experienced instruction that is based on recent developments in SLA. Additionally, there are very few opportunities for pedagogical training for teachers of biblical and ancient languages.[2] Therefore, it is not uncommon for instructors to teach the way they were taught. Training instructors to appropriate these developments in SLA would be a fruitful endeavor. Teacher training could come in the form of workshops, conferences, and clinics. However, adding language pedagogy classes to ancient language programs of study, especially at the graduate and post-graduate level, could have a large impact.

Instructors also need support and encouragement. Modern language instructors have several guilds that provide opportunities for enrichment, collaboration, and research.[3] Few options exist for biblical and ancient languages, particularly for those interested in language pedagogy. As noted in the introduction, the Evangelical Theological Society

---

[2] A few teacher training opportunities in recent years include pedagogy workshops for both Hebrew and Greek instructors at Fresno Pacific University in conjunction with the Biblical Language Center, a Hebrew pedagogy workshop offered by Paul Overland at Ashland Theological Seminary, and a Latin immersion and pedagogy training by the Septentrionale Americanum Latinitatis Vivae Institutum (SALVI).

[3] For example, the American Association of Applied Linguistics (AAAL), the American Council on the Teaching of Foreign Languages (ACTFL), and the Modern Language Association (MLA). For a more comprehensive list, see http://languageconsortium.org/professional-organizations/.

has an Applied Linguistics and Biblical Language Group. The National Association of Professors of Hebrew also sponsors conferences and pedagogical sessions at the Society of Biblical Literature. For Latin, instructors have the Septentrionale Americanum Latinitatis Vivae Institutum (SALVI). However, more could be done, perhaps even an independent society for teachers of ancient languages who are interested in collaborating in empirical research, educating instructors, and sharing pedagogical innovations.

Where Do I Go from Here?

As an individual instructor reading this volume, it is my hope that you gain a greater appreciation for the SLA principles addressed. However, you may also be wondering how to implement these principles in your own course. For some people, the changes I am suggesting could seem overwhelming, so let me offer a few pieces of advice.

One Thing at a Time

My first suggestion is to start where you are and start small. Don't expect to change the entire language course in one academic year. Instead, try to change only one or two aspects of the course each time you teach it. Try to change one activity each time around, or you may want to try to apply one principle at a time. Make use of the examples at the end of each chapter in this volume. Each time you go through the course, it will get easier.

Prepare

As you think about the changes you want to make to your course, my second suggestion would be that you educate and prepare yourself. You can do this in several ways. First, you will want to read SLA literature on the principle you plan to incorporate. Each chapter of this book ends with a select bibliography for this purpose. Educate yourself on the research and the rationale behind the principle. Then, second, you can look for ways to implement the principle. The examples near the end of each chapter are intended for this purpose, but you might also consider perusing modern language textbooks for examples to adapt for your L2.

Look for items such as classroom activities, homework assignments, or supplemental materials like graded readers. Finally, I would encourage you to attend a teacher training workshop. While there are a few that specifically target biblical and ancient language instructors (see above), don't be afraid to attend a modern language pedagogy workshop. Learn from others who are applying SLA principles to their teaching—in any language.

Develop Speaking and Listening Skills

Many instructors are intimidated by an approach to language learning that involves interaction, that is, speaking and listening. As noted above, many of us only learned how to read L2, so our speaking and listening skills are underdeveloped. Let me suggest a few ways to overcome this challenge. First, I would encourage you to spend time listening to L2.[4] Listen to audio recordings in the car or while you are taking a walk. Listen to recordings of literature while you read the text at the same time. Like your students, you will need plenty of comprehensible input to help you develop proficiency.

Another way to develop your speaking and listening skills would be to take a language class that incorporates speaking and listening. Some classes are available in person (some in Israel!) and some online, using synchronous instruction through real-time video interaction.[5] However, even a local class on the modern counterpart to your language, such as Modern Greek, can help to improve your listening and speaking fluency.

Have Fun!

My last bit of advice would be for you to make the learning enjoyable—for you and for your students. Bring down the affective filter (see

---

[4] There are plenty of free audio recordings available online. See, e.g., the Hebrew Bible read by Israel Radvinsky (https://www.youtube.com/watch?v=iEXOlP-6WkQ), the Greek New Testament (https://www.youtube.com/playlist?list=PLk3Pw QOcbBq2U2r7 xsulg8e2Lvs0_QFU5), and Classical Greek and Latin recitals by Harvard faculty (https://classics.fas.harvard.edu/greek-audio and https://classics.fas .harvard.edu/latin-audio).

[5] See, e.g., the those offered by the Biblical Language Center, Biblingo, the Polis Institute, and Vivarium Novum, and the Septentrionale Americanum Latinitatis Vivae Institutum (SALVI).

chapter 12) by finding what works best for you and for them. If you are getting anxious about speaking and interacting and incorporating too many SLA principles all at once, then back off a little until it feels comfortable and enjoyable again. Then, when you are ready, try to challenge yourself again. My hope and prayer is that more and more students will find the biblical and ancient languages useful and enjoyable through pedagogy that is informed and enriched by SLA principles.

Blessings to you as you teach!

GLOSSARY OF TERMS

GLOSSARY OF TERMS

access: the act of drawing upon language forms and structures that have been previously acquired in order to communicate meaning through language output

accuracy: the correctness of an utterance (written or spoken)

advance organizer: anything that will help prime a learner's prior knowledge to help him or her connect the information in the text with information he or she already has stored in long-term memory, which aids with making inferences and promotes interpretation

Affective Filter Hypothesis: the idea that learners have a mental filter that prevents them from fully processing and utilizing the comprehensible input they receive, especially when they are unmotivated, anxious, or lacking in self-confidence

attentional resources: the limited amount of mental capacity, including working memory, that a learner can utilize for processing language data during acquisition

Audio-Lingual Method: an environmentalist method for language instruction that developed in the early twentieth century; with this method, language instruction focuses on getting the student to imitate and practice the same structures over and over until they are habits; teachers are expected to be explicit and focus their instruction mainly on the more difficult structures

automaticity: mental processing that is fast, involuntary, independent of distractions, unconscious, and done without the use of mental algorithms or sets of rules

ballistic processing: unstoppable or involuntary processing; one characteristic of automaticity

chunk: an unanalyzed word or phrase, usually beyond the student's current level of grammar and vocabulary understanding, initially memorized for use in a specific, frequently occurring situation

code-switching: going back and forth between L2 and L1 during a conversation or in writing

Cognitive Anti-Method: an innatist language teaching method that attempts to recreate natural learning processes in the classroom

Cognitive-Code Method: an innatist language teaching method that contends that students need to understand and analyze language rules to develop competence

Communicative Approach: a philosophy of language instruction that incorporates various principles and strategies under its umbrella, particularly those focused on using language for communication; instructors using this approach focus on developing the communicative competence of their learners, while emphasizing the cognitive abilities that learners bring to the process

communicative drills: language learning activities in which a student must attend to meaning to complete the activity, and the content of the student's response is not already known to the person asking the question

comprehensible input: language input that can be understood

consciousness-raising: as one option for form-focused instruction, this strategy aims at helping the learner focus on the formal properties of a language in an attempt to help the learner understand grammar and learn it as explicit knowledge

contextual clues: using visual aids, gestures, and other clues to make language input comprehensible for the learner

controlled grammar practice: consciously rehearsing structures until they are internalized

Critical Period Hypothesis: the idea that it is only possible for an individual to acquire a language (L1 or L2) to native-like levels during a limited developmental period in his or her lifespan, usually only through puberty

cross-modal processing: listening and attending to auditory information that occurs in conjunction with other modalities, such as vision and touch

direct consciousness-raising tasks: using explanations to describe the form and function of the target structure(s) (see also **consciousness-raising** and **explicit grammar instruction**)

environment analysis: an inventory of external factors that can affect the goals of a course, usually completed by the instructor as part of the design process of the course

environmentalist approach: an approach to language learning, developed in the early twentieth century that sees language as an abstract system and learning as a stimulus-response-reinforcement process; this approach focuses on the external aspects of language learning, including imitation and practice to form habits of language

explicit corrective feedback: explicit instruction given to a learner when he or she makes an error in language production, usually in an effort to help the learner correct the mistake (see also **feedback** and **reactive form-focused instruction**)

explicit grammar instruction: intentionally teaching grammar rules as explicit knowledge, using grammatical metalanguage

explicit language knowledge: language knowledge that is conscious and articulated, often in the form of rules about how the language works or behaves

extensive reading: reading large quantities of extended texts that are at or below the learner's current reading ability in order to promote fluency by increasing the quantity of comprehensible input the learner receives

feedback: providing error correction to a learner to help move the learner toward greater proficiency (see also **explicit corrective feedback** and **reactive form-focused instruction**)

flow: a psychological construct that refers to the feeling of being completely absorbed in the present moment, usually while participating in an activity that is self-rewarding

fluency: the ease and speed with which an individual can produce language output or comprehend language input

foreign language anxiety: a feeling of stress or apprehension that is associated with L2 contexts

form-focused instruction: language instruction that focuses on grammatical accuracy

four strands of language learning: the four main instructional components that should make up a language course, namely, meaning-focused input, language-focused learning, meaning-focused output, and fluency activities

Grammar-Translation Method: an approach to language instruction that focuses on memorization of vocabulary and paradigms with translation serving as the main form of student practice and assessment

imaging: a learner's creation of a visual image for learning vocabulary to help in the learning process and improve recall

immersion in the classroom: a teaching strategy that uses as much L2 in the classroom as possible and as little L1 as possible

implicit language knowledge: language knowledge that is unconscious and intuitive

indirect consciousness-raising tasks: inviting learners to generate their own descriptions of L2 grammar, given a series of examples (see also **consciousness-raising**)

information exchange tasks: a type of language learning activity in which the interlocutors share with each other information that the other(s) did not already know

information gap tasks: a type of language learning activity in which each of the participants is given information that other participants in the activity do not have; participants must share the information they have for the group to successfully complete the activity

innatist approach: an approach to language learning formulated in reaction to the environmentalist approach to language learning; this approach holds that all children are born with a Language Acquisition Device, which allows them to learn any language (see also **Language Acquisition Device and Universal Grammar**)

input: language data a learner receives that has some kind of communicative intent, including spoken and/or written language

input enhancement: a process used to make specific target items in language input more salient for a learner; examples of input enhancement include using italics, bolding, or voice inflection

input flood: intentionally embedding a target structure in a text (written or oral) as frequently as possible to increase the ratio of target structure occurrences to non-target structure occurrences, with the goal of making the target structure more salient and more likely to be processed

instance processing: using a token or instance stored in memory to solve a problem rather than an algorithm or set of rules

instantiation: when learning vocabulary, a learner intentionally recalls a specific experience, instance, or example of the meaning of the word to help improve recall

intake: language data in the L2 input that the leaner attends to and processes for form and/or meaning; intake is a subset of language input in that not all input is absorbed as intake

interaction: using L2 to communicate with another person; an integral part of meaning-focused instruction

interactionist approach: an approach to language learning that seeks to use discourse and functional aspects of the language to teach communicative competence in social settings

Keyword Technique: a mnemonic device for learning vocabulary in which the student thinks of an L1 word that sounds like the L2 word being learned and then creates a visual image that combines the two words

Languaculture: a term coined by Michael Agar that communicates the intimate relationship between language and culture

Language Acquisition Device (LAD): an innate, internal ability possessed by all children that allows them to learn any language, promoted by Noam Chomsky and later replaced by Universal Grammar (UG) (see also **Universal Grammar**)

language-processing: an option for form-focused instruction in which specific L2 structures are intentionally reinforced through language use (see also **form-focused instruction**)

load independent processing: the ability to process language input automatically without the interference of other processes or distractions that are going on simultaneously

meaning proposition encoding: the process by which meaning is extracted from words and structures while words and syntax are being parsed

meaning-focused instruction: instruction that treats L2 as a tool for communication and relies on input and interaction as the primary means of instruction

meaningful drills: language learning activities for which there is only one correct answer, but the student must attend to meaning to complete the activity

mechanical drills: language learning activities that a student can complete without attending to meaning and for which there is only one correct answer

metalanguage: language and vocabulary used for talking about language

modification of input: making language input comprehensible for a language learner by slowing down, enunciating, adjusting vocabulary usage, adjusting syntax, providing more repetition, and/or modifying discourse structure

monitoring: ensuring that an utterance (written or spoken) is grammatically correct and socially appropriate before producing it; one component of producing language output

needs analysis: an inventory of what students need to learn in a given course, usually completed by the instructor as part of the design process of the course

negotiation of meaning: using repetition, requests for clarification, restating, and circumlocution during a conversation to ensure that the interlocutors understand each other

output: language data a learner produces that has some kind of communicative intent, including spoken and/or written language

output hypothesis: the idea that producing language output (spoken or written) constitutes an important part of the process of learning a second language in certain circumstances

phonetic processing: discerning sounds and discriminating various sounds from one another

proactive form-focused instruction: intentionally teaching grammar rules, either explicitly or implicitly; differentiated from reactive form-focused instruction, which is an attempt to correct learner errors (see also **form-focused instruction**)

processing instruction (PI): an instructional approach specifically designed to improve the quality of input delivered to learners with the goal of helping the students overcome inefficient processing strategies; each PI lesson includes explicit grammar instruction, information about processing strategies, and structured input activities (see also **explicit grammar instruction, processing strategies,** and **structured input**)

processing strategies: the way(s) in which a learner derives meaning from language input; some processing strategies are more effective than others, according to Processing Instruction research (see also **Processing Instruction**)

production strategies: strategies and skills that allow someone producing language output to be able to string together forms in appropriate ways

proficiency: in language learning, the automatic and implicit knowledge of phonetics, prosody, phonology, morphology, and syntax, along with mastery of vocabulary and sociolinguistic competence

reactive form-focused instruction: explicit corrective feedback from an instructor to a learner on his or her performance, especially when a mistake is made; differentiated from proactive form-focused instruction, which is the intentional teaching of grammar rules (see also **form-focused instruction, feedback,** and **explicit corrective feedback**)

recast: restating a learner's incorrect utterance in a way that corrects the mistake

salience: in language learning, the degree to which a student notices a particular target word or structure; students are more likely to process those forms that are noticed

scaffolding: a learning situation in which a knowledgeable participant creates a supportive environment in which a novice may participate and improve his or her skills and knowledge, moving to higher levels of competence

simplification of input: making language input comprehensible for a language learner by slowing down, enunciating, adjusting vocabulary usage, adjusting syntax, providing more repetition, and modifying discourse structure

situation model of reader interpretation: a model of reader comprehension in which the reader constructs meaning, making extensive use of the reader's prior knowledge of the topic, which usually involves spatial, visual, and even personal and emotional information

sociolinguistic competence: the ability to use language correctly in a given sociocultural situation

structured input activities: student activities that are used as part of a Processing Instruction lesson; these activities must follow a very specific set of guidelines that help a student overcome inefficient processing strategies (see also **Processing Instruction** and **processing strategies**)

structured output activities: language learning activities in which participants must access a targeted form or structure to express meaning and exchange information that was not previously known

syntactic parsing: the ability to recognize and assign meaning to sentence-level, rather than word-level, markers such as word order, determiners (the, a, this, those, etc.), subordinate clauses, and tense

task: in language instruction, an activity that requires students to use L2, with a focus on meaning and completion of a goal (see also **task-based syllabus**)

task-based syllabus: an instructional course design that uses the task as the unit of progression (see also **unit of progression** and **task**)

text model of reader comprehension: a model of reader comprehension in which the reader derives meaning only as it is represented in the text

Total Physical Response (TPR): a method of language instruction in which the instructor gives commands to the learners in L2, and the learners demonstrate comprehension by responding through actions

TPR Storytelling: an expansion of Total Physical Response (TPR) that encourages learners to develop reading and writing skills in addition to listening and speaking skills (see also **Total Physical Response**)

unit of analysis: (see **unit of progression**)

unit of progression: in course development, the type of unit around which the course is organized, for example, grammatical structures, vocabulary items, topics, or tasks

Universal Grammar (UG): an innate, internal ability possessed by all children that allows them to learn any language, replacing the Language Acquisition Device (LAD) in some theories of language acquisition (see also **Language Acquisition Device**)

visual textual enhancement: marking a target structure in written language input to make it more salient for a language learner; examples include color coding, italics, and boldface font

word integration: (see **syntactic parsing**)

Zone of Proximal Development (ZPD): in the process of learning, the level at which a learner demonstrates what he or she can potentially do, with evidence coming from what he or she can do with assistance from an expert or through collaboration with peers

BIBLIOGRAPHY

Agar, Michael. *Language Shock: Understanding the Culture of Conversation*. New York: Morrow, 1994.

Ajabshir, Zahra Fahker. "The Relative Efficacy of Input Enhancement, Input Flooding, and Output-based Instructional Approaches in the Acquisition of L2 Request Modifiers." *Language Teaching Research* (2020): 1–23.

Aleph with Beth. "Welcome to Biblical Hebrew." https://hebrew .bibleling.org/?fbclid=IwAR2PKKvxpdpU1UO061yHdjHu1o0F HOxlc8j14rGE8sTcaGf9mOXIS5UQ0nk#/.

Aleph with Beth in partnership with GlossaHouse. https://www. glossahouse.com/aleph-with-beth.

Allen, Pauline, and Bronwen Neil. *Greek and Latin Letters in Late Antiquity: The Christianisation of a Literary Form*. Cambridge: Cambridge University Press, 2020.

Alpha with Angela. https://www.youtube.com/channel/UCe0ilqwSO8 XVnCw4m3UYC1Q.

American Council on the Teaching of Foreign Languages. "Facilitate Target Language Use." https://www.actfl.org/resources/guiding -principles-language-learning/target-language.

American Council on the Teaching of Foreign Languages. "ACTFL Proficiency Guidelines 2012." https://www.actfl.org /publications/guidelines-and-manuals/actfl-proficiency-guidelines-2012.

American Council on the Teaching of Foreign Languages. "Facilitate Target Language Use." https://www.actfl.org/resources/guiding -principles-language-learning/target-language.

Anderson, John R. "Acquisition of Cognitive Skill." *Psychological Review* 89 (1982): 369–406.

Anderson, John R. *Learning and Memory: An Integrated Approach*. 2nd ed. New York: Wiley, 2000.

Anderson, John R. *The Architecture of Cognition*. Cambridge: Harvard University Press, 1983.

Anderson, Richard C., Kathleen C. Stevens, Zohara Shifrin, and Jean H. Osborn. "Instantiation of Word Meanings in Children." *Journal of Reading Behavior* 10.2 (1978): 147–57.

Arevart, Supot, and Paul Nation. "Fluency Improvement in a Second Language." *RELC Journal* 22 (1991): 84–94.

Artigal, Josep. "Some Considerations on Why a New Language is Acquired by Being Used." *International Journal of Applied Linguistics* 2 (1992): 221–40.

Asher, James J. "Children's First Language as a Model for Second Language Learning." *The Modern Language Journal* 56.3 (1972): 133–39.

Asher, James J. *Learning Another Language through Actions*. 6th ed. Los Gatos, CA: Sky Oak Productions, 2000.

Augustine. *The Confessions of Saint Augustine*. Translated by John K. Ryan. New York: Image Books, 1988.

Baddeley, Alan. *Essentials of Human Memory*. Classic Edition. London: Psychology Press, 2014.

Baddeley, Alan. "Working Memory: An Overview." Pages 1–31 in *Working Memory and Education*. Edited by S. Pickering. Burlington, MA: Academic Press, 2006.

Baddeley, Alan. *Working Memory, Thought, and Action*. New York: Oxford University Press, 2007.

Baddeley, Alan, and Graham Hitch. "Working Memory." Pages 47–89 in vol. 8 of *The Psychology of Learning and Motivation*. Edited by G. H. Bower. New York: Academic Press, 1974.

Beaton, Alan. *Dyslexia, Reading and the Brain: A Sourcebook of Psychological and Biological Research*. Hove, East Sussex: Psychology Press, 2004.

Benati, Alessandro. "Classroom-oriented Research: Processing Instruction (Findings and Implications)." *Language Teaching* 52.3 (2019): 343–59.

Biblical Language Center. https://www.biblicallanguagecenter.com.

Birdsong, David. "Interpreting Age Effects in Second Language Acquisition." Pages 109–27 in *Handbook of Bilingualism: Psycholinguistic Approaches*. Edited by J. Kroll and A. M. B. de Groot. Oxford: Oxford University Press, 2005.

Birdsong, David. "Introduction: Whys and Why Nots of the Critical Period Hypothesis for Second Language Acquisition." Pages 1–22 in *Second Language Acquisition and the Critical Period Hypothesis*. Edited by D. Birdsong. Mahwah, NJ: Erlbaum, 1999.

Birdsong, David, ed. *Second Language Acquisition and the Critical Period Hypothesis*. Mahwah, NJ: Erlbaum, 1999.

Blake, Mary E., and Patricia L. Majors. "Recycled Words: Holistic Instruction for LEP Students." *Journal of Adolescent and Adult Literacy* 39.2 (1995): 132–37.

Bloom, Kristine C., and Thomas J. Shuell. "Effects of Massed and Distributed Practice on the Learning and Retention of Second-Language Vocabulary." *Journal of Educational Research* 74.4 (1981): 245–48.

Bloomfield, Leonard. *Language*. New York: Holt, Rinehart & Winston, 1933.

Bower, Kim. "Explaining Motivation in Language Learning: A Framework for Evaluation and Research." *Language Learning Journal* 47.5 (2019): 558–74.

Brown, A. Philip, II, Bryan W. Smith, Richard J. Goodrich, Albert L. Lukaszewski. *A Reader's Hebrew and Greek Bible*. 3rd ed. Grand Rapids: Zondervan, 2020.

Brown, H. Douglas. "Requiem for Methods." *Journal of Intensive English Studies* 7 (1993): 1–12.

Brown, H. Douglas, and Heekyeong Lee. *Teaching by Principles: An Interactive Approach to Language Pedagogy*. 4th edition. White Plains, NY: Pearson Education, 2015.

Bruner, Jerome S. *The Process of Education*. Cambridge: Harvard University Press, 1977.

Buescher, Kimberly D. "Developing Second Language Narrative Literacy Using Concept-Based Instruction and a Division-of-Labor Pedagogy." PhD dissertation, The Pennsylvania State University, 2015.

Buescher, Kimberly. "A Sociocultural Approach to Second Language Literacy Pedagogy." Pages 378–87 in *The Routledge Handbook of Sociocultural Theory and Second Language Development*.

Edited by J. P. Lantolf, M. E. Poehner, and M. Swain. New York: Routledge, 2018.

Bullard, Jeremy. "The 100 'Simplest' Chapters of the Hebrew Bible." *Hebrew Higher Education* 21 (2019): 1–8.

Buth, Randall, Brian Schultz, Scott McQuinn, and Benjamin Kantor. *Living Biblical Hebrew*. Jerusalem: Biblical Language Center, 2019.

Bygate, Martin, ed. *Learning Language Through Task Repetition*. Philadelphia: John Benjamins, 2018.

Byram, Michael, and Anwei Feng. "Culture and Language Learning: Teaching, Research and Scholarship." *Language Teaching* 37.3 (2004): 149–68.

Cain, Kate. "Children's Reading Comprehension: The Role of Working Memory in Normal and Impaired Development." Pages 61–91 in *Working Memory and Education*. Edited by S. Pickering. Burlington, MA: Academic Press, 2006.

Chastain, Kenneth *Developing Second Language Skills: Theory and Practice*, 2nd ed. Chicago: Rand McNally, 1976.

Chaudron, Craig. *Second Language Classrooms: Research on Teaching and Learning*. Cambridge: Cambridge University Press, 1988.

Chomsky, Noam. *Syntactic Structures*. The Hague: Mouton de Gruyter, 1957.

Chow, Bonnie Wing-Yin, and Catherine McBride-Chang. "Phonological Processing Skills and Early Reading Abilities in Hong Kong Chinese Kindergarteners Learning to Read English as a Second Language." *Journal of Educational Psychology* 97.1 (2005): 81–87.

Chung, Mihwa. "The Effect of a Speed Reading Course: A Replication." *Asian Journal of English Language Teaching* 20 (2010): 95–116.

Chung, Mihwa, and Paul Nation. "The Effect of a Speed Reading Course." *English Teaching* 61 (2006): 181–204.

The Consortium for Language Teaching and Learning. "Multiple Language Organizations." http://languageconsortium.org/ professional-organizations/.

Cook, John A., and Robert D. Holmstedt, *Beginning Biblical Hebrew: A Grammar and Illustrated Reader*. Grand Rapids: Baker, 2013.

Cook, Vivian. "Using the First Language in the Classroom." *Canadian Modern Language Review* 57 (2001): 402–23.

Cook, Vivian. *Second Language Learning and Language Teaching*. 5th ed. New York: Routledge, 2016.

Criado, Raquel. "Towards the Validation of a Scale for Measuring the Load of Form Focus and Meaning Focus of Textbook Activities in Foreign Language Teaching." *Revista Electrónica de Lingüística Aplicada (RAEL)* 1.15 (2016): 129–49.

Cuevas, Joshua. "Is Learning Styles-Based Instruction Effective? A Comprehensive Analysis of Recent Research on Learning Styles." *Theory & Research in Education* 13.3 (2015): 308–33.

Dallaire, Hélène M. *Biblical Hebrew: A Living Language*. 2nd ed. Hélène M. Dallaire, 2017.

Dalton-Puffer, Christiane. "Questions as Strategies to Encourage Speaking in Content-and-Language-Integrated Classrooms." Pages 187–213 *Current Trends in the Development and Teaching of the Four Language Skills*. Edited by E. Usó-Juan and A. Martínez-Flor. Berlin: De Gruyter, 2006.

Damasio, Antonio R. *Descartes' Error: Emotion, Reason, and the Human Brain*. London: Penguin, 1994.

de Graaff, Rick, and Alex Housen. "Investigating the Effects and Effectiveness of L2 Instruction." Pages 726–55 in *The Handbook of Language Teaching*. Edited by M. Long and C. Doughty. Oxford: Blackwell, 2009.

de Jong, Nel, and Charles A. Perfetti. "Fluency Training in the ESL Classroom: An Experimental Study of Fluency Development and Proceduralization." *Language Learning* 61.2 (2011): 533–68.

de Saussure, Ferdinand, Charles Bally, and Albert Sechehaye. *Cours de Linguistique Générale*. Paris: Payot, 1916.

DeKeyser, Robert. "Beyond Focus on Form: Cognitive Perspectives on Learning and Practicing Second Language Grammar." Pages 42–63 in *Focus on Form in Classroom Second Language*

Acquisition. Edited by C. Doughty and J. Williams. Cambridge: Cambridge University Press, 1998.

DeKeyser, Robert. "Implicit and Explicit Learning." Pages 313–48 in *The Handbook of Second Language Acquisition.* Edited by C. Doughty and M. Long. Malden, MA: Blackwell, 2003.

DeKeyser, Robert M. "The Robustness of Critical Period Effects in Second Language Learners." *Studies in Second Language Acquisition* 22 (2000): 499–533.

DeKeyser, Robert. "Skill Acquisition Theory." Pages 94–112 in *Theories in Second Language Acquisition.* 2nd ed. Edited by B. VanPatten and J. Williams. New York: Routledge, 2015.

Department of the Classics. Harvard University. "Greek Audio." https://classics.fas.harvard.edu/greek-audio.

Department of the Classics. Harvard University. "Latin Audio." https://classics.fas.harvard.edu/latin-audio.

deSilva, David A. *Honor, Patronage, Kinship, and Purity: Unlocking New Testament Culture.* 2nd ed. Downers Grove, IL: Intervarsity, 2022.

Donato, Richard. "Collective Scaffolding in Second Language Learning." Pages 33–56 in *Vygotskian Approaches to Second Language Research*, ed. J. P. Lantolf and G. Appel. Norwood, NJ: Ablex, 1994.

Dörnyei, Zoltán. "Attitudes, Orientations, and Motivations in Language Learning: Advances in Theory, Research, and Applications." *Language Learning* 53 (2003): 3–32.

Dörnyei, Zoltán. "Conceptualizing Motivation in Foreign Language Learning." *Language Learning* 40 (1990): 46–78.

Dörnyei, Zoltán. *Motivational Strategies in the Language Classroom.* Cambridge: Cambridge University Press, 2001.

Doughty, Catherine, and Jessica Williams, eds. *Focus on Form in Classroom Second Language Acquisition.* Cambridge: Cambridge University Press, 1998.

Dresler, Martin, William R. Shirer, Boris N. Konrad, Nils C. J. Müller, Isabella C. Wagner, Guillén Fernández, Michael Szisch, Michael D. Greicius. "Mnemonic Training Reshapes Brain

Networks to Support Superior Memory." *Neuron* 93 (2017): 1227–35.

Egan, Richard W., Jerry Fjermestad, and Davida Scharf. "The Use of Mastery Quizzes to Enhance Student Preparation." *Journal of Higher Education Theory and Practice* 17.8 (2017): 36–42.

Ehrman, Madeline, and Betty Lou Leaver. "Cognitive Styles in the Service of Language Learning." *System* 31 (2003): 391–415.

Eisterhold, Joan Carson. "Reading-Writing Connections: Toward a Description for Second Language Learners." Pages 88–101 in *Second Language Writing: Research Insights for the Classroom*. Edited by B. Kroll. Cambridge: Cambridge University Press, 1990.

Elgort, Irina. "Deliberate Learning and Vocabulary Acquisition in Second Language." *Language Learning* 61.2 (2011): 367–413.

Elley, Warwick B. "Vocabulary Acquisition from Listening to Stories." *Reading Research Quarterly* 24.2 (1989): 174–87.

Ellis, Nick C. "At the Interface: Dynamic Interactions of Explicit and Implicit Language Knowledge." *Studies in Second Language Acquisition* 27 (2005): 305–52.

Ellis, Nick C., ed. *Implicit and Explicit Learning of Languages*. London: Academic Press, 1994.

Ellis, Nick C. "Memory for Language." Pages 33–68 in *Cognition and Second Language Instruction*. Edited by P. Robinson. New York: Cambridge University Press, 2001.

Ellis, Nick C. "Vocabulary Acquisition, Word Structure, Collocation, Word-Class, and Meaning." Pages 122–39 in *Vocabulary: Description, Acquisition and Pedagogy*. Edited by N. Schmitt and M. McCarthy. Cambridge: Cambridge University Press, 1997.

Ellis, Rod. "The Definition and Measurement of L2 Explicit Knowledge." *Language Learning* 54 (2004): 227–75.

Ellis, Rod. "Designing a Task-Based Syllabus," *RELC Journal* 34.1 (2003): 64–81.

Ellis, Rod. "Explicit Knowledge and Second Language Learning and Pedagogy." Pages 143–53 in vol. 6 of *Encyclopedia of Language and Education*. Edited by J. Cenoz and N. H. Hornberger. New York: Springer, 2008.

Ellis, Rod. *Instructed Second Language Acquisition: Learning in the Classroom.* Applied Language Studies. Oxford: Blackwell, 1990.

Ellis, Rod. *Language Teaching, Research, and Pedagogy.* Malden, MA: Wiley-Blackwell, 2012.

Ellis, Rod. "Principles of Instructed Language Learning." *System* 33 (2005): 209–24.

Ellis, Rod. "Principles of Instructed Second Language Learning." Pages 31–45 in *Teaching English as a Second or Foreign Language.* 4th ed. Edited by M. Celce-Murcia, D. M. Brinton & M. A. Snow. Boston: Heinle and Heinle, 2013.

Ellis, Rod. *The Study of Second Language Acquisition.* 2nd ed. Oxford Applied Linguistics. Oxford: Oxford University Press, 2008.

Ellis, Rod. *Task-Based Language Learning and Teaching.* Oxford: Oxford University Press, 2003.

Ellis, Rod. "Teaching and Research: Options in Grammar Teaching." *TESOL Quarterly* 32.1 (1998): 39–60.

Ellis, Rod. "A Theory of Instructed Second Language Acquisition." Pages 79–114 in *Implicit and Explicit Learning of Languages.* Edited by Nick C. Ellis. London: Academic Press, 1994.

Ellis, Rod, Shawn Loewen, Catherine Elder, Rosemary Erlam, Jenefer Philp, and Hayo Reinders. *Implicit and Explicit Knowledge in Second Language Learning, Testing and Teaching.* Bristol, UK: Multilingual Matters, 2009.

Eubank, Lynn, and Kevin R. Gregg. "Critical Periods and (Second) Language Acquisition: Divide et Impera." Pages 65–99 in *Second Language Acquisition and the Critical Period Hypothesis.* Ed. D. Birdsong. Mahwah, NJ: Lawrence Erlbaum, 1999.

Farley, Andrew P. *Structured Input: Grammar Instruction for the Acquisition-Oriented Classroom.* Boston: McGraw-Hill, 2005.

Faust, Avraham, and Shlomo Bunimovitz. "The Four Room House: Embodying Iron Age Israelite Society." *Near Eastern Archaeology* 66.1/2 (2003): 22–31.

Fischler, Ira. "Attention and Language." Pages 381–99 in *The Attentive Brain.* Edited by R. Parasuraman. Cambridge: MIT Press, 1998.

Foster, Pauline, and Amy Snyder Ohta. "Negotiation for Meaning and Peer Assistance in Second Language Classrooms." *Applied Linguistics* 26 (2005): 402–30.

Francese, Christopher. *Core Latin and Ancient Greek Vocabularies.* Carlisle, PA: Dickinson College Commentaries, 2020.

Gabryś-Barker, Danuta, and Joanna Bielska, eds. *The Affective Dimension in Second Language Acquisition.* Bristol, UK: Multilingual Matters, 2013.

Gardner, Howard. *Multiple Intelligences: New Horizons.* New York: Basic Books, 2006.

Gardner, R. C. *Social Psychology and Second Language Learning: The Role of Attitude and Motivation.* London: Arnold, 1985.

Garnham, Alan, and Jane Oakhill. "The Mental Models Theory of Language Comprehension." Pages 313–39 in *Models of Understanding Text.* Edited by B. Britton and A. Graesser. Mahwah, NJ: Erlbaum, 1996.

Gass, Susan M. *Input and Interaction and the Second Language Learner.* Mahwah, NJ: Erlbaum, 1997.

Gershman, Susan Jane. "Foreign Language Vocabulary Learning under Seven Conditions." PhD diss., Columbia University, 1970.

Goldman, Susan R., Richard M. Golden, and Paul van den Broek. "Why are Computational Models of Text Comprehension Useful?" Pages 27–51 in *Higher Level Language Processes in the Brain.* Edited by F. Schmalhofer and C. Perfetti. Mahwah, NJ: Erlbaum, 2007.

Grabe, William. "Fluency in Reading—Thirty-five Years Later." *Reading in a Foreign Language 22* (2010): 71–83.

Grabe, William. *Reading in a Second Language: Moving from Theory to Practice.* Cambridge: Cambridge University Press, 2009.

Grabe, William. "Research on Teaching Reading." *Annual Review of Applied Linguistics 24* (2004): 44–69.

Greenspahn, Frederick E. "Why Hebrew Textbooks Are Different from Those for Other Languages." *SBL Forum.* n.p. [cited July 2005]. Online: http://sbl-site.org/Article.aspx?ArticleID=420.

Gregersen, Tammy, and Elaine K. Horwitz. "Language Learning and Perfectionism: Anxious and Non-Anxious Language Learners'

Responses to Their Own Oral Performance." *Modern Language Journal* 86.4 (2002): 562–70.

Gregersen, Tammy. "Language Learning Vibes: What, Why and How to Capitalize for Positive Affect." Pages 89–98 in *The Affective Dimension in Second Language Acquisition*. Edited by D. Gabryś-Barker and J. Bielska. Bristol, UK: Multilingual Matters, 2013.

Groton, Anne H., and James M. May. *Thirty-Eight Latin Stories Designed to Accompany Wheelock's Latin*. 5th ed. Wauconda, IL: Bolchazy-Carducci, 2004.

Gruber-Miller, John, ed. *When Dead Tongues Speak: Teaching Beginning Greek and Latin*. Oxford: Oxford University Press, 2006.

Hadley, Alice Omaggio. *Teaching Language in Context*. 3rd ed. Boston: Heinle & Heinle, 2001.

Haier, Richard J., Benjamin V. Siegel Jr., Andrew MacLachlan, Eric Soderling, Stephen Lottenberg, Monte S. Buchsbaum, "Regional Glucose Metabolic Changes After Learning a Complex Visuospatial/Motor Task: A Positron Emission Tomographic Study," *Brain Research* 570 (1992): 134–43.

Halcomb, T. Michael W. *800 Words and Images: A New Testament Greek Vocabulary Builder*. Wilmore, KY: GlossaHouse, 2013.

Halcomb, T. Michael W., and Fredrick J. Long. *Speak Koine Greek: A Conversational Phrasebook*. Wilmore, KY: GlossaHouse, 2014.

Halcomb, T. Michael W., and Jordan Day. *The Path to Learning Greek*. Wilmore, KY GlossaHouse, 2013.

Hall, James W. "On the Utility of the Keyword Mnemonic for Vocabulary Learning." *Journal of Educational Psychology* 80.4 (1988): 554–62.

Hall, Joan Kelly, and Lorrie Stoops Verplaetse. "The Development of Second and Foreign Language Learning through Classroom Interaction." Pages 1–20 in *Second and Foreign Language Learning Through Interaction*. Edited by J. K. Hall and L. S. Verplaetse. Mahwah, NJ: Lawrence Erlbaum, 2000.

Hall, Joan Kelly and Lorrie Stoops Verplaetse, eds. *Second and Foreign Language Learning Through Classroom Interaction*. Mahwah, NJ: Erlbaum, 2000.

Halliday, M. A. K. *Learning How to Mean: Explorations in the Development of Language*. London: Arnold, 1975.

Hansen, Dee, Elain Bernstorf, and Gayle M. Stuber. *The Music and Literacy Connection*. 2nd ed. Lanham, MD: Rowman & Littlefield, 2014.

Hatch, Evelyn. "Simplified Input and Second Language Acquisition." Pages 64–86 in *Pidginization and Creolization as Language Acquisition*. Edited by R.W. Andersen. Cambridge, MA: Newbury House, 1983.

Herschensohn, Julia. *Language Development and Age*. Cambridge: Cambridge University Press, 2007.

Hinkel, Eli. "Current Perspectives on Teaching the Four Skills." *TESOL Quarterly* 40 (2006): 109–31.

Horwitz, Elaine K., Michael B. Horwitz, and Joann Cope. "Foreign Language Classroom Anxiety." *Modern Language Journal* 70.2 (1986): 125–32.

Hu Hsueh-chao, Marcella, and Paul Nation. "Unknown Vocabulary Density and Reading Comprehension." *Reading in a Foreign Language* 13.1 (2000): 403–30.

Hulme, Charles, Margaret Snowling, Marketa Caravolas, and Julia Carroll. "Phonological Skills Are (Probably) One Cause of Success in Learning to Read: A Comment on Castles and Coltheart." *Scientific Studies of Reading* 9 (2005): 351–65.

Hulstijn, Jan H. "Intentional and Incidental Second Language Vocabulary Learning: A Reappraisal of Elaboration, Rehearsal and Automaticity." Pages 258–86 in *Cognition and Second Language Instruction*. Edited by P. Robinson. Cambridge: Cambridge University Press, 2001.

Hulstijn, Jan H. *Language Proficiency in Native and Non-Native Speakers: Theory and Research*. Language Learning and Language Teaching 41. Philadelphia: John Benjamins, 2015.

Imhof, Margarete. "What is Going on in the Mind of a Listener? The Cognitive Psychology of Listening." Pages 97–126 in *Listening and Human Communication in the 21st Century*. Edited by A. D. Wolvin. Malden, MA: Blackwell, 2010.

Jacobs, George M., and Thomas S. C. Farell, "Paradigm Shift: Understanding and Implementing Change in Second Language Education." *TESL-EJ* 5.1 (2001): 1–16.

Jenkins, Joseph R., and Robert Dixon, "Vocabulary Learning." *Contemporary Educational Psychology* 8 (1983): 237–60.

Johnson, David W., and Roger T. Johnson. *Learning Together and Alone: Cooperative, Competitive, and Individualistic Learning*. 4th ed. Boston: Allyn and Bacon, 1991.

Johnson, Keith. "Mistake Correction." *English Language Teaching Journal* 42 (1988): 89–96.

Julius Caesar. C. Iuli Commentarii Rerum in Gallia Gestarum VII A. Hirti Commentarius VII. T. Rice Holmes. Oxonii. e Typographeo Clarendoniano. 1914. Scriptorum Classicorum Bibliotheca Oxoniensis. Available at: http://www.perseus .tufts.edu/hopper/text?doc=urn:cts:latinLit:phi0448.phi001.perseus-lat1:2.1.1.

Kintsch, Walter. *Comprehension: A Paradigm for Cognition*. Cambridge: Cambridge University Press, 1998.

Kintsch, Walter, Vimla L. Patel, and K. Anders Ericsson. "The Role of Long-Term Working Memory in Text Comprehension." *Psychologia* 42 (1999): 186–98.

Kintsch, Walter, and Katherine A. Rawson. "Comprehension." Pages 209–26 in *The Science of Reading*. Edited by M. Snowling and C. Hulme. Malden, MA: Blackwell, 2005.

Kittel, Bonnie Pedrotti, Victoria Hoffer, and Rebecca Abts Wright. *Biblical Hebrew: Text and Workbook*. 2nd ed., fully revised by Victoria Hoffer. New Haven: Yale University Press, 2005.

Koda, Keiko. *Insights into Second Language Reading*. Cambridge: Cambridge University Press, 2005.

Koine Greek. "Hear the New Testament (and Other Texts) Read in Koine." https://www.koinegreek.com/audio.

Kozulin, Alex, and Erica Garb. "Dynamic Assessment of EFL Text Comprehension." *School Psychology International* 23.1 (2002): 112–27.

Kozulin, Alex, and Erica Garb. "Dynamic Assessment of Literacy: English as a Third Language." *European Journal of Psychology of Education* 19.1 (2004): 65–77.

Krahnke, Karl J., and Mary Ann Christison. "Recent Language Research and Some Language Teaching Principles." *TESOL Quarterly* 17.4 (1983): 625–49.

Krashen, Stephen D. "The Comprehension Hypothesis Extended." Pages 81–94 in *Input Matters in SLA*. Edited by T. Piske & M. Young-Scholten. Bristol, UK: Multilingual Matters, 2009.

Krashen, Stephen D. "The Input Hypothesis and Its Rivals." Pages 45–77 in *Implicit and Explicit Learning of Languages*. Edited by N. C. Ellis. New York: Academic Press, 1994.

Krashen, Stephen D. *The Input Hypothesis: Issues and Implications*. London: Longman, 1985.

Krashen, Stephen D. *Principles and Practice in Second Language Acquisition*. New York: Pergamon, 1982.

Krashen, Stephen D., and Tracy D. Terrell. *The Natural Approach: Language Acquisition in the Classroom*. Hayward, CA: Alemany, 1983.

Kroll, Barbara. "Techniques for Shaping Writing Course Curricula: Strategies in Designing Assignments." Pages 423–45 in *Current Trends in the Development and Teaching of the Four Language Skills*. Edited by E. Usó-Juan and A. Martínez-Flor. Berlin: De Gruyter, 2006.

Kumaravadivelu, B. "The Postmethod Condition: (E)merging Strategies for Second/Foreign Language Teaching." *TESOL Quarterly, 28* (1994): 27–48.

Lantolf, James P. "Second Language Learning as a Mediated Process." *Language Teaching* 33 (2000): 79–96.

Lantolf, James P. "Sociocultural Theory and L2: State of the Art." *Studies in Second Language Acquisition* 28 (2006): 67–109.

Lantolf, James P. *Sociocultural Theory and Second Language Learning*. Oxford: Oxford University Press, 2000.

Lantolf, James P., and Tracy G. Beckett "Sociocultural Theory and Second Language Acquisition." *Language Teaching* 42.4 (2009): 459–75.

Lantolf, James P., and Steven L. Thorne. *Sociocultural Theory and the Genesis of Second Language Development*. Oxford: Oxford University Press, 2006.

Larsen-Freeman, Diane, and Michael H. Long. *An Introduction to Second Language Acquisition Research*. Applied Linguistics and Language Study. London: Longman, 1991.

LaSor, William Sanford. *Handbook of Biblical Hebrew*. Grand Rapids: Eerdmans, 1978.

Laufer, Batia, and Geke C. Ravenhorst-Kalovski. "Lexical Threshold Revisited: Lexical Text Coverage, Learners' Vocabulary Size and Reading Comprehension." *Reading in a Foreign Language* 22.1 (2010): 15–30.

Laufer, Batia, and Belaa Rozovski-Roitblat. "Incidental Vocabulary Acquisition: The Effects of Task Type, Word Occurrence and Their Combination." *Language Teaching Research* 15.4 (2011): 391–411.

Lee, Eunbae, and R. Lainie Wilson Harris. "The Effects of Online Glossary Quizzes and Student Autonomy on Domain Vocabulary Learning in Business Law." *Journal of Computing in Higher Education* 30.2 (2018): 326–43.

Lee, James F. "Comprehensible Input." In *The TESOL Encyclopedia of English Language Teaching*. Edited by John I. Liontas. New York: Wiley & Sons, 2018.

Lee, James F., and Bill VanPatten. *Making Communicative Language Teaching Happen*. 2nd ed. Boston: McGraw-Hill, 2003.

Levelt, Willem J. M. *Speaking: From Intention to Articulation*. Cambridge: MIT Press, 1989.

Levi, Tziona, and Matthew E. Poehner. "Employing Dynamic Assessment to Enhance Agency Among L2 Learners." Pages 295–309 in *The Routledge Handbook of Sociocultural Theory and Second Language Development*. Edited by J. P. Lantolf, M. E. Poehner, and M. Swain. New York: Routledge, 2018.

Levin, Joel R., Christine B. McCormick, Gloria E. Miller, Jill K. Berry, and Michael Pressley. "Mnemonic Versus Nonmnemonic Vocabulary-Learning Strategies for Children." *American Educational Research Journal* 19.1 (1982): 121–36.

Lightbown, Patsy M. "Getting Quality Input in the Second/Foreign Language Classroom." Pages 187–97 in *Text and Context: Cross-Disciplinary Perspectives on Language Study*. Edited by C.

Kramsch and S. McConnell-Ginet. Lexington, MA: Heath & Co., 1992.

Lightbown, Patsy, and Nina Spada. *How Languages are Learned*. 3rd ed. Oxford: Oxford University Press, 2006.

Liu, Na, and I. S. P. Nation. "Factors Affecting Guessing Vocabulary in Context." *RELC Journal* 16.1 (1985): 33–42.

Lloyd, Mair E., and Steven Hunt, eds. *Communicative Approaches for Ancient Languages*. London: Bloomsbury Academic, 2021.

Long, Michael H. "A Role for Instruction in Second Language Acquisition: Task-Based Language Teaching." Pages 77–99 in *Modelling and Assessing Second Language Acquisition*. Edited by K. Hyltenstam and M. Pienemann. Clevedon, England: Multilingual Matters, 1985.

Long, Michael H. "Does Second Language Instruction Make a Difference?" *TESOL Quarterly* 17 (1983): 359–82.

Long, Michael H. "Focus on Form: A Design Feature in Language Teaching Methodology." Pages 39–52 in *Foreign Language Research in Cross-cultural Perspectives*. Edited by K. de Bot, R.B. Ginsberb, and C. Kramsch. Amsterdam: John Benjamins, 1991.

Long, Michael H. *Second Language Acquisition and Task-based Language Teaching*. New York: Wiley & Sons, 2015.

Loschky, Lester. "Comprehensible Input and Second Language Acquisition." *Studies in Second Language Acquisition* 16.3 (1994): 303–23.

MacIntyre, Peter D., and R. C. Gardner. "The Subtle Effects of Language Anxiety on Cognitive Processing in the Second Language." *Language Learning* 44.2 (1994): 283–305.

Madlener, Karin. *Frequency Effects in Instructed Second Language Acquisition*. Boston: De Gruyter, 2015.

Magnan, Sally Sieloff. "The Unqualified Promise of Teaching for Communicative Competence: Insights from Sociocultural Theory." Pages 350–79 in *Sociocultural Theory and the Teaching of Second Language*. Edited by J. P. Lantolf and M. E. Poehner. London: Equinox, 2008.

Martínez-Flor, Alicia, and Esther Usó-Juan, and Eva Alcón Soler, "Towards Acquiring Communicative Competence through

Speaking," Pages 139–57 in *Current Trends in the Development and Teaching of the Four Language Skills*. Edited by E. Usó-Juan and A. Martínez-Flor. Berlin: De Gruyter, 2006.

Martínez-Flor, Alicia, and Esther Usó-Juan. "Towards Acquiring Communicative Competence through Listening." Pages 29–46 in *Current Trends in the Development and Teaching of the Four Language Skills*. Edited by E. Usó-Juan and A. Martínez-Flor. Berlin: De Gruyter, 2006.

Mashrah, Hind Talal. "The Role of Implicit Negative Feedback in Language Development—Some Reflections." *International Journal of English Language and Translation Studies* 5.1 (2017): 1–7.

McDaniel, Mark A., and Michael Pressley. "Putting the Keyword Method in Context." *Journal of Educational Psychology* 76.4 (1984): 598–609.

McQuinn, Scott. "Toward a Principled Communicative Methodology for Teaching the Biblical Languages." Master's thesis, Fresno Pacific University, 2017.

Metzger, Bruce M. *Lexical Aids for Students of New Testament Greek.* Grand Rapids: Baker, 1998.

Min, Hui-Tzu. "EFL Vocabulary Acquisition and Retention: Reading Plus Vocabulary Enhancement Activities and Narrow Reading." *Language Learning* 58.1 (2008): 73–115.

Mitchel, Larry A. *A Student's Vocabulary for Biblical Hebrew and Aramaic, Updated Edition: Frequency Lists with Definitions, Pronunciation Guide, and Index*. Grand Rapids: Zondervan, 2017.

Moore, Karen, and Gaylan DuBose. *Latin Alive!* Camp Hill, PA: Classical Academic Press, 2008.

Mounce, William D. *Basics of Biblical Greek Grammar*. 4th ed. Grand Rapids: Zondervan, 2019.

Mounce, William D. *A Graded Reader of Biblical Greek*. Grand Rapids: Zondervan, 1996.

Nakamura, Jeanne, and Mihaly Czikszentmihalyi. "The Experience of Flow: Theory and Research." Pages 279–96 in *Oxford Handbook of Positive Psychology*. 3rd edition. Edited by C. R. Synder, S. J. Lopez, L. M. Edwards, and S. C. Marques. Oxford: Oxford University Press, 2021.

Nation, I. S. P. *Learning Vocabulary in Another Language.* 2nd ed. Cambridge: Cambridge University Press, 2013.

Nation, I. S. P. *Teaching and Learning Vocabulary.* Boston: Heinle & Heinle, 1990.

Nation, I. S. P. "Teaching and Learning Vocabulary." Pages 581–596 in *Handbook of Research on Second Language Teaching and Learning.* Edited by E. Hinkel. Mahwah, NJ: Erlbaum, 2005.

Nation, I. S. P. *Teaching ESL/EFL Reading and Writing.* New York: Routledge, 2009.

Nation, I. S. P., and John Macalister. *Language Curriculum Design.* New York: Routledge, 2010.

Nation, Paul. "The Four Strands." *International Journal of Innovation in Language Learning and Teaching* 1.1 (2007): 2–13.

Nation, Paul. "Improving Speaking Fluency." *System* 17.3 (1989): 377–84.

Nation, Paul, ed. *New Ways in Teaching Vocabulary.* TESOL, 1994.

Nation, Paul. "Reading Faster." *International Journal of English Studies* 9.2 (2009): 131–44.

Newmark, Leonard, and David A. Reibel. "Necessity and Sufficiency in Language Learning." *International Review of Applied Linguistics in Language Teaching* 6 (1968): 145–64.

Noonan, Jennifer E. "Recent Teaching Grammars for Biblical Hebrew: A Review and Critique." *Ashland Theological Journal* 43 (2011): 99–118.

Noonan, Jennifer E. "Teaching Biblical Hebrew Grammar." Pages 317–35 in *"Where Shall Wisdom Be Found?" A Grammatical Tribute to Professor Stephen A. Kaufman on the Occasion of His Retirement from Hebrew Union College-Jewish Institute of Religion.* Edited by H. Dallaire, B. J. Noonan, and J. E. Noonan. Winona Lake, IN: Eisenbrauns, 2017.

Noonan, Jennifer, and Paul Overland. "Teaching Biblical Hebrew to Oral-Preference Learners." *Hebrew Higher Education* 19 (2017): 121–34.

Norris, John M., and Lourdes Ortega. "Effectiveness of L2 Instruction: A research Synthesis and Quantitative Meta-analysis." *Language Learning* 50 (2000): 417–528.

Ohta, Amy Snyder. "A Longitudinal Study of the Development of Expression of Alignment in Japanese as a Foreign Language." Pages 103–20 in *Pragmatics in Language Teaching*. Edited by K. R. Rose and G. Kasper. New York: Cambridge University Press, 2001.

Ohta, Amy Snyder. "Rethinking Interaction in SLA: Developmentally Appropriate Assistance in the Zone of Proximal Development and the Acquisition of L2 Grammar." Pages 51–78 in *Sociocultural Theory and Second Language Learning*. Edited by J. P. Lantolf. Oxford: Oxford University Press, 2000.

Ohta, Amy Snyder. *Second Language Acquisition Processes in the Classroom: Learning Japanese*. Mahwah, NJ: Lawrence Erlbaum, 2001.

Overland, Paul. "Can Communicative Methods Enhance Ancient Language Acquisition?" *Teaching Theology and Religion* 7.1 (2004): 51–57.

Overland, Paul. *Learning Biblical Hebrew Interactively*. Rev. ed. Sheffield: Sheffield Phoenix, 2016.

Overland, Paul. *Millim: Words for Conversation in the Biblical Hebrew Classroom*. Wilmore, KY: GlossaHouse, 2019.

Overland, Paul, Steve Cook, Jennifer Noonan, Benjamin Noonan, Robert (Bob) Stallman. "Communicative Methods for Teaching Biblical Hebrew." *The Wabash Center Journal on Teaching* 2.2 (2021): 109–30.

Overland, Paul, Lee Fields, and Jennifer Noonan. "Can Communicative Principles Enhance Classical Language Acquisition?" *Foreign Language Annals* 44.3 (2011): 583–98.

Piazza, John P. "Simple Latin Online Reading Resources." http://johnpiazza.net/latin/online-reading/.

Pickering, Martin J., and Matthew J. Traxler. "Parsing and Incremental Understanding During Reading." Pages 238–58 in *Architectures and Mechanisms for Language Processing*. Edited by M. Crocker, M. Pickering, and C. Clifton. Cambridge: Cambridge University Press, 2000.

Pienemann, Manfred. "An Outline of Processability Theory and Its Relationship to Other Approaches to SLA." *Language Learning* 65.1 (2015): 123–51.

Pienemann, Manfred. *Language Processing and Second Language Development: Processability Theory.* Amsterdam: John Benjamins, 1998.

Poehner, Matthew E., and James P. Lantolf. "Dynamic Assessment in the Language Classroom." *Language Teaching Research* 9 (2005): 233–65.

Pressley, Michael, Joel R. Levin, Nicholas A. Kuiper, Susan L. Bryant, and Sarah Michener. "Mnemonic Versus Nonmenemonic Vocabulary-Learning Strategies: Additional Comparisons." *Journal of Educational Psychology* 74 (1982): 693–707.

Quast, Jennifer Elizabeth. "Using Processing Instruction to Teach Biblical Hebrew Grammar." PhD dissertation, Hebrew Union College-Jewish Institute of Religion, 2009.

Radvinsky, Israel. "Bible (Hebrew) 01: Genesis by Hebrew Bible, read by Israel Radvinsky (1948-2007)." https://www.youtube.com/watch?v=iEXOlP-6WkQ.

Rapp, David N., Paul van den Broek, Kristen L. McMaster, Panayiota Kendeou, and Christine A. Espin. "Higher-Order Comprehension Processes in Struggling Readers: A Perspective for Research and Intervention." *Scientific Studies of Reading* 11 (2007): 289–312.

Rasinski, Timothy V. *The Fluent Reader: Oral Reading Strategies for Building Word Recognition, Fluency, and Comprehension.* New York: Scholastic Books, 2003.

Ray, Blaine, and Contee Seely. *Fluency through TPR Storytelling: Achieving Real Language Acquisition in School.* 2nd ed. Berkeley: Command Performance Language Institute, 1998.

Rebuschat, Patrick, ed. *Implicit and Explicit Learning of Languages.* Amsterdam: John Benjamins, 2015.

Rebuschat, Patrick. "Measuring Implicit and Explicit Knowledge in Second Language Research." *Language Learning* 53.3 (Sept. 2013): 595–626.

Richards, Jack C., and Theodore S. Rodgers. *Approaches and Methods in Language Teaching: A Description and Analysis*. Cambridge: Cambridge University Press, 1986.

Robinson, Peter. "Individual Differences, Cognitive Abilities, Aptitude Complexes and Learning Conditions in Second Language Acquisition." *Second Language Research* 17 (2001): 368–92.

Roediger, Henry L., and Lyn M. Goff. "Memory." Pages 250–64 in *A Companion to Cognitive Science*. Edited by W. Bechtel and G. Graham. Malden, MA: Blackwell, 1998.

Roediger, Henry L., III, Yana Weinstein, and Pooja K. Agarwal. "Forgetting: Preliminary Considerations." Pages 1–22 in *Forgetting*. Edited by S. Della Sala. Hove, East Sussex: Psychology Press, 2010.

Saffire, Paula. "Ancient Greek in Classroom Conversation." Pages 158–89 in *When Dead Tongues Speak: Teaching Beginning Greek and Latin*. Edited by J. Gruber-Miller. Oxford: Oxford University Press, 2006.

Saffire, Paula, and Catherine Freis. *Ancient Greek Alive*. Chapel Hill: University of North Carolina Press, 1999.

Scarcella, Robin C., Elaine S. Andersen, and Stephen D. Krashen, eds. *Developing Communicative Competence in a Second Language*. New York: Newbury House, 1990.

Scheumann, Jesse R., and Christine Lynn Hiegel. *Jonah: An Illustrated Hebrew Reader's Edition*. Wilmore, KY: GlossaHouse, 2017.

Scheumann, Jesse R., and Merissa Scheumann. *According to Their Kinds: A Biblical Hebrew Picture Dictionary*. Wilmore, KY: GlossaHouse, 2019.

Schmidt, Richard. "Attention." Pages 3–32 in *Cognition and Second Language Instruction*. Edited by P. Robinson. Cambridge: Cambridge University Press, 2001.

Schmidt, Richard W. "The Role of Consciousness in Second Language Learning." *Applied Linguistics* 11.2 (1990): 129–58.

Schmidt Richard W., and Sylvia Nagem Frota. "Developing Basic Conversational Ability in a Second Language: A Case Study of an Adult Learning of Portuguese." Pages 237–326 in *Talking to*

Learn: Conversation in Second Language Acquisition. Edited by R. Day. Rowley, MA: Newbury House, 1986.

Schwandt, John D. *An Introduction to Biblical Greek: A Grammar with Exercises.* Bellingham, WA: Lexham, 2020.

Schwartz, Bonnie D., and Rex A. Sprouse. "L2 Cognitive States and the Full Transfer/Full Access Model." *Second Language Research* 12 (1996): 40–72.

Schwieter, John W., and Alessandro Benati, eds. *The Cambridge Handbook of Language Learning.* Cambridge: Cambridge University Press, 2019.

Segalowitz, Norman. "Access Fluidity, Attention Control, and the Acquisition of Fluency in a Second Language." *TESOL Quarterly* 41.1 (2007): 181–186.

Segalowitz, Norman. "Automaticity and Second Languages." Pages 382–408 in *The Handbook of Second Language Acquisition.* Edited by C. Doughty and M. Long. Malden, MA: Blackwell, 2003.

Sfard, Anna. "On Two Metaphors for Learning and the Dangers of Choosing Just One." *Educational Researcher* 27.2 (1998): 4–13.

Sharwood Smith, Michael. "Consciousness-Raising and the Second Language Learner." *Applied Linguistics* 2 (1981): 159–69.

Sharwood Smith, Michael. "Input Enhancement in Instructed SLA: Theoretical Bases." *Studies in Second Language Acquisition* 15.2 (1993): 165–79.

Sharwood Smith, Michael. "Speaking to Many Minds: On the Relevance of Different Types of Language Information for the L2 Learner," *Second Language Research* 7.2 (1991): 118–32.

Simcock, Moina. "Developing Productive Vocabulary Using the 'Ask and Answer' Technique." *Guidelines* 15.2 (1993): 1–7.

Simon, Ethelyn, Irene Resnikoff, Linda Motzkin, Susan Noss. *Tall Tales Told in Biblical Hebrew.* Oakland, CA: EKS, 1994.

Sinclair, John McH., and Antoinette Renouf. "A Lexical Syllabus for Language Learning." Pages 140–60 in *Vocabulary and Language Teaching.* Edited by R. Carter and M. McCarthy. London: Longman, 1988.

Singer, Murray, and Jose Leon. "Psychological Studies of Higher Language Processes: Behavioral and Empirical Approaches." Pages

9–25 in *Higher Level Language Processes in the Brain*. Edited by F. Schmalhofer and C. Perfetti. Mahwah, NJ: Erlbaum, 2007.

Skehan, Peter. *A Cognitive Approach to Language Learning*. Oxford: Oxford University Press, 1998.

Skinner, B. F. *Verbal Behavior*. New York: Appleton-Century-Crofts, 1957.

Sonbul, Suhad, and Norbert Schmitt. "Direct Teaching of Vocabulary after Reading: Is It worth the Effort?" *ELT Journal* 64.3 (2010): 253–60.

Storch, Neomy. "Patterns of Interaction in ESL Pair Work." *Language Learning* 52 (2002): 119–58.

Stowers, Stanley Kent. *Letter Writing in Greco-Roman Antiquity*. Philadelphia: Westminster Press, 1986.

Swain, Merrill. "Communicative Competence: Some Roles of Comprehensible Input and Comprehensible Output in Its Development." Pages 235–53 in *Input in Second Language Acquisition*. Edited by S. M. Gass & C. G. Madden. Rowley, MA: Newbury House, 1985.

Swain, Merrill. "The Output Hypothesis: Theory and Research." Pages 471–83 in *Handbook of Research in Second Language Teaching and Learning*. Edited by E. Hinkel. Mahwah, NJ: Lawrence Erlbaum, 2005.

Swain, Merrill. "Three Functions of Output in Second Language Learning." Pages 125–44 in *Principle and Practice in Applied Linguistics: Studies in Honour of H. G. Widdowson*. Edited by G. Cook and B. Seidlhofer. Oxford: Oxford University Press, 1995.

Sylwester, Robert. "How Emotions Affect Learning." *Educational Leadership* 52.2 (1994): 60–64.

Tabor, James, and Randall Buth. *Living Koine Greek*. Jerusalem: Biblical Language Center, 2002.

Tasos, Anton. "Majority Text—The Original Greek New Testament." https://www.youtube.com/playlist?list=PLk3PwQOcbBq2U2r7xsulg8e2Lvs0_QFU5.

Terrell, Tracy David. "Acquisition in the Natural Approach: The Binding/Access Framework." *The Modern Language Journal* 70.3 (1986): 213–27.

Thomas, Margaret Hanratty, and John N. Dieter. "The Positive Effects of Writing Practice on Integration of Foreign Words in Memory." *Journal of Educational Psychology* 79.3 (1987): 249–53.

Thompson, Jeremy P. "Learning Biblical Hebrew Vocabulary: Insights from Second Language Vocabulary Acquisition." PhD dissertation, University of Stellenbosch, 2010.

Thompson, Jeremy P. "Word-list Size and Biblical Hebrew Vocabulary Learning." *Hebrew Higher Education* 14 (2012): 47–61.

Tinkham, Thomas. "The Effects of Semantic and Thematic Clustering on the Learning of Second Language Vocabulary." *Second Language Research* 13.2 (1997): 138–63.

Traupman, John C. *Conversational Latin for Oral Proficiency*. 4th ed. Wauconda, IL: Bochazy-Carducci, 2007.

Trenchard, Warren C. *The Complete Vocabulary Guide to the Greek New Testament*. Rev. ed. Grand Rapids: Zondervan, 1998.

Turnbull, Miles, and Katy Arnett. "Teachers' Uses of the Target and First Languages in Second and Foreign Language Classrooms." *Annual Review of Applied Linguistics* 22 (2002): 204–18.

Usó-Juan, Esther, and Alicia Martínez-Flor. "Approaches to Language Learning and Teaching: Towards Acquiring Communicative Competence Through the Four Skills." Pages 3–25 in *Current Trends in the Development and Teaching of the Four Language Skills*. Edited by E. Usó-Juan and A. Martínez-Flor. Berlin: De Gruyter, 2006.

Usó-Juan, Esther, and Alicia Martínez-Flor. *Current Trends in the Development and Teaching of the Four Language Skills*. Berlin: De Gruyter, 2006.

Usó-Juan, Esther, Alicia Martínez-Flor, and Juan Carlos Palmer-Silveira. "Towards Acquiring Communicative Competence through Writing." Pages 383–400 in *Current Trends in the Development and Teaching of the Four Language Skills*. Edited by E. Usó-Juan and A. Martínez-Flor. Berlin: De Gruyter, 2006.

Vainikka, Anne, and Martha Young-Scholten. "The Gradual Development of L2 Phrase Structure." *Second Language Research* 12 (1996): 7–39.

Van Pelt, Miles V., and Gary D. Pratico. *Graded Reader of Biblical Hebrew: A Guide to Reading the Hebrew Bible*. 2nd ed. Grand Rapids: Zondervan, 2020.

Vance, Donald R. *A Hebrew Reader for Ruth*. Peabody, MA: Hendrickson, 2003.

Vandergrift, Larry. "Listening to Learn or Learning to Listen?" *Annual Review of Applied Linguistics* 24 (2004): 3–25.

VanPatten, Bill. *From Input to Output: A Teacher's Guide to Second Language Acquisition*. Boston: McGraw-Hill, 2003.

VanPatten, Bill. "Grammar Instruction for the Acquisition Rich Classroom." *Foreign Language Annals* 26 (1993): 435–50.

VanPatten, Bill. *Input Processing and Grammar Instruction: Theory and Research*. Norwood, NJ: Ablex, 1996.

VanPatten, Bill. "Input Processing in Second Language Acquisition." Pages 5–31 in *Processing Instruction: Theory, Research, and Commentary*. Edited by B. VanPatten. Mahwah, NJ: Erlbaum, 2004.

VanPatten, Bill. "Processing Instruction: An Update," *Language Learning* 52 (2002): 755–803.

VanPatten, Bill. *Processing Instruction: Theory, Research, and Commentary*. Mahwah, NJ: Erlbaum, 2004.

VanPatten, Bill. "Thirty Years of Input (or Intake, the Neglected Sibling)." Pages 287–311 in *Social and Cognitive Factors in Second Language Acquisition*. Edited by B. Swierzbin, F. Morris, M. Anderson, C. Klee, and E. Tarone. Somerville, MA: Cascadilla, 2000.

VanPatten, Bill, and Alessandro G. Benati. *Key Terms in Second Language Acquisition*. London: Continuum, 2010.

VanPatten, Bill, and Teresa Cadierno. "Explicit Instruction and Input Processing." *Studies in Second Language Acquisition* 15 (1993): 225–43.

VanPatten, Bill, Erin Collopy, Joseph E. Price, Stefanie Borst, Anthony Qualin. "Explicit Information, Grammatical Sensitivity, and the First-Noun Principle: A Cross-Linguistic Study in Processing Instruction." *Modern Language Journal* 97.2 (2013): 504–25.

VanPatten, Bill and Soile Oikkenon. "Explanation Versus Structured Input in Processing Instruction." *Studies in Second Language Acquisition* 18.3 (1996): 495–510.

VanPatten, Bill, and Jessica Williams, eds. *Theories in Second Language Acquisition*. Mahwah, NJ: Erlbaum, 2007.

Vidal, Karina. "A Comparison of the Effects of Reading and Listening on Incidental Vocabulary Acquisition." *Language Learning* 61.1 (2011): 219–58

Vygotsky, Lev. *Thought and Language*. Translation newly revised and edited by Alex Kozulin. Cambridge: MIT Press, 1986.

Wang, Alvin Y., and Margaret H. Thomas. "Effect of Keywords on Long-Term Retention: Help or Hindrance?" *Journal of Educational Psychology* 87.3 (1995): 468–75.

Wang, Alvin Y., Margaret H. Thomas, Carolyn M. Inzana, and Laurie J. Primicerio, "Long-Term Retention under Conditions of Intentional Learning and the Keyword Mnemonic," Bulletin of the Psychonomic Society 31.6 (1993): 545–47.

Watson-Gegeo, Karen Ann. "Mind, Language, and Epistemology: Toward a Language Socialization Paradigm for SLA." *The Modern Language Journal* 88 (2004): 331–50.

Webb, Stuart. "The Effects of Repetition on Vocabulary Knowledge." *Applied Linguistics* 28.1 (2007): 46–65.

Webber, Nancy E. "Pictures and Words as Stimuli in Learning Foreign Language Responses." *Journal of Psychology* 98 (1978): 57–63.

Wells, Gordon. "The Complementary Contributions of Halliday and Vygotsky to a 'Language-Based Theory of Learning.'" *Linguistics and Education* 6 (1994): 41–90.

West, Travis. *Biblical Hebrew: An Interactive Approach*. Wilmore, KY: GlossaHouse, 2016.

Weyrick, David, and David Baker. "An Investigation of Biblical Language Study from 1986–1991 at Ashland Theological Seminary." *Bulleting of Higher Hebrew Education* 5–6 (1992–1993): 56–67.

Whalen, Karen, and Nathan Ménard. "L1 and L2 Writers' Strategic and Linguistic Knowledge: A Model of Multiple-Level Discourse Processing." *Language Learning* 45.3 (1995): 381–418.

White, Lydia. *Second Language Acquisition and Universal Grammar.* Cambridge: Cambridge University Press, 2003.

Willis, Dave, and Jane Willis. *Doing Task-Based Teaching.* Oxford: Oxford University Press, 2007.

Wong, Wynne. *Input Enhancement: From Theory and Research to the Classroom.* Boston: McGraw-Hill, 2005.

Zwaan, Rolf A., and Gabriel A. Radvansky. "Situation Models in Language Comprehension and Memory." *Psychological Bulletin* 123 (1998): 162–85.

Zwaan, Rolf A., and David N. Rapp. "Discourse Comprehension." Pages 725–64 in *Handbook of Psycholinguistics*, 2nd ed. Edited by M. Traxler and M. A. Gernsbacher. Burlington, MA: Academic Press, 2006.

AUTHOR INDEX

SUBJECT INDEX

NOTES

NOTES

NOTES

NOTES

NOTES